LUMBER AND POLITICS

LUMBER AND POLITICS
The Career of Mark E. Reed

ROBERT E. FICKEN

FOREST HISTORY SOCIETY, INC. / Santa Cruz, California
UNIVERSITY OF WASHINGTON PRESS / Seattle and London

The Forest History Society is a nonprofit, educational institution dedicated to the advancement of historical understanding of man's interaction with the North American forest environment. It was established in 1946. Interpretations and conclusions in FHS publications are those of the authors; the institution takes responsibility for the selection of topics, the competence of the authors, and their freedom of inquiry.

Work on this book and its publication were supported by grants to the Forest History Society.

Library of Congress Cataloging in Publication Data
Ficken, Robert E
  Lumber and politics.
  Bibliography: p.
  Includes index.
  1. Reed, Mark E. 2. Lumber trade—Washington (State) —History. 3. Washington (State)—Politics and government. 4. Businessmen—United States—Biography. I. Forest History Society. II. Title.
HD9757.W2F2   338.7′63′49820924 [B]   78-21756
ISBN 0-295-95655-0 (Univ. of Wash. Press)

For Lorraine

Acknowledgments

This book, like all historical exercises, could not have been written without the assistance of many individuals and institutions. Elwood R. Maunder of the Forest History Society first suggested that I write a book on the career of Mark Reed and was an invaluable source of support throughout my work on the project. William G. Reed shared his close knowledge of his father's life and provided access to the records of the Simpson Timber Company.

A number of libraries and historical societies made their collections of historical documents available to me. I am especially indebted to Richard C. Berner and his staff in the Manuscripts Collection of the University of Washington Library. The people in the Northwest Collection, the newspaper center, and the interlibrary loan office of the University of Washington Library provided essential and helpful services. I am also grateful for the help of the Washington State Historical Society, the Oregon Historical Society, the Washington State Archives in Olympia, and the Manuscripts Division of the Washington State University Library. Robert Monroe of the University of Washington Library and Donnie Crespo of the Weyerhaeuser Company Archives helped in the gathering of illustrations.

I have been fortunate in the careful reading given the manuscript by several individuals. Professor Robert E. Burke of the University of Washington brought his editorial skill and historical insight to bear on the manuscript with beneficial results. Woody Maunder, Betty Mitson, and Harold K. Steen of the Forest History Society also provided detailed and helpful critiques of all or part of the manuscript. The resultant book is better for their effort. Remaining factual or interpretative errors, of course, remain the fault of the author.

I also owe a great debt to my wife, Lorraine K. Ficken, for her patience and understanding, without which this book could not have been completed.

Contents

Illustrations

LUMBER AND POLITICS

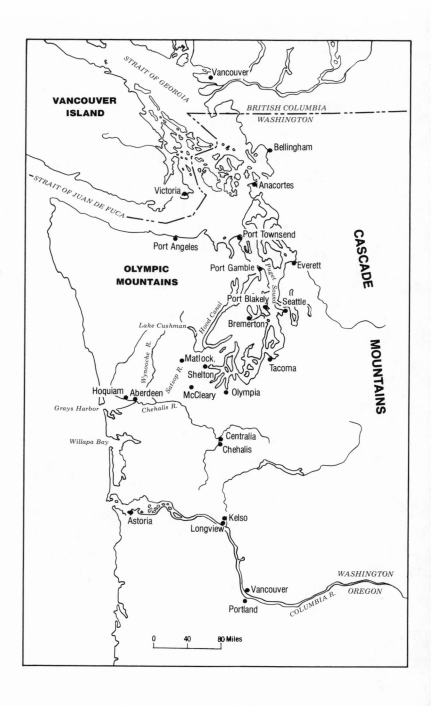

STRAIT OF GEORGIA

VANCOUVER
ISLAND

Vancouver

BRITISH COLUMBIA
WASHINGTON

Bellingham

STRAIT OF JUAN DE FUCA

Victoria

Anacortes

Port Townsend

Port Angeles

OLYMPIC
MOUNTAINS

Port Gamble

Everett

CASCADE

Port Blakely

Seattle

Lake Cushman

Bremerton

Hood Canal

Puget Sound

Wynooche R.

Satsop R.

Matlock

Tacoma

Shelton

Hoquiam
Aberdeen

McCleary

Olympia

MOUNTAINS

Grays Harbor

Chehalis R.

Willapa Bay

Centralia
Chehalis

Astoria

Kelso
Longview

WASHINGTON
OREGON

Vancouver

COLUMBIA R.

Portland

0   40   80 Miles

Introduction

History, it is often noted, is not what happened in the past but what we are able to find out about what happened in the past. The historian, in his re-creation of the past, is dependent on, and limited by, the evidence available to him. Thus, the end product of the historian's work may well be only a dim reflection of actual people and events, filtered down through time and the vagaries of documentation. As one result of this process many important personalities fail to receive due recognition because the evidence dealing with their careers has been destroyed or is otherwise unavailable to the historian. But with new evidence historians can correct these oversights and by providing information on the careers of important historical figures help present a more coherent picture of the past.

One such figure in the history of both the state of Washington and the Northwest forest industry was Mark E. Reed. The driving force behind the development of the Simpson Logging Company in the years after World War I, Reed was also prominent in banking and investment circles and was the most important political leader in the state during the 1920s. He was, one colleague recalled, "the biggest influence in the state . . . during his active years," while a Seattle newspaper began a 1926 series on "The Men Who Make Our State" with a profile of Reed. Despite these facts, Mark Reed is relatively unknown, seldom being mentioned by historians, and an account of his career is long overdue.[1]

In his business affairs Mark Reed symbolized the basic trend in modern American business: that leading toward ever larger and more efficient organization. The Northwest lumber industry was in a constant state of chaos; few lumbermen thought of the future, even fewer planned for it. Reed was one of the few leaders of the industry to attempt to bring some semblance of order out of this chaos. He sought to do so initially by establishing a mill organization to supplement the logging activities of Simpson. This made Reed's operation one of the most efficient and profitable in a notoriously inefficient business. With the coming of the Great Depression and its devastating impact on the fortunes of lumbermen, he took the lead in efforts to work out cooperative schemes within the industry and then an actual merger of many of its most important components. Reed's most salient characteristic was his ability to see the big picture—to see, one might say, the forest for the trees.

This characteristic also manifested itself in Reed's significant achievements as a reformer. Although a conservative, he was by no means opposed to change, assuming leadership in a number of campaigns to correct some of the abuses of modern industrialism. While still a private citizen, he pressed for the passage of Washington's workmen's compensation act. Then, as a prominent state legislator, he was the person most responsible for the state's first medical insurance legislation and for important increases in compensation payments. These efforts were not motivated by simplistic concerns of a philanthropic nature. Rather, by improving the conditions of labor, they helped encourage development of a stable work force while discouraging the growth of radicalism. They helped to create a more ordered community. And they did not involve the surrender of any of the ultimate decision-making powers of the businessman over his operation.[2] Reed showed that a businessman could be a reformer and that conservatism was not inimical to reform.

In politics Mark Reed was an enthusiastic Republican in an era when that party dominated the state. Indeed, he liked to say that the only constructive thing ever accomplished by the Democrats was passage of the Federal Reserve Act, and that, he noted, was the brainchild of Republican Senator Nelson Aldrich.[3] (This affiliation did not prevent Reed from aiding Democratic candidates when doing so benefitted his business or political interests.) The most important Republican in the state, Reed probably could have been governor if he had wished. Instead, he exercised power as leader of the state house of representatives, as the principal adviser of one governor and the main opponent of another, and as manager of the presidential campaigns of Calvin Coolidge and Herbert Hoover in the state. Reed stood for an orderly administration of the party and the state government. This, he believed, was the best course for the state and for business, whose welfare he considered to be practically synonymous.

Reed was thus a conservative and a reformer, a pursuer of self-interest, and a promoter of his version of the public interest. One of the first important citizens of the state to be born in Washington, his life spanned the development of the Puget Sound region from a few small settlements to an urban-industrial complex. The study that follows is based in large part on materials not previously available to historians. It is hoped that the study will demonstrate the importance of this major figure. And it is hoped that, through an account of the career of Mark Reed, new perspectives will be gained on the history of his state and industry.

CHAPTER 1

Reed and Simpson:
The Formative Years

Olympia, Washington Territory, two days before Christmas, 1866. In a small house near the territorial capitol building, Elizabeth Finley Reed gives birth to a son, Mark Edward, the fifth child of her marriage to Thomas Milburne Reed. (Of the previous four, only one, Thomas M. Reed, Jr., had survived infancy.) The arrival of a new son in the midst of the holiday season is no cause for rejoicing, however, as Elizabeth Reed dies four days later from the complications of birth. "The infant scarce ushered into life," laments the Olympia *Pacific Tribune*, "is deprived of that nourishment, which, while it yields vitality, gives impress to the future man." Mark Reed, though, grows up with the Pacific Northwest to become one of the most important figures in the economic and political history of Washington.[1]

1

Tom Reed, the widowed husband and father, had been born in Kentucky in 1825 to parents of Scotch-Irish background. In typical frontier fashion he left home at the age of eighteen with ten dollars in his pocket and worked as a country school teacher and general-store clerk. Along with many of his youthful compatriots he abandoned these pursuits for the lure of the California gold rush in 1849. After several attempts at mining in Sacramento and El Dorado counties, Reed became a store-keeper in El Dorado, where he served in a number of local political offices. He returned briefly to Kentucky in 1853 for his marriage to Elizabeth Finley, bringing his bride back to California by the Cape Horn route.

Unsuccessful in the gold fields, Reed moved to Washington Territory in 1857 as Wells Fargo agent for Olympia. He spent most of his time during the early 1860s occupied with mining ventures in far-off Idaho, at the time part of Washington. He represented Lewiston in the territorial legislature at Olympia in 1862 and 1863, serving as speaker of the house. In 1864 he served in the new Idaho legislature and also as prosecuting attorney of Nez Perce County. Reed returned to Olympia in 1865, where he secured a clerkship in the U.S. Surveyor's office. A thin man with large facial features and a wispy goatee, he was highly regarded by his contemporaries and was active in territorial political and social affairs, helping to organize the first Grand Masonic Lodge in Washington and serving as its secretary until his death in 1905.[2]

Olympia at the end of the Civil War was the leading community in the territory. A thousand people lived along tree-shaded streets on a mile-long peninsula formed by Budd Inlet. At the southern end of Puget Sound, Olympia had not yet been overshadowed by its younger neighbors to the north, Seattle and Tacoma. It dominated the area's economic and political life and offered access to rich fisheries and abundant forests. And it was a site of great natural attractiveness. "The scenery to be viewed from Olympia is grand in the extreme," one observer extolled. "The placid waters of the Sound in front, bordered on either side by the dark green of the heavy forests . . . surmounted in the distance by the snow-clad summits of the Olympic Mountains, form a picture of most enchanting beauty."[3]

There is little evidence with which to reconstruct the first three decades of Mark Reed's life in Olympia. Tom Reed married two more times, and Mark was apparently raised by these stepmothers. While there is no direct documentation for such speculation, the circumstances of his mother's death must have had a profound impact on young Mark, depriving him of much childhood security and contributing to the reticence that characterized his adult years.[4]

Tom Reed became deputy U.S. surveyor in 1872, and his frequent absences from home deprived Mark of an additional force for stability. These absences came to an end in 1877 when the elder Reed was appointed territorial auditor, but political success was not accompanied by financial security. Tom operated a store in Olympia and speculated in railroads and real estate, including construction of one of the town's first apartment buildings. His business affairs never really panned out, however, and frequently hampered his son's advancement.[5]

As a schoolboy Mark worked in his father's store and in a printing office. He attended the University of Washington briefly in 1884, but financial stringency forced him to drop out and return to Olympia. There he assumed management of his father's bankrupt grocery store. Mark then departed for Oakland, California to attend the California Military Academy, from which he graduated in 1887 with a profound respect for the value of discipline and an ordered existence. Military training, Reed later insisted, "tends to impress upon the youth the necessity of obeying their superiors and brings to their attention their obligation to promptly act when a definite purpose is set before them for consummation." An early biographer has suggested that this experience "was probably the basis of the regimentation of his logging and other enterprises."[6]

Following graduation, Mark spent two years working in mercantile establishments in Los Angeles and San Francisco. He returned to Olympia in 1889, a rather thin young man in his early twenties with large features and a bushy walrus mustache covering his upper lip. Washington had just become a state, with the capital in Olympia. Tom Reed had been a delegate to the constitutional convention and had then been elected the state's first auditor, winning more votes than any other Republican candidate for state office.[7]

Mark worked as a deputy to his father until 1892. During this period he also studied law with Olympia attorney James A. Haight. Offering the security of organization and logical argument, this work, like his military experience, influenced him greatly. "I am thankful for my law training," Reed recalled years later. "It helped me out of many a spot. Every young business man should have some knowledge of the law." He did not complete his studies, however, looking elsewhere for his opportunity in life.[8]

As Tom Reed's son, Mark was one of the leading young men of Olympia. He served as an officer in Washington's first

National Guard unit and became a leader in local Masonic Lodge activities. He also managed to accumulate a small amount of savings from his job as deputy auditor, as well as stock in the Capital National Bank. But he was unsure of himself, his feelings of insecurity heightened by the contrasting achievements of his brother, Thomas M. Reed, Jr. The latter was ten years older than Mark and had graduated from the University of California and then attended law school at Princeton. A prominent Puget Sound attorney, Tom, Jr. was named to the Thurston County bench in 1893 by Governor John McGraw.⁹

If he was going to match the success of his brother, Mark Reed realized that he probably could not do so in Olympia. The state capital boasted of its telephone and electric trolley systems, and community boosters rhapsodized over the "beautiful, level town site, sloping gradually back from the water." But Olympia had been bypassed by the new transcontinental railroads, while ship captains preferred to call at the more northerly Puget Sound ports, and the town was stagnating. The population of Seattle increased tenfold during the 1880s and doubled again the following decade, and Tacoma expanded at an equal rate. Olympia, on the other hand, was losing people, the population in 1900 barely exceeding four thousand.¹⁰

Olympia offered little opportunity in the early 1890s, but the vast forests of the surrounding region presented an altogether different prospect to the young man. The lumber industry of Washington had boomed mightily in the previous decade, output increasing ten times between 1879 and 1889. This expansion had a profound impact on tiny Mason County, to the west of Olympia on the southwestern shore of Puget Sound. Originally named Sawamish County, it was renamed Mason County in 1864 after an important territorial political figure, Charles H. Mason. The county's economy, based on a few primitive water-powered sawmills and some isolated small farms, remained backward for many years. The principal town, Shelton, contained only ten houses in 1888. But the lumber boom brought prosperity to the area. One hundred million feet of logs were produced in Mason County in 1892, and Shelton had expanded to over a hundred dwellings.¹¹

Logging in the woods of Mason County seemed an ideal

endeavor to Reed, one that had the potential of considerable success and allowed him to remain close to Olympia as well. In 1893 he formed a partnership with Ike Ellis, an experienced logger, and invested his savings in timberland on Cranberry Creek near Shelton. The firm of Reed and Ellis constructed a mile-long wooden-pole railroad along which oxen pulled cars laden with logs to the creek, where they were dumped and then towed to Oakland Bay. Unfortunately, the enterprise fell victim to the severe national depression beginning in 1893 and became, according to Stewart Holbrook, "one of the quickest logging failures in Puget Sound history." Reed himself blamed the outcome on prevailing Puget Sound log scaling practices, which allowed purchasing sawmills to determine the number of board feet in a shipment of logs and thus the amount of money owed the logger. Reed and other logging operators were convinced that this system allowed the mills to cheat them.12

His first experience in the logging business a distinct failure and his savings gone, Reed returned to Olympia with at least an intimate acquaintance with the problems of the industry to show for his effort. Through the political influence of his father and brother he secured a position as secretary of the state land commission. In this position he looked after the day-to-day affairs of an agency that administered five hundred thousand acres of land, handling with dispatch the voluminous correspondence of the commission. The commissioners were impressed with Reed's energy and applauded his "exceptional fidelity and executive ability." But the election of Populist John Rogers to the governorship in 1896 meant that Republican officeholders like Reed were out of a job.13

Reed was forced to work for a time as a logger, an experience that gave him a good deal of sympathy for the hard life of the working men in the woods. "I built my own bunk," he told a reporter years later, "and we carried our blankets rolled up on our backs and furnished the bed clothing for our bunks." Although he acquired valuable insights, this was an extremely frustrating period. After he attained success, Reed urged that "any young man who shows a disposition to get out and help himself" should be aided by "his older fellowmen who have had to fight the same kind of battle." Trying experiences, though, were invaluable as builders of character. Those who "were compelled through force of circumstance to depend more or less on their own efforts" became better, more reliable men as a result. These were trying years, he reflected with hindsight, "but I was sure I had a definite future."[14]

Now thirty years of age, Reed had yet to find success or security, but he had obtained training that would help mold his business career. His exposure to military and legal discipline enhanced his penchant for order and efficiency. And his experience with the state land commission and as logging operator and working man awakened him to the opportunities available in the young state's burgeoning lumber industry, as well as to the weaknesses of that industry. In early 1897 Olympia banker C. J. Lord, an old family friend, sent Reed to take over a bankrupt logging camp in Mason County. While undertaking this task, Reed became acquainted with Sol Simpson, one of the most important loggers in the state. Their meeting brought to an end Reed's search for meaningful endeavor and opened the way to business success and political power.[15]

                              2

Like his new young friend, Sol Simpson had struggled to achieve success. Born in Quebec in 1843 to a New England family, Simpson moved to Nevada in the 1860s, where he engaged in mining ventures and graded roads. He married the daughter of the superintendent of the federal mint and, shortly after the birth of their first daughter, Irene, in 1877, the family moved to Seattle. There Simpson operated a contracting firm, grading city streets and railroad lines for the coal mines south and east of the city. In 1886 he was hired by Captain William Renton of the Port Blakely Mill Company to grade that firm's railroad into its huge timber holdings in Mason County.[16]

Having begun operations in 1864, the Port Blakely Mill Company was one of the major mills established on Puget Sound by San Francisco interests to satisfy the booming demand for lumber in California in the decades following the gold rush. By 1882 its Bainbridge Island mill was the largest on the Pacific Coast, with a daily capacity of two hundred thousand board feet. The company was an innovative force in the industry, buying up timberlands away from the Sound in anticipation of the time when waterfront stands of timber would be depleted. And, beginning in the mid-1880s, it pioneered in the construction of logging railroads to reach these heretofore isolated trees and bring the "round stuff" (logs) out to tidewater.[17]

Western Washington was tree country, with nearly three hundred billion feet of standing timber. Ideal climate and soil conditions had produced vast stands of Douglas fir, cedar, hemlock, and spruce over the centuries. "It is difficult to conceive of forests more magnificent," one visitor marveled. The forests of the region, another observer reported, "are bewildering, stultifying to the mind, in their magnitude and denseness and stupendous individual growths." A third commentator noted "a confused impression," gotten while sailing down Puget Sound, "of a limitless forest of great density, upon which the energy of man may be expended for centuries without any appreciable effect." Another writer, alive to economic realities, observed that "there are dollars in the knotless stems when sawed, and of the latter feature only the lumberman thinks."[18]

This dollar feature dominated the thoughts of lumbermen as the market prospered in the 1880s, due in large part to the expansion of demand in California and railroad construction in the Northwest. "Though the country is new, and much of the choicest timber land is not easily accessible," the Portland *West Shore* reported in 1888, "the lumber output of the northwest is enormous, and constantly increasing." In that year the mills of Washington and Oregon could produce three million board feet a day. By the turn of the century Washington had become the nation's leading lumber producer, a position it held for over thirty years, and two-thirds of the wage earners in the state were dependent on the industry. The state's mills alone had a daily capacity of over nine million feet. "The lumber business of Washington," the Olympia *Washington Standard* commented, "is represented by figures that are almost incomprehensible."[19]

Washington's forest industry was in the midst of this rapid development when Sol Simpson arrived at Kamilche on Little

Skookum Inlet, seven miles south of Shelton, with his equipment, a crew of experienced road builders, and a few horses. A
forceful, innovative man, the wiry Simpson quickly impressed
his new associates. "Mr. Simpson is a pleasant man easy to get
along with . . . a man who is conscientously honest," a Port
Blakely official recorded. By 1888 the railroad was hauling out
nearly two hundred thousand feet of logs a day. In that same
year Simpson was elevated to the position of superintendent of
all operations on the Blakely. (The railroad was officially the
Puget Sound and Grays Harbor Railroad but was commonly
known as the Blakely.)[20]

Simpson adopted a number of policies on the Blakely that he
later followed in his own company and that would be continued
by Mark Reed. Alive to the newest techniques, he was probably
the first logger to use horses in place of oxen in the woods and
was then among the first to use donkey engines for the yarding
of logs. At a time when operations were becoming increasingly
expensive as loggers moved away from tidewater, he sought to
make his operations more efficient. And, plagued as all operators of the time were by the proclivity of workers to quit in
favor of better paying or less exhausting jobs in the coal mines,
or to leave work for a bust in town, Simpson searched for
means of encouraging the development of a more stable work
force. He hoped to transform the "boomer" (the man who stays
on the job only a short time) into a "homeguard" (the long-term
employee) by attracting family men to his camps. "It would be
greatly to the advantage of the Company," an associate wrote,
"to encourage men of that class and by that means we would
gradually become more independent of the floating class of
labor."[21]

Simpson did not plan to stay with Port Blakely. Toward the
end of the 1880s he began buying timberland, apparently with
money borrowed from Captain Renton. In 1890 he resigned and
set up S. G. Simpson and Company, with headquarters in the
small town of Matlock in the western part of the county. Few
records of this company's activities remain. It does seem to have
been prosperous, however, and it was closely connected with
the Port Blakely Mill Company. In July 1893, for example,

Simpson cut seven million feet of logs, all destined for the Port Blakely mill on Bainbridge Island.[22]

In 1895 Simpson, Alfred H. Anderson, and four Port Blakely stockholders formed the Simpson Logging Company. Anderson was an early representative of a major trend in the Northwest industry in the closing years of the century: the infusion of new capital from the timber-denuded Great Lakes states. He had come to Washington in the mid-1880s to manage timber holdings of his father-in-law, Benjamin Healy, a prominent Wisconsin businessman. These properties included an interest in the Peninsular Railroad, which ran west from Shelton to near Simpson's Matlock operations. The newly formed Simpson Company was capitalized at fifty thousand dollars, with Sol Simpson contributing his assets, and Anderson, a timber tract owned by Healy. "Really the tangible assets consisted of 'chips and whetstones' in the language of the streets," Mark Reed later recalled in what became something of a company legend. Although Sol Simpson was the active force in the company, two-thirds of its financing came from the Port Blakely interests, and each shareholder received a sixth of the venture.[23]

As this arrangement indicates, the Simpson Logging Company was something of a subsidiary of the Port Blakely organization. This fact was further demonstrated by Port Blakely's payment to Simpson of a lower price for its logs than it paid other loggers and by its claim of first call on Simpson's output. Only those logs not desired by the mill could be sold elsewhere. Sol Simpson chafed under these restrictions, particularly as the Simpson Logging Company prospered. By 1898 he had five hundred men at work in eight camps along eighty miles of railroad and was, according to the Shelton newspaper, "probably the largest individual employer of labor in Washington."

Finally, Simpson could stand this situation no longer, and in 1902 he informed Port Blakely that he had "taken the liberty to advance the price of logs to the Blakely Mill the same as other Mill Co's are paying." He asserted his belief that it was "but a fair proposition for us" to receive the market price from Port Blakely. Simpson concluded that he was "always willing that the mill should have the *call* on anything the Simpson Logging Co has but sure think they should give us the same as they pay other loggers, and the same price we are offered by other mills." The Simpson Logging Company continued to be closely related to Port Blakely, but it had taken an important step toward achieving a wholly independent status, a status that befitted its growing position in the woods.[24]

3

Simpson had become one of the most important logging operations in the state by the time Mark Reed came to work for the company in late 1897. He worked initially as a foreman at Camp One on the shore of Lake Newatzel. No evidence remains of this period of work, except for a story recalled by oldtimers that Reed had knocked out a drunken teamster named Jack Hogan who had beaten a fourteen-year-old skid greaser. Hogan came after Reed with a shotgun but managed to kill another man instead and was sentenced to the state penitentiary at Walla Walla for his outburst.[25]

In 1898 Reed was brought into Shelton to manage the Lumberman's Mercantile Company, in which Sol Simpson and A. H. Anderson owned a major interest. "Mark is a man of rare business attainments," Olympia editor John Miller Murphy wrote, "and we predict he will make a faithful and efficient record in the responsible position to which he has been assigned." The Lumberman's Mercantile, with fifty thousand dollars worth of merchandise in its two-story, red-frame building on Railroad Avenue, was the largest general store in the county. As manager, Reed held a responsible position, one that occasionally had its exciting moments. The store caught fire in March 1899, for instance, and according to a newspaper account: "Manager Reed and a clerk each picked up the small extinguishers and after a few anxious minutes had the fire in subjection. . . . After they had time to think [it] over, the boys were worse scared and haven't got over their scare yet. Under the counter was a can or two of black powder, on the shelves were a lot of shot gun cartridges, and in the rear was a half dozen boxes of dynamite—a deadly combination for Shelton."[26]

Reed quickly became one of the most important of the town's

eight hundred residents, a reflection of his membership in a prominent Olympia family and his status as local representative of Mason County's leading employer. With a friend, he rented a home from oysterman Joe Deer and, reported the local paper, "opened up a bachelor's hall." He represented Shelton at the 1899 legislative ball in Olympia, "at which," the *Mason County Journal* observed, "the elite of the state were present, or rather those of the elite who could afford tickets at $5 each." But Reed's activities were by no means limited to the store or to Shelton.[27]

Although continuing to hold the position of store manager, Reed became a general troubleshooter for Sol Simpson. He was given the responsibility for reorganizing the railroad properties Simpson and Anderson had brought into the new company so that they could be operated in the most efficient manner. And he aided the two men in establishing the Phoenix Logging Company, which operated along Hood Canal in the northern part of the county and was for years an important Simpson affiliate.[28]

Reed also helped form the Puget Sound Timbermen's Association, an organization of independent loggers to counter the economic power of the sawmills and push for reform of scaling practices. The official mill scale was invariably less than that of the logger, and as we have seen, Reed blamed the collapse of Reed and Ellis on this factor. The loggers secured passage of legislation establishing state and county scalers, who would presumably be impartial. This did not end all scaling problems, as loggers continued to express dissatisfaction with the results obtained by the men performing this important task. Reed himself complained a few years later to Edwin G. Ames of the Puget Mill Company that "there are but very few scalers on the Sound today who are competent to scale a raft of logs, and on whose judgment I would feel like standing behind as being a fair and equitable scale between the parties." But at least the alleged unfair practices of the mills were brought to an end. And Reed for the first time operated as a political spokesman for the industry.[29]

When Sol Simpson purchased controlling interest in the Capital National Bank of Olympia from C. J. Lord in early 1900,

Reed was dispatched to run the bank. "While we may reget to see Manager Reed leave Shelton," newspaper publisher Grant Angle observed, "the call is a deserved promotion with increased remuneration, and possibly even better things in store, and therefore he is to be congratulated." Six months later, however, Reed returned to Shelton when Lord reacquired control of the bank.[30]

No sooner had Reed returned to Shelton, though, than he was off to Alaska, following the footsteps of his brother, who had gone north in quest of a fortune during that territory's gold rush. Sol Simpson had formed the White Star Steamship Company in order to take advantage of the great demand for passage to Alaska and had also invested in banking and retail activities in Nome. Reed was sent to Nome to serve as White Star agent and to look after Simpson's investments in that remote and colorful community. He spent much of 1900 and 1901 in Nome, giving up the mayoralty of Shelton, to which he had been elected in late 1900. Alaskan life could be arduous, for reasons of climate if for nothing else. But Reed enjoyed Alaska, finding there considerable challenge.[31]

He returned to Seattle in April 1901 to marry Simpson's daughter Irene, and the couple honeymooned aboard ship bound for Nome. Irene was a spirited young woman who, while growing up, had liked to ride on horseback through the woods near her father's logging camps and had often acted as a nurse when workers were injured. As Sol Simpson became wealthy, she had come to enjoy the relative sophistication of Seattle society and hoped to remain in the Puget Sound metropolis following her marriage. The marriage cemented Reed's alliance with the Simpson family and, combined with his ability, destined him for eventual control of the logging company.[32]

Reed's Alaskan venture came to an end when the steamer carrying Irene back to Seattle for a visit in the late summer of 1901 limped into port after losing its rudder at sea. Sol Simpson, who had for several days feared that his daughter was lost, ordered Reed to "close up everything in Nome to the best of your ability and come home as soon as possible." Simpson did not wish to risk another such traumatic experience. "I don't care what becomes of Alaska," he exclaimed. "Not all the gold of Nome would induce me to take another chance." Upon his return from the north, Reed supervised the Seattle end of the steamship business and gradually assumed day-to-day management of his father-in-law's other properties as well.[33]

Sol Simpson's health declined rapidly, and he was forced to spend an increasing amount of time at southern California health resorts. With Simpson more and more out of the picture, Reed took over direct control of the Simpson Logging Company, with its three hundred employees and five camps producing up to three hundred thousand feet of logs a day. He also became general manager of the Peninsular Railroad. The road hauled more logs than any other logging railroad in the state, serving the Simpson camps and those of the other principal operations in the area, the Mason County Logging Company and the Western Washington Logging Company.[34]

Shortly after returning from California, Sol Simpson died at Reed's Shelton home in May 1906. "He was almost the only one of the old-time loggers who had weathered the storms which beset the industry under old methods," the *Mason County Journal* observed, "and had reached a prosperous and influential position." A. H. Anderson, who had not previously taken an active part in the company's management, became president. Reed continued as manager and, because Anderson was occupied with a myriad of outside activities, undertook an even more direct supervision of the business. He moved its operating offices from Matlock, establishing headquarters for the first time in Shelton.[35]

Reed's first significant move following the death of Simpson was to acquire the stock owned by the Port Blakely investors. Traveling to California, he made the purchase with the aid of a $360,000 loan from the Dexter Horton National Bank of Seattle. (This transaction apparently initiated Reed's long involvement with the state's largest bank.) Reed received a one-twelfth interest in the company as his commission for handling the arrangements, and the rest of the stock was divided equally between Anderson and the Simpson family, the latter represented by the Simpson Investment Company. The Simpson Logging Company thus became wholly the property of the two families, a situation that would ultimately become unique among major forest products companies.[36]

A year later Reed became involved in his first major political controversy and, not for the last time, was a target for critics of the state's handling of timber sales. The nation was in the midst of the progressive era, and in Washington public suspicion was directed at the so-called timber barons, who were allegedly always on the outlook, said one writer, for "some scheme for squeezing tribute out of the state for the benefit of private business." The progressives focused their attention on the state land commission, charging that it had sold timber for less than market value because of corrupt relationships between the commissioners and lumbermen. (At the time of statehood, the federal government had turned over huge amounts of timberland to Washington state, to be used to finance public education and the construction of state buildings.)

In March 1907 a special legislative committee investigated the sale of a Mason County timber section to the Simpson Logging Company. Reed and Anderson, it was hinted, had bribed Land Commissioner E. W. Ross to sell the timber for twelve thousand dollars, which was three thousand dollars below the price dictated by the state cruise. Reed, appearing before the committee, denied the allegations and offered to open company books to prove his contention. Admitting that Anderson had sent him fifteen thousand dollars to cover the purchase, Reed said that the difference was meant to provide leeway in the event other bids were offered. When this proved unnecessary, Reed claimed he kept the three thousand dollars as a commission for his trip to California to buy out the Port Blakely interests. This explanation was not entirely satisfactory to committee members, but the investigation soon fizzled out and no action was taken. The incident appears to have been the only time in Reed's career when his personal integrity was seriously questioned. Detesting publicity, especially of this sort, Reed shied away in the future from dealings with the land commission, acquiring only an occasional stand of state timber.[37]

Records of Reed's operation of the company over the next few years are sketchy, making it difficult to reconstruct his activities. It does seem that Simpson made only limited economic progress during these years of stagnant lumber markets following the Panic of 1907. Increased railroad freight rates to the east exacerbated the problems caused by falling demand in the traditional California and Pacific Rim cargo markets. The productive capacity of the industry had meanwhile expanded considerably, the number of Washington sawmills capable of turning out over twenty million feet a year having doubled between 1900 and 1905. The scramble of these large operations for what was left of a constantly declining market produced economic disaster. Seventy percent of the mills in the Northwest, the *Timberman* estimated in 1908, had been forced to close down.[38]

Business was stagnating, but Reed's personal life was prospering. Mark and Irene's first son, Sol Simpson Reed, was born in May 1902, and two more boys, Frank and Will, had arrived by 1908 to complete the family. The Reeds lived in a modest frame house with a picket fence in front, a couple of blocks north of Railroad Avenue and the Lumberman's Mercantile Company. Although his father "was the boss of everything," William G. Reed has recalled, "we lived in a house that wasn't any bigger than anybody else's." Family life was pleasant, although Mark was often absent on business and when home, notes his youngest son, his "word was absolute law." In summer the family moved out into the cool forest, living in tents at an abandoned logging camp.[39]

There was no question that Reed was the most prominent person in Shelton, which had grown to over twelve hundred people by 1910 and boasted of an electric light system and a municipal waterworks. While he usually did not socialize with the townspeople (never, for example, becoming involved in the local Masonic Lodge), he was genial and willing to listen to problems and do what he could for the welfare of the community. He could even unbend to the extent of running in the "fat man's race" at Shelton's Fourth of July picnic in 1915. Nor was he inclined to flaunt his increasing financial worth. The first automobiles, for instance, appeared on Shelton streets in 1906, but Reed did not acquire one himself until 1911.[40]

Reed's attitude toward Shelton was rather unique. Lumbermen had traditionally been interested only in the rapid exploitation of the available natural resource so that they could retire with their millions to California. They paid scant attention to the welfare of the towns where they operated or to that of the workers who cut the logs and sawed the lumber. But Reed, finding in his business, in his family, and in Shelton the security and stability he had lacked for so many years, was interested in building a community. He constantly stressed to his growing sons and to business associates that nothing must be done to undermine the future of Shelton, that the town must be regarded as a permanent institution. Thus, when a fire in August 1914 destroyed most of the business establishments in Shelton, Reed rushed home from Seattle, his chauffeur covering the hundred-mile distance in under three hours, to announce that he would see to the immediate construction of a new fireproof business block.[41]

Reed's appearance reflected his growing prestige and sense of security. Gone were the walrus mustache and the uncertain look in his eyes, while his face and body filled out in the husky fashion that in those days betokened a man of substance. Reed was "over six feet tall, big-boned; he had a deep, musical voice and a very pleasant manner of talking to you," one close associate recalled. He could put people at ease with "a twinkle in his eye that . . . was always there until he got exercised about something, and then he could look pretty stern." Another subordinate remembered that "when something went against his grain, the sky shook and the lightening was there and the thunder. . . . But he was a very fair man and a very kindly man."

He was still not one of the major figures in the lumber industry, however. Reed operated on the fringes of significant influence, serving as a trustee of the Lumbermen's Club of Seattle and forging strong friendships with such important figures as George S. Long of the Weyerhaeuser Timber Company and Edwin G. Ames of the Puget Mill Company. His picture, though, did not appear in any of the region's lumber trade journals until 1914. In part, this lack of attention from the business press was a recognition of the fact that he was not officially the head of his company. It also reflected the reticence that kept him from attending most lumber industry conventions and his distaste for publicity—personality factors that were reinforced by the influence of Sol Simpson, who had shared these qualities.[42]

A. H. Anderson died at the Waldorf-Astoria Hotel in New York in April 1914. With his death, Reed became president of the Simpson Logging Company and a variety of other organizations. These other businesses included the Phoenix Logging Company, the Peninsular Railroad, and the State Bank of Shelton, as well as the Simpson and Anderson estate companies. The five-million-dollar Anderson estate was the largest aggregate of private capital in the Northwest, making Reed one of the region's major financial figures. He also headed the Shelton Navigation Company, which operated steamers on the lower Sound and, in the absence of railroad connections, provided the only public transportation for Mason County residents. Reed's name and picture began to appear frequently in business publications, reflecting his new importance. In the same year, 1914, Reed embarked as well on another course that would complement his economic standing with political power.[43]

4

Considering the political careers of his father and brother, it was perhaps inevitable that Mark Reed would also become actively involved in politics. "He just loved the political atmosphere," one associate later recalled of Reed. After coming to Shelton, Reed was active in local Republican party affairs, serving briefly as mayor and attending county and state party gatherings. As the most prominent resident of the small town he was looked to for leadership. With his Olympia connections he was presumed to possess political influence in the state capital that could benefit the community. Reed, for his part, asserted that he had an obligation to take part in politics. "Personally, I think every good citizen has a duty to uphold in the community," he said. "Some of us, due to a more fortunate position, have a larger duty than others, but we all can, and should, help."[44]

Reed also realized that political activity could benefit his business interests. For one thing, the growing tax burden could be brought under control. In a 1914 speech at the dedication of Shelton's new town hall (financed by a donation from the widow of Sol Simpson), Reed argued that he and other tax-payers were "oppressed with the consciousness that the ten-dency of the times is not to upbuild but rather to confiscate." Tax collections in the country, he pointed out, had risen from $47,000 in 1904 to $233,000 in 1913. (The property tax, assessed and raised at the county level, was the mainstay of the state's revenue structure.) This "stupendous sum" represented "practically an increase of 500 per cent in nine years." The person who did not pay taxes, Reed continued, should not rest content with the thought that this was none of his or her concern. The tax burden operated to "increase land values, discourage investment and settlement, repel industrial enter-prise and finally produce a stagnant condition which puts labor out of commission."[45]

Other problems facing the timber industry, including labor unrest and the potentially expensive question of accident prevention and compensation, could also be solved or at least ameliorated through participation in politics. Reed was con-vinced that society was endangered by the growing discontent of labor in the forests and mills of the Northwest, where the radical Industrial Workers of the World had achieved consider-able success in securing the allegiance of workers. Both employer and employee had an interest in attacking the causes of this discontent, for the latter to secure a better life and for the former to secure a more efficient utilization of his property by preventing strikes and reducing the frightening rate of accidents and their attendant impact on production and on expensive litigation. By securing increased cooperation between management and labor Reed hoped to achieve that "orderly system of association" he believed to be the ideal society.[46]

Reed began to devote considerable energy to politics in 1910, when he was elected mayor of Shelton for the second time and also managed a successful local option election. The six Shelton saloons, Reed and other local employers argued, undermined the stability of the work force, leading to accidents, reduced output and absenteeism. Once in office, however, Reed changed his mind about prohibition because of the financial impact of the saloon close-down. He was forced to hire Shelton's first full-time policeman as a result of "the very unsatisfactory conditions incident to the attempted enforcement of the local option law," but the law could still not be enforced. Local option, moreover, endangered the morals of the community because liquor could be imported, and as a result the town's youth was becoming "dissipated and demoralized to a greater extent than would be possible if the open saloon was at hand under strict regulation." Regulated saloons, Reed also pointed out, would pay taxes, relieving some of the burden carried by other property owners.[47]

The desire to do something about taxes and labor problems influenced Reed's decision to run for the state legislature in 1914, as did his concern that the progressive movement, with its regulatory commissions, initiatives, referendums, and direct primaries, had gone too far. Reed was friendly with many of Washington's progressives, but abhorred their impact on the state. The progressive reforms, he asserted, were "disturbing our political life." The direct primary, for instance, had destroyed party discipline and encouraged officeholders to curry favor with their constituents by increasing expenditures of public money. The legislature's proclivity for "'freak' legislation," he wrote Edwin G. Ames, deserves "our most serious and deliberate consideration." Businessmen had paid too little attention to state politics, Reed believed, and must change this stance if their interests were to be protected.

Compounding the problems of progressivism for Reed was the fact that Mason County was represented in the state house of representatives by a Socialist, W. H. Kingery, the only member of that party ever to sit in the legislature. Reed was determined to eliminate this embarrassment to his local political influence. Reed was also encouraged to run by Democratic Governor Ernest Lister, an old friend, who was urging moderate and public spirited businessmen of all parties to take part in politics, much to the chagrin of more partisan members of the Democratic party.[48]

Reed's candidacy for the house of representatives won the approbation of local conservative elements. Reed was the community's "most representative citizen," the *Mason County Journal* claimed, and, the "splendid progress" registered in Shelton's life was "due to his good business ability and public spirit." If the people wished to bring an end to "high taxes, extravagant and wasteful laws" and were "really in earnest in their desire that the same conservative judgment be used in making laws as in the conduct of successful business affairs," they would cast their ballots for him. The Olympia *Recorder*, stressing that "men of this type are needed in the legislature," applauded Reed's "intimate knowledge of the needs of this section of the state, long and successful experience in large business affairs," and his high standing "throughout all this section of the state."

While Kingery campaigned vigorously on a reform platform, Reed relied on his name, prestige, and the not unimportant fact that a large percentage of the voters worked for him. His only public effort during the campaign was publication of a letter denying Socialist charges that he would favor the timber interests in Olympia. "I will work and vote against any measure," he promised, "which would tend to discriminate in favor of any class of property in the matter of taxation, and this applies to timber." Reed was elected with eleven hundred votes to six hundred for Kingery. He would face opposition only once in the next seven elections.[49]

As he continued to do every odd-numbered year for the coming decade-and-a-half (the legislature met in regular session every other year), Reed rearranged his schedule in January 1915 in order to spend sixty days in Olympia. "I have been rushing from one thing to another trying to get ready to move over to Olympia," he wrote on a similar occasion a few years later, "and frankly it does seem almost impossible to find the breaking off point." Reed was one of the 110 Republicans who dominated the other 29 Democratic and Progressive members of the house and senate in 1915, but he differed from his colleagues in a number of respects. At forty-eight he was several years older than the typical house member. He was one of only nine native Washingtonians in the house. And he was one of only ten lumbermen in the legislature (as compared to thirty-seven lawyers and thirty-three farmers), a figure that still gave the industry its largest representation since the early 1890s. Despite his atypical background, Reed was appointed to the most important house committees: rules, appropriations, roads, and banking. (Another freshman member, timberman Roland H. Hartley of Everett, who became governor in the following decade, received only minor committee posts.) The appointments reflected Reed's growing stature as a businessman and the recognition that his frequent dealings with the likes of George Long and Edwin G. Ames qualified him as the designated spokesman in the legislature for the views of big business.[50]

"The reduction of taxes is one of the chief aims of Representative Reed," Grant Angle wrote as Reed departed for Olympia, "and he will work along lines that will bring about a reform in that direction." This was indeed Reed's prime objective. He was one of the strongest advocates of legislation requiring all taxing districts to establish budget systems and to avoid going into debt. He also fought for a bill that would charge the estates of insane persons for their care in state institutions. On other matters, he introduced legislation making it illegal to bring liquor into logging camps if they were posted against its use, this despite his growing disenchantment with the prohibition movement. Of major local interest, he secured an appropriation for construction of the Olympic Highway through southeastern Mason County, for the first time providing the area with decent road access to the outside world, and was instrumental in passage of legislation protecting the important lower Puget Sound oyster reserves.[51]

In this first session he was a narrowly conservative and highly effective legislator. "No member of the state legislature," the Shelton *Journal* enthused, "has made a better record for the securing of benefits for the home community," while the *State Capital Record* reported that "Reed is rated as one of the best men who ever sat in the legislature." In concert with another new member, Ed Sims of Port Townsend, Reed had quickly become one of the most powerful figures in the house. The *Journal* informed its readers that he had been "one of the really 'big men' of the legislature, one of the small coterie of leaders who are responsible for the results shown."[52]

This rapid achievement of influence resulted in part from Reed's membership on key committees, especially rules, and from his method of operations. "The real work is in committees," Reed pointed out, although he went on to claim that "the power and influence of the rules committee is greatly over-estimated." The committee did control whether or not a given measure reached the floor, Reed conceded, but a simple major-ity of house members could force it to release any bill. Of course, such action was extremely rare, and Reed's position on the committee gave him considerable behind-the-scenes influ-ence over the course of business in the house. Members often claimed that their pet bills were sidetracked in the rules committee, particularly during the hectic closing days of a session.[53]

Reed disliked bringing pressure to bear on legislators, a course of action that the huge Republican house majority made unnecessary in any event. Rather, he preferred to operate in an informal and subtle fashion. House and senate members, he commented, "need relaxation after a long, hard drag through-out the day." He might, for example, invite legislators to a leisurely dinner at which there would be no mention of legisla-tive business. "An informal dinner of such a nature," Reed observed, "lays the foundation for an obligation which very often works out more advantageously than attempting to bring about a direct commitment at the time of the gathering." When he did argue for a particular position, he did so in low-key fashion, emphasizing the need for a realistic approach to the problems of the state. "Keen in analysis, slow of speech, but accurate in conclusion," two legislative commentators wrote, Reed was "almost invariably able to convince the House with his careful, direct logic."[54]

As a result of his legislative success a Reed-for-governor boom developed in southwestern Washington. "The office of governor would not be any too large for Mr. Reed," the Elma *Chronicle* observed, "and he would undoubtedly make a first rate executive." This paper joined "his many friends . . . all over the state" in "hoping that he can be induced to throw his hat in the ring" for the governorship in 1916. While visiting Shelton, House Speaker W. W. Conner noted that Reed's "friends are trying to get him into the race" and suggested that "he would make a pretty [good] race if he ever got into it as he is well known all over the state." But Reed, as he would do later when more inviting gubernatorial prospects opened up, refused to run for governor, stating that he had no plans for continued involvement in public life.[55]

Reed returned to the legislature in 1917 though, and, Ed Sims having declined to run for re-election, was chosen house majority leader. In this position, he abandoned the parochial limits of the previous session to push through major reform legislation. Along with many other lumbermen, Reed had lobbied the legislature for passage of the state's workmen's compensation act in 1911, one of the first in the nation. The act, however, compensated injured workers only for lost salary, providing no funds for medical expenses. Now Reed sponsored the state's first medical insurance act, establishing a state medical board to administer employer-employee contributions and pay the doctors' bills for injured workers. The legislation also provided for an accident prevention program. The measure, Reed believed, represented a fair compromise with legislation supported by organized labor requiring employers to foot the entire cost of the insurance fund. The legislature had defeated more stringent first-aid legislation in 1915, a failure Reed regarded as a serious error. Employers "made a mistake," he had informed Governor Lister, "in not granting concessions to the 'other side' which would have minimized some of the antagonism" on the part of labor. The Reed bill passed both houses by large margins and was recognized as a major reform, one that benefitted workers and helped educate employers to the advantages of safety.[56]

This achievement, as well as Reed's overall ability and integrity, won him plaudits from a variety of observers. The Montesano *Vidette* observed that Reed was "the cleanest floor leader that the House has seen in years. . . . Brains and integrity are his virtues." Conservative lumberman Edwin G. Ames expressed the wish that "more men of your class and ability could be induced to spend time" in the legislature. If that was possible, Ames asserted, businessmen "would not look forward with dread to coming sessions of law-making bodies." At the other end of the ideological spectrum, Representative Victor Zednick of Seattle, a labor spokesman, said that the Reed first-aid bill was "a step in the right direction." Prior to the session, political writer Jay Thomas noted in the *Washington State Weekly*, progressive legislators had distrusted Reed as a "'representative of the big interests.'" However, they all now recognized his "ability . . . and have become impressed with his fairness."[57]

Reed's work in the legislative session was overshadowed by the climactic events of the early spring of 1917, as the United States neared active participation in World War I. The involvement of the nation in the war would have a great impact on the lumber industry. And it would again place Reed in a position of responsible leadership, a position commensurate with his new importance as a business and political leader.

5

As the nation approached war, Mark Reed avoided emotionalism, continuing his level-headed approach to public issues. He dissuaded the legislature from censuring the chairman of the University of Washington's German department for alleged unpatriotic remarks, arguing that Americans must avoid jingoism. He denounced Washington Senator Wesley Jones's involvement in efforts to prevent President Woodrow Wilson from arming American merchant vessels for protection against German submarines. "It is to the disgrace of Washington," Reed charged, "that a citizen of this state, for whom I have voted every time, should be instrumental in holding back approval" of Wilson's proposal. "Let us get behind the president and let him know that we shall be there all the time."[58]

When war was finally declared, Reed told a rally in Shelton that all Americans "should do their mite" to help bring victory. He pledged that all Simpson employees who entered the service would get their jobs back after the war and that "reasonable provision" would be made for their families while they were away. Reed took an active part in local Red Cross efforts as Mason and adjoining Thurston and Grays Harbor counties raised their share of the one million dollars asked of the state for the Red Cross. He also served as a member of the county defense council. In May 1917 he traveled to the East on behalf of Washington lumbermen to secure contracts for construction of wooden ships. The demands of war, it appeared, were certain to be a vital factor in the economy of the Northwest.[59]

The timber industry, along with most sectors of the nation's economy, had been in the doldrums when the war began in Europe in 1914. "So far as business is concerned," Edwin G. Ames reported, "it never was so bad before in my thirty-five years' experience." Eighty-five percent of the industry's workers in Washington and Oregon, he estimated, were unemployed. The Puget Mill Company was running at 40 percent of capacity and the Port Blakely Mill was shut down altogether. According to Reed the price of logs had fallen from twelve dollars in 1908 to eight dollars by the end of 1914. There were ten million feet of unsold logs in the Olympia and Shelton area. The trade, Reed remarked after a trip to San Francisco, was "very sluggish" and was not likely to pick up until the war in Europe came to an end.[60]

But the war proved to be a considerable economic stimulus, bringing renewed prosperity to the woods and logging towns. "The lumber market continues to grow encouraging," the Shelton newspaper observed in late 1915, "and locally the logs are towed away as fast as they reach water and are rafted." Despite opposition from some mills, Reed raised log prices to ten dollars and kept all Simpson camps going with full crews in order to keep up with orders. "The lumber business today is better than it has been in a decade," exulted the *West Coast Lumberman*. "For the first time in several years," Grant Angle wrote, "the operators say they have no fear of over production, and the only cloud in the lumber heaven is the lack of ships to send forth the manufactured lumber."[61]

With the United States entering the war the heavens seemed to become even clearer, especially as the stands of long-fibered spruce on the Olympic Peninsula were deemed essential for the government's airplane production plans. The war, Edmond S. Meany of the University of Washington commented, "has made the harvest of Spruce the dominant item in this timber region."[62] But clouds were beginning to form, threatening the prosperous weather. Demand was high, but labor was being drained off by the draft as well as the shipyards and other war industries. As a result, the supply of labor became tight. Workers, long chafing under low wages and the squalor of the camps and mills, were prepared to take advantage of this rare opportunity to better the conditions of their working lives.

These conditions did not seem bad to many observers. Olympia editor John Miller Murphy rhapsodized on the logging camp "with its carpet of fragrant pine needles, its canopy of green branches and the little brook of clear spring water flowing past the door of the cook house." City dwellers traveled for hours, he noted, to reach such places, "yet this is the place where the men congregate at night, and after the evening meal gather around the fire and swap stories, totally oblivious of their surroundings and the beauties of nature." Another writer observed that there was "a certain rough, crude poetry and romance about the lives of the men" in the woods. Even an experienced observer like Stewart Holbrook could refer to the "rough yet romantic glamor" of the logging camps.[63]

Such viewpoints did not accurately portray the conditions in the woods. A study completed in 1918 indicated that half of the logging camps lacked wooden bunks, and an equal percentage were without showers and were bug-infested. Another commentator wrote of the "filthy bunk-houses of the lumber camps, the desolation of the soggy woods, and the constant peril from crashing trees and flashing ropes." Forester George Drake recalled that the typical logging camp was "pretty rugged. . . . where we slept at night was one big old log cabin with about fifty men in it. . . . You were overcome with the odor of drying socks and crawled into bed with the bedbugs."[64]

The industry, with its reliance on railroads and other machinery, was expensive to operate and profits were not often high. Lumbermen therefore believed that expenses had to be cut to a minimum where possible, which usually meant wages and camp amenities. Many operators, moreover, had risen from the ranks of the buckers and fallers and could see no reason why conditions should be improved. One employer contended that he had "worked out of it into something better," so "why should any husky man make such a 'holler' about working conditions?" Simple greed, of course, was another factor in the refusal of employers to spend money on their workers.[65]

A few companies made an effort to provide decent quarters for their employees. Mark Reed, for instance, remembered the unpleasantness of his own early experience in the woods, recalling a visit to a logging camp where he had to sleep on a pile of boards previously occupied by a group of hogs. "That night the hard boards and the odor of the hogs kept me awake for a long time; and I vowed then that if I ever had charge of a real camp I would provide decent furnishings for the men who worked in the woods." Simpson camps were considered to be well above average. The company, Grant Angle extolled, "has always been a little ahead of other lumbering concerns in the introduction of modern methods of operation, such as . . . clean, sanitary camps and the best of cooks and food." In 1917 the company built a portable camp on twelve railroad cars at a cost of $25,000. (Logging camps had to be frequently moved, reducing the feasibility of expensive fixed camps.) The train contained such amenities as steam heat, electric lights, drying rooms, a dining car, and separate sleeping quarters.[66]

A list of rules was posted prominently in each Simpson logging camp, rules that were found by the *Timberman* to be so "splendid" that it published them for the education of its readers. Aside from regulations admonishing employees to observe safety precautions and not to bring liquor into camp, the list laid down company policy on camp conditions. Cooks were ordered to "feed the men good, wholesome food, in abundance and [to] be attentive and obliging to their wants." Foremen were instructed to "see that the bunk houses and all surroundings are kept clean and sanitary" and to make sure that "the toilets are properly enclosed and kept fly proof." Any employee who had a complaint about conditions was urged to come into town and bring his grievance directly to the attention of Reed. Such concern was not typical of the industry as a whole.[67]

Early in July 1917 the mills and camps of western Washington were hit by the most severe strike in their history. A series of local strikes by the Industrial Workers of the World east of the mountains spread across the Cascades. The I.W.W. had been founded in 1905 by Big Bill Haywood and a group of other radical labor leaders. Its oft-stated goal was no less than the overthrow of capitalism, a goal loudly proclaimed in violent rhetoric. Thanks to the failure of most lumbermen to provide decent wages and working conditions, the Wobblies had acquired a large following in the Northwest by the summer of 1917. They were joined in their walkout by the much smaller Timber Workers Union, an affiliate of the conservative American Federation of Labor. Within two weeks 90 percent of the operations west of the Cascades were closed down. In Mason County all logging, with the exception of one Simpson side, came to an end.[68]

"Probably fifty percent of our men are I.W.W.'s," Reed wrote of his workforce. "This does not mean that fifty percent of our men are bad at heart, but there is a full ten percent of this fifty percent that are antagonistic and disloyal and constantly keep their propaganda before the loyal men." Grant Angle backed up this assessment of the local situation. "Less than half the men" on strike were Wobblies, he contended, while "the others have been intimidated, or else have funds and prefer to take it easy until things quiet down or work is necessary again."[69]

Disregarding the deplorable conditions that had produced the unrest, the operators were determined to break the strike and to break the I.W.W. as well, which was more of a threat to property than the A.F.L. Businessmen and other conservatives were driven to distraction by what was known as the "Wobbly horrors." The *West Coast Lumberman* called for the arrest and deportation of "these alien fomenters of unrest" and the *Timberman* denounced the "nefarious teachings of the I.W.W., with their utter disregard for the laws of either God or man." Wobblies, according to Grant Angle, hoped as their "chief aim in life . . . to secure a living off others and with as little work as possible." In the process, said the *American Lumberman*, the "labor agitators have succeeded in striking down a great industry and rendering it helpless."[70]

Although varying from place to place, the demands of the strikers centered on a call for the eight-hour day, which soon became the focus of the entire dispute. "The sentiment involved in this demand," Reed later recalled, "grew so extensively that it became the practically universal desire of the men employed in the lumber industry that they be granted an eight hour working day." But the employers were adamantly opposed.[71]

In response to the strike, lumber manufacturers met in Seattle and formed the Lumbermen's Protective Association, pledging a half-million dollars to fight the eight-hour day. Reed was named to an executive committee, headed by E. S. Grammer of the Puget Mill Company, charged with keeping day-to-day watch on the situation. Lumbermen would be willing to accept a national eight-hour day, one operator contended, "but simply cannot grant a regional eight-hour day without wrecking the industry." Reed was in complete agreement, insisting that retention of the present wage scale while abandoning the traditional ten-hour day would bring the industry to its knees because it could no longer compete with the South, where labor was cheap. Laboring men, for their part, would not accept reduced wages in return for fewer hours. Efforts of state and federal officials to mediate the dispute came to naught.[72]

The strikers suddenly returned to work in early September. Conservatives momentarily rejoiced over the apparent crushing of the unions. "The lumbermen and millowners of Washington," the Seattle *Argus* applauded, "in defeating the strike of the I.W.W. have performed a patriotic action for which they deserve the thanks of all classes of people." Grant Angle exulted over the apparent fact that the "I.W.W. is about eliminated from control." Two Simpson camps were soon going full tilt, while the other five were able to start up at reduced strength.[73]

The elation proved to be short-lived, however, as the workers had merely switched tactics, abandoning the picket lines and adopting the "strike on the job." Through sabotage, complete devotion to safety regulations and instructions (which tended to slow down production), and other methods, the strikers were able to tie up operations. Spruce production was limited to less than three million feet a month, much less than the ten million feet required by the government for its airplane program. And the workers were able to draw their paychecks as well. Such circumstances proved even more frustrating to the operators than the strike of the summer months.[74]

Colonel Brice P. Disque, a thirty-eight-year-old army officer of considerable energy and devotion to his assigned task, arrived on the scene at this point. For several months Disque had monitored Northwest labor conditions for the War Department. His job now was to bring an end to the labor dispute so that the maximum amount of spruce production could be achieved. With this goal uppermost in his mind, Disque came under the influence of three academic figures: Carleton H. Parker, iconoclastic economics professor at the University of Washington; President Henry Suzzallo of the same institution, chairman of the state defense council; and James Scherer of the national defense council. These three men, especially Parker, preached that only by eradicating abusive working conditions could the I.W.W. be immobilized and lumber output maximized. Advised by Parker, Disque determined that army personnel should be provided to make up the industry's labor shortage and that means should be found to improve the lot of workers. Thus were born two unique organizations: the army's Spruce Production Division and the Loyal Legion of Loggers and Lumbermen, the latter a cooperative effort among army, employers, and workers to bring a modicum of reform to the woods and mills and to increase output.[75]

The lumbermen were greatly impressed by Disque. George Long, manager of the vast Weyerhaeuser timber interests, referred to him as "a very fine practical man." Disque, in turn, found the lumbermen to be congenial associates and gradually drifted away from the influence of Parker. The Colonel, Reed was told by Hoquiam logger Alex Polson, was becoming dependent on "good practical men, not theorists."[76]

Reed was one of Disque's closest advisers. At the first meeting between the colonel and important industry leaders, in Portland in late October 1917, Reed was named to a committee with Polson and J. J. Donovan of the Bloedel-Donovan Lumber Mills to work out the organization of the Loyal Legion, then served as a Four L director. A month later Disque named Reed, Long, J. H. Bloedel, and Timothy Jerome of the Merrill and Ring Lumber Company to a special advisory council. Disque later extolled Reed and the others for the "intimate, trusting, and honest relations" they had maintained with him. Although the

Simpson Logging Company had little spruce on its lands, Reed also served as a member of the Spruce Production Board, in that capacity spending a great deal of time at Portland headquarters during the winter and spring of 1918.[77]

Working with Colonel Disque, Reed became a strong advocate of the eight-hour day, agreeing with Senator Miles Poindexter of Washington that this would undercut the appeal of the I.W.W. Dropping the traditional ten hours might well hurt the mills, Reed conceded, by increasing their cost of production and making it more difficult for them to compete with other lumber-producing regions. But Simpson was strictly a logging concern, and the situation was considerably different in the great outdoors. "It is impossible," Reed pointed out, "to work longer than eight hours a day actually on the job in a logging camp for a very considerable portion of the year." Even during the long days of summer efficiency began to fall off as workers toiled along toward the ten-hour mark. It was "very difficult to maintain a successful operation" under the long hours, Reed concluded, recognizing that Simpson had little to lose and much to gain by conceding the eight-hour day. Not only would the major problem of labor discontent be resolved, but efficiency stood to improve as well.[78]

The problem was to convince the other operators to go along, for it was crucial that the industry maintain a united front. "I certainly am at a loss to know how to handle this labor situation," Reed wrote Henry Suzzallo. "The stand taken by some of the employers is very disheartening to say the least." Concentrating on the Olympia-Grays Harbor area, Reed held a series of conferences with employers, urging acceptance of his position. Some operators, he reported, were granting wage increases of as much as $1.50 a day. "This is evidently done for the purpose of forestalling any action that some of us might take on the eight hour day." He had hoped that "for the wellbeing of the industry ... we could bring about a united and concerted action," but "radicals" among the employers seemed determined to "make trouble, and I do not hesitate to say if that is what they are looking for, their search will not be in vain."[79]

Opponents remained intransigent and responded with scorn

as rumors of imposition of the eight-hour day by government fiat filtered out of the nation's capital. The Wilson administration would reduce the working day, the *Argus* exclaimed, "at a time when every loyal citizen should be exerting himself to the utmost to produce the sinews of war." Such an order, Senator Wesley Jones charged, "can have but one unfortunate effect and that is to dampen the patriotism of our people and make them feel that in this hour of the nation's trial they are singled out and compelled to bear a burden which their competitors . . . are not required to bear." The *West Coast Lumberman* observed that the shorter work day "could not increase the output of lumber on the Pacific Coast but would decrease production, and certainly, this is not a result which the government seeks."[80]

Despairing of united industry action, Reed, with the approval of Disque, increased the pressure on recalcitrant operators. Calling a meeting of Mason County's principal loggers in mid-February 1918, he won their agreement to the eight-hour day. (The actual working day could extend beyond that point, but overtime would have to be paid.) Wages would remain at the prevailing rate, $3.75 to $8.00 a day depending upon skill, but a decrease in the workday amounted to an increase in wages per hour worked. Disque, for his part, indicated that he would direct the soldiers of the Spruce Division and the efforts of the Loyal Legion toward companies adopting similar positions. Lumbermen holding out would presumably have to cope with the Wobblies without the assistance of the military.[81]

This pressure had its effect. At a dramatic meeting in Portland in late February, the employers agreed to accept the eight-hour day, ending what the *West Coast Lumberman* called "the greatest and most important fight that Pacific Northwest lumbermen ever waged for any cause." Although the step meant a significant increase in the cost of production and a few lumbermen reacted with complete disgust, most accepted the eight-hour day as a necessary evil. At least, George Long noted, there was a "gleam of sunshine" in that it might portend the end of worker discontent and "a more honest effort" in the mills and woods.[82]

Disque moved to supplement what historian Harold Hyman has called a "large victory" for timber workers with a series of reforms designed to improve camp conditions to the level of those enjoyed by army privates, an interesting insight on prevailing standards. By the end of the war in the fall of 1918, one hundred thousand workers were registered in a thousand Four L locals. Backed by thirty thousand Spruce Division soldiers in the woods and in the mills and barracks at Vancouver, Washington, these men had increased the output of spruce to twenty million feet a month. Furthermore, the back of Wobbly strength in the industry had been broken. "I do not anticipate any disturbance of any kind in our camps," a Simpson foreman reported to Reed, "as our men are, in the main, very loyal and apparently will not tolerate any interruption in this pursuit of their patriotic duty."[83]

Despite his successes, Disque became the target of considerable criticism. Some conservatives accused the colonel of being extravagant and of fostering, rather than lessening, worker discontent. The American Federation of Labor and its supporters, on the other hand, contended that he was a tool of the lumber barons and, having achieved the defeat of the I.W.W., was thwarting legitimate organizing efforts of the patriotic Timber Workers Union. Wesley Jones argued on the floor of the Senate that Disque had wasted large sums of money, and that experienced local men rather than an outside army officer should be in charge of the spruce program.

Reed defended Disque against his critics. "When the quality of the material is considered and compared with that which was furnished by private operators before the Government took charge of this work," the Shelton logger informed Jones, "we feel confident that the Government is getting value received." Disque, moreover, had taken the labor situation in hand, "with the result that the operations of the I.W.W. are largely curbed and offset and we are today getting better results in the way of production than we have for a year past." Finally, the Colonel had "done wonders in bringing about a better feeling between employers and employees." Reed admired Disque, for they both believed that paternalistic reform would ameliorate the festering problems of the lumber industry in the interest of efficient production and an orderly society.[84]

When the legislature assembled in Olympia at the end of the

war, Reed again demonstrated his belief in the positive benefits of reform. In a series of private meetings with William Short, head of the state Federation of Labor, Reed worked out a joint labor program. Short agreed to support anti-syndicalism legislation designed to eliminate the I.W.W., and Reed sidetracked efforts by some legislators, in the aftermath of the Seattle general strike of 1919, to outlaw strikes. With the rate of accidents in industry having increased 145 percent since 1911, Reed backed a modest increase in workmen's compensation benefits. Finally, in a measure that earned him the plaudits of most labor elements, he secured legislation that recognized the legality of trade unions and, borrowing from the federal Clayton Act, restricted the granting of injunctions against union activity.[85]

Reed had proven himself to be an enlightened and intelligent employer. Troubled by many of the side-effects of industrialism, by the brutality and squalor present in so many of the logging camps and lumber mills, and by the frightful safety hazards of Washington's most important industry, he strived to ameliorate the sorry situation. Reed, writes one historian, "hoped to foster a better society through beneficial labor legislation."[86] But altruism was not the principal element in his calculation. Reform, by increasing morale, by reducing time lost through accidents, and by contributing generally to more efficient operations increased productivity while decreasing costs, resulting in a more profitable operation. Reed's genius was his ability to grasp such concepts and his willingness to put them into effect.

Mark Reed was fifty-two years old at the end of the war. Born on the frontier, he had, after considerable floundering in his early years, achieved prominence in an industry that had grown from near nonexistence at the time of his birth to a position of supreme economic importance in the state. He had found security in a stable community and as head of an important business organization. Like his father he had become a significant figure in Washington politics. Moreover, he had demonstrated a breadth of vision, a grasp for the common interests of business and society, not usually associated with the oft-despised timber barons. He was by the time of the First

World War a figure to be reckoned with in the Northwest. But the most important achievements of his career, both in the lumber industry and in politics, were still ahead.

CHAPTER 2

Building Shelton

The Simpson Logging Company, as the name suggests, re-stricted itself to the cutting and sale of logs, leaving the manu-facture of lumber to its customers. Like most logging operators, Sol Simpson and A. H. Anderson meant to liquidate their company once the available timber was removed. These plans promised disaster for Shelton and Mason County. Shelton was in effect a company town, dominated by Simpson and its related business enterprises. Thanks to the vision of Mark Reed, how-ever, Shelton was not to suffer the fate of other logging towns, the remains of which dot the landscape of western Washington. Reed was determined to make Simpson over into a permanently operating company, one he could pass on to his sons. And, regarding Shelton as a home and community rather than merely as a source of labor, he was equally determined to place the future of the town on a sound footing. Both goals required that Simpson become a more fully-integrated company, sawing its own logs into lumber in its own mills. In the process of expanding the scope of Simpson's operations, Mark Reed built Shelton into a stable commonwealth in the woods. Reed, two local historians have written, "must be styled as 'father' of Shelton's industrial progress."[1]

1

Mark Reed managed his business affairs, his son William G. Reed notes, "in ways which were more reflective of his person-ality and desire than they were of standard business organiza-tion." Reed's typical day in Shelton began with a tour of the workshops, followed by disposition of correspondence at the Simpson office on the second floor of the Lumberman's Mer-cantile Company. A shave and then a session of poker at a nearby cigar store completed the morning. After lunch and a nap at home he would return to the office for conferences with key subordinates, then conclude the day with inspections of the State Bank of Shelton, where he personally reviewed all loan applications, and the Lumberman's store. "He probably spent no more than a couple of hours a day on what a modern business executive would think of as general management" of the Simpson Logging Company, his son observes. But this was enough, in the less-structured business world of the day, to keep close tabs on operations.[2]

Much of Reed's time following the end of World War I was devoted to the continuing problem of labor unrest. At first it seemed as if the radical labor movement had been eliminated. The reforms instituted by Colonel Disque had apparently destroyed the I.W.W. in the woods and mills. Nationally, the Wobbly leadership had either been jailed, deported, or had fled the country. And the public outcry against the infamous Centralia "massacre" of the fall of 1919, coupled with the hysteria of the "red scare" of that same year, had seemingly forever destroyed the reputations of the remaining radicals. Finally, the labor shortage that had been so skillfully exploited by the Wobblies during the war appeared to be a thing of the past.

True, some conservatives like Edwin G. Ames grumbled that "there is a shortage of men and women, young and old, who are willing to do certain classes of work which they had been brought up to do before the war." But this shortage, while perhaps vexing to those seeking domestic help or hoping to fill other menial positions, was not present in the lumber industry. As the shipyards and other war industries closed down, the discharged workers flocked to their prewar jobs in the mills and logging camps. The industry itself, however, was experiencing the impact of the postwar depression, forcing a reduction in available jobs at a time when the size of the work force was increasing. Lumber production on the West Coast fell from ten billion feet in 1920 to seven billion in 1921, while the national lumber price index dropped by half. Log prices took a corresponding nosedive.[3]

"So plentiful are the loggers now," the *Mason County Journal* reported, "that already more than fifty men have returned to town unable to get jobs in the camps and more men are arriving daily from down Sound cities." Competition for jobs was intense, and employers could dispense with those who had been involved with the Wobblies during the war. "The logging operators can choose their men," editor Grant Angle observed, "and eliminate the I.W.W., the trouble-makers and the sabotage actors who played havoc with the industry and made operations as costly as possible." With radicalism apparently eliminated and prices on the downswing, the Simpson Logging Company instituted a 20 percent reduction in wartime wage rates.[4]

Reed took the lead in efforts to overcome the depressed conditions. In early 1921 he made a sharp cut in Simpson log prices, forcing other loggers to do the same and stabilizing the market at the lower level. He detested price cutting, but believed that if it was necessary it should be done as rapidly as possible. The episode demonstrated the leadership exerted by Reed in the industry. Demand began to pick up almost immediately, as Reed had anticipated, and the postwar doldrums came to an end.[5]

The lumber market improved considerably in 1922, production for the year matching 1920 levels. Washington lumber payrolls reached record highs in 1923. "With all camps operating," Reed observed, "satisfactory help is getting very scarce and the radical riff-raff help is expensive at any price." Pressure developed on the wage front under these circumstances. "We are facing a problem in the logging end of the game," Reed wrote in April 1922, "which is somewhat disconcerting in that it looks as if we would have to readjust wages upwards within the near future." Still, he speculated, we might "get better results if we increase our wage schedule somewhat." Simpson employees were given an increase in the summer of 1922 to near the wartime level. But the Wobblies were beginning to stir from the ashes of their defeat. "Labor trouble has started," the Loyal Legion of Loggers and Lumbermen warned its corporate sponsors.[6]

Wobbly activity was limited primarily to sabotage and other tactics of the 1917 "strike on the job" variety, since the radicals lacked the strength to call a general walkout. "The I.W.W. have commenced to use quick silver by placing it in locomotive boilers, which puts them out of business in 36 hours," U.S. Marshal Ed Benn reported, advising Reed to "be on your guard." Railroad spikes placed in Simpson logs delivered at the mills were found only after they had severely damaged saws. "It would seem to us that this is a deliberate attempt on the part of the radical employees to make trouble," Reed answered one irate customer. "Very likely this has happened in our camp as they would be more likely to find railroad spikes around there than they would around your mill."

An alarming increase in forest fires took place. J. J. Donovan of the Bloedel-Donovan Lumber Mills, for one, was convinced that "a lot of these fires are incendiary." Donovan described an incident on timberland owned by a man named Moore. The logging engineer had discovered "a man busily engaged in gathering brush and bark to feed this new fire, and when the engineer called to him the answer was a shot, and the man ran." The "devil is still at large," Donovan observed in disgust.

Machinery at the Phoenix Logging Company was damaged, Reed wrote, "under very suspicious circumstances." Simpson camp foremen were ordered to "keep close watch on your equipment and take every precaution to prevent depradation by these agitators." Reed wished to avoid unnecessary alarm, but "to be forewarned is to be forearmed."[7]

The Wobblies attempted a strike in early 1923, but achieved only limited success. Simpson lost about one-fourth of its crew and the Phoenix operations lost nearly half, but only one or two camps in Mason County were forced to halt logging. "The leaders of the IWW," Ed Benn noted, wanted to bring on a large-scale strike, "but do not seem to be making satisfactory headway." Reed agreed, observing that while the "'wobblies' certainly are getting busy," it did not seem "that they are as strong as they were." Much to the relief of the operators, "they do not have so strong a hold on the logging industries in this section as they had in 1917." Still, it was important to keep close watch on the situation, for it would be impossible to avoid all trouble.[8]

Reed kept informed through correspondence with other logging operators, through bulletins from the state Federation of Industries, and through informants within the radical camp.

He also received copies of confidential Justice Department reports from his friend Ed Benn. One such report detailed a series of I.W.W. meetings in Seattle at which Wobbly attorney George Vanderveer and other speakers extolled the "strike on the job" and called for a takeover of American industry by workers. "Never before in the history of Wobblyism in this part of the country," the agent breathlessly recounted, had he heard such "violent and hostile speeches; loud and revolutionary demonstrations, urgent demands for direct action and scornful disregard for law and order of any kind."

Another Justice Department report received by Reed examined the work of a Spanish-American War veteran named Fritiof Werenskjold, described by the government agent as "the main leader among the Scandinavian I.W.W. in Seatle." This gentleman and his cohorts operated the Harmony Singing Society in a house near Lake Washington. There, Werenskjold "shoots his Wobblyism into" his followers. The society presented plays and poetry readings in which the "owners of industries are pictured as bloodthirsty devils who ruin the lives of young women and who for their own gain and profit permit even murder to be committed among the 'wage slaves.'" These performances, the report concluded, amounted to an especially nefarious activity of the Wobblies.[9]

What Reed made of these rather inane accounts is unclear, but he did not respond to the Wobbly situation in the hysterical fashion of many other businessmen. J. J. Donovan, for example, argued that the agitation called for "especially drastic action." He recommended that the state execute those persons convicted of setting forest fires. "Unfortunately," he complained in reference to the Centralia massacre, "in this country ex-soldiers of the war can be shot down in the open streets without anything serious happening to their murderers."[10]

A number of people hoped to take advantage of the situation by pushing schemes cloaked in the legitimacy of patriotism. The Reverend Mark A. Matthews, famed Seattle preacher and foe of liquor and radicalism, urged Reed to install radios in his camps and to help finance broadcasts from the First Presbyterian Church in Seattle so that his men could enjoy "every benefit of the Gospel and of true Americanism." Matthews claimed to be doing his utmost to "counteract the influence of the anarchist, the red socialist, and the communist, and the bolshevist." Reed answered that "groan boxes" (camp terminology for radios) had already been installed and declined to contribute to the reverend's plan.[11]

A more persistent solicitation of funds came from John Anderson of Portland, operator of the somewhat bizarre "Anderson System" or "blue box movement." His work consisted of gathering used magazines deposited in blue boxes on the streets of Portland, Seattle, and Tacoma and shipping them to isolated logging camps. "An agency must exist," he insisted, "that will prevent the men feeding on the vicious literature" of the I.W.W. "and other destructive forces, which must be counteracted." Good reading material would produce in the men "confidence instead of suspicion—love instead of hate—the brotherhood of man—instead of class consciousness." Anderson solicited all the logging operators for contributions, usually after he had shipped magazines to their camps. In this fashion he raised nearly ten thousand dollars yearly during the early 1920s.

Anderson also toured the logging camps, giving religious speeches. In 1922 he made 160 such appearances, "causing 190 people to accept Jesus Christ as their personal savior. By doing so they became fully 100% Americans." In addition, he sponsored a women's chorale group, which gave concerts in the camps. "The ladies in the company have been wonderfully received in the various camps where they have been singing," and the men clamored for return engagements, Anderson claimed.

Reed fumed over the unsolicited shipment of magazines. Although he considered Anderson to be a charlatan, he nevertheless sent an occasional fifty dollars to Portland. Finally, in late 1924, he ordered Anderson to halt his activities in Simpson camps. The company would provide its own reading material, and Reed refused to "be placed under obligation to make any particular contribution without first having knowledge of the obligation that is about to be created." Anderson, however, persisted in his shipments and solicitations. As late as 1929, Reed, now quite exasperated, insisted that Anderson "not make any shipments of literature to our camps. . . . We further do not think it is advisable to make the contribution that you suggest."[12]

While avoiding hysteria and the blandishments of people like Matthews and Anderson, Reed approached the revived problem of labor agitation in the same sensible manner he had exhibited in the previous decade. He continued his efforts to improve the stability of Simpson's work force. "We are trying to do the right thing by our men," he commented, "by giving them the best wages, the best accomodations [sic] and the best 'grub.'" In this fashion they would be less susceptible to the appeal of the Wobblies. "Get an I.W.W. settled down, married and owning a little property," Grant Angle contended, and "he loses his I.W.W. leanings usually."[13]

Reed supported the philosophy of the Loyal Legion of Loggers and Lumbermen that there was a "mutuality of interest as between employer and employee." But he did not care to be associated with the Loyal Legion itself once the wartime emergency was over. There were Four L locals in most of the Simpson camps, but employees were not pressed to join the organization, and participation was not as extensive as in other companies. Reed himself had resigned from the Four L board of directors in 1919, and had gradually reduced Simpson financial support so that by the mid-1920s neither the company nor its employees had much involvement with the Legion. Although believing in the goals of the Legion, Reed did not want any outside interference in the operation of his business affairs. The businessman's right to complete control of decision-making, he believed, was sacrosanct. Besides, there was no need for the reformism of the Legion at Simpson.[14]

There was no need for labor unions, either, although Reed was on friendly terms with conservative state labor leaders and had supported the right of workers to organize. The efforts of Reed, and Sol Simpson before him, to improve working conditions had been designed in part to forestall the development of unionism. These efforts were accelerated in the aftermath of the war, as Reed countered the Wobbly appeal with an effective dosage of paternalism. "Employee-management relations were almost a father and son relationship," William G. Reed recalled.

"The whole organization knew him and had a high degree of personal admiration for him." Employees often brought their personal problems to Reed, seeking his advice. "A choker-setter would come into him and say gee, Mr. Reed, I am having a lot of trouble with my wife and . . . I think maybe she is going out with another guy and I'm thinking about shooting her, what do I do." Reed would dispense his advice and the worker would leave with the satisfaction that his employer sympathized with his difficulties. Reed stressed to his sons and to his subordinates that the company's employees, like the town of Shelton, must be regarded as a community. When possible, job openings were filled by hiring relatives of men already working for the company. "He certainly instilled in me very early the feeling of the oneness of everybody who worked in the company," the younger Reed notes.[15]

Camp conditions continued to be the focus of attention. Steam heat, electric lights, and hot and cold running water were common amenities in Simpson camps, so common that old-fashioned operators complained that Reed was pampering his men. The allegiance of family men was encouraged by construction of schools in the camps and by endeavoring to keep married men at work on maintenance tasks when logging operations were closed down. Simpson's Camp One "is as good a place to live and work as any logging camp I have ever visited," John B. Fitzgerald, editor of the *Four L Bulletin*, observed. "It is a car-camp, equipped with shower baths, running water, electric lights, etc. The food is excellent, [and] there is a good school." A writer for the *Camp and Mill News* reported that "comfortable quarters and good men to work under, together with clean, wholesome food, make this operation a good place to work in." One camp cook was even offered a job as pastry chef at Seattle's exclusive Olympic Hotel.[16]

The Simpson Logging Company also established a group insurance plan for its employees. Depending upon time spent with the company, each worker received up to fifteen hundred dollars' worth of life insurance. In 1920 Reed financed a third of the cost of Shelton's first hospital. Previously, he observed, "it was necessary to take the injured workmen to the hospital in Olympia . . . a hard jaunt for an injured man." But the new hospital's ambulance could run "quickly to the camps and the danger and much of the suffering is eliminated." The hospital was established as a nonprofit corporation, to be managed by a board of directors made up of employer and employee representatives. It meant a major advance in the lives of Simpson employees in particular and Mason County residents in general.[17]

A few Simpson workers charged that these efforts were merely cynical attempts to paper over the fundamentally different interests of management and labor, to in effect make wage slaves of the men. Some readers, too, will find nothing but cynicism in Reed's actions, ignoring his broad vision of society and his commitment to the stability of the local community. Most of Reed's workers appreciated his interest in their welfare, however, and Simpson was known throughout the industry for its loyal "home guard" work force. Reed's policies seemed to have succeeded so well that William G. Reed was "shocked" when unionism came to Simpson in 1934, "as it never occured to me that anybody in the company would think about joining a union. . . . [It was] like having your daughter turn up with a Democratic party button."[18]

In addition to reforming working conditions, Reed resisted the urgings of some lumbermen to return to the old ten-hour day and to cut wages drastically. On this latter point he was seconded by his friend Alex Polson of Hoquiam, a pioneer logger who was alive to the most advanced thinking in the industry. "There is no time in the history of the nation," Polson pointed out, "when there was [sic] more homes being built than there is at the present time . . . and the great reason for it is that labor is getting better wages than was ever known in the history of this land." Polson was convinced that employers "should make every effort to maintain" high wages. This was necessary for the stability of the industry, respecting both its labor force and its markets.[19]

Reed altered other employment practices, however. Since many I.W.W. sympathizers had been hired through Seattle employment agencies, he determined to "leave Seattle alone for a while." Simpson began drawing men from Tacoma, Centralia, and Portland. "We are particularly interested in building up a loyal Americanized crew," Reed informed one Portland employment agent, "and every effort that can be advanced by our employment service to weed out the 'red element' will be more than appreciated." Another Portland agent wrote Reed that, as an American Legion member, "its [sic] against my principals [sic] to even consider sending you a man unwilling to become an American citizen and live up to the American ideas and principals."[20]

The agitators were reputed to be for the most part foreigners, and many believed that the ultimate solution to the problem would be to erect bars against immigration. "There is no room for the alien who comes with hatred for this country and its laws in his heart," the *Four L Bulletin* cried, "his mouth frothing with sedition and his hand filthy with sabotage." For a time Reed seemed to be veering toward this position. "Unfortunately a large percentage of the labor used in our lumbering operations are foreigners," he stated, "and many of them have no intention of ever becoming citizens." Alex Polson agreed, taking the point of view that was becoming predominant among conservatives. Immigrants from southern and eastern Europe, he contended, "are not educated as to the high standards of our principals." They inevitably proved to be "easily led by the red tongued disloyal orator in the disruption of this government, which in turn will close every factory in our land."[21]

But Reed was only voicing his pique, as he continued to uphold the traditional industrial viewpoint that immigrants were a good source of cheap labor. An "ill-advised permanent" restriction of immigration "would be disastrous to our industries, as well as all other industries of the country." There was already a shortage of common labor, and the skilled workers of the future had to be derived from the common labor pool. Therefore, "if the source of the labor supply which we have enjoyed in the past is cut off entirely the situation is liable to go from bad to worst." Advocates of restriction were "just playing into the hands of Sam Gompers," the president of the American Federation of Labor. Foreigners predominated among the radicals, but the solution was to make good Americans out of them, not to keep them out of the country in the first place.[22]

The agitation of 1922 and early 1923 died out and, except for an occasional isolated act of sabotage, the Northwest lumber industry was without further labor disruption until the Great Depression. This development had more to do with the weakness of the I.W.W., which never recovered from its defeat during the war, than with any other factor. "The majority of the men are inclined towards getting a job and staying on it," one correspondent informed Reed in early 1924. "The sympathy which was evident for the 'wobblies' last season at this time, has changed to a disgusted opinion of all that means shut-downs and hardship caused by strikes and striking on the job."[23]

The attitude of much of the industry to labor agitation typified the manner in which most problems were handled. Lumbermen were preoccupied with hysteria and could do little more than muddle about in an ineffective manner, letting the problem more or less take care of itself. They were indecisive, slow to recognize the real causes of their problems and virtually incapable of taking sound steps toward the solution of those problems. Mark Reed was one of the few operators able to grasp reality, avoid emotionalism, and attempt constructive action, however much that action might differ from the time-honored but outdated methods of the industry.

2

Once the immediate postwar slump had passed, conditions in the Northwest became for a time rather prosperous. Washington lumber production increased from five billion feet in 1921 to nearly nine billion in 1922. "Building was suspended during the war period," Reed later recalled, "and it was necessary to catch up." Increased lumber production, of course, meant good times for loggers. Simpson put over 150 million feet of logs in the water each year during the early 1920s. Fir sold for $12, $17, and $24 per thousand feet, depending on grade, and high-quality cedar brought $30 per thousand.[24]

Simpson, as an independent logger, had no formal connections with a mill organization, as the company had had earlier with the Port Blakely Mill Company. Still, Simpson could rely on steady customers because of the quality of its product. "We like your logs better than any logs we get," one mill owner wrote, "and would like to take our supply largely from your camps." In addition, the Simpson Logging Company was a major stockholder in at least two mills—the Clear Fir Lumber

Company of Tacoma and the Buchanan Lumber Company of Olympia (sometimes referred to as the "Reed and Buchanan plant")—which meant that these organizations would normally be steady customers.[25]

Moreover, Simpson had a number of steady arrangements with other mill companies. The Anacortes Box and Lumber Company, for example, contracted in mid-1922 to take all of Simpson's hemlock and maintained this agreement for several years. Simpson was also the main source of supply for the Henry McCleary Timber Company's Olympia sawmill. (This lumber was subsequently returned to neighboring Grays Harbor County for manufacture at the McCleary door factory.) Two or three rafts a month were sent on a regular basis to the Clark-Nickerson mill at Everett.[26]

Because of Simpson's independent status, cooperation with these mills on matters of price and supply was important in order to protect and enhance their competitive positions in the lumber market, thereby assuring a steady demand for logs. On prices Reed noted, "it has always been our policy to look at these questions not alone from the logging standpoint but from the viewpoint of cooperation." It was "to the advantage of both parties" for the logger and the mill owner to cooperate in efforts to place the latter "in a position to go after business in competitive territory." Aside from quality, this was another reason why mill operators liked to do business with Reed, for they were not used to such cooperation on the part of their suppliers. "If the rest of the loggers in the State were as big as you are," one wrote to Reed, "there would be no trouble to solve our economic problems."[27]

Reed was somewhat circumspect in establishing relations with sawmills, since trust was an important factor in such relationships. (Logs were usually sold on credit, with a 2 percent discount for payments made within ten days.) He frequently utilized his banking connections to learn the credit status of prospective customers. On one occasion, for example, he was informed by his friend C. J. Lord, president of the Capital National Bank, that the finances of an Olympia mill were "not in shape to warrant a credit" of the amount proposed. "They have not been quite making both ends meet." The parties to a business agreement must have confidence in each other, Reed believed. Only in this fashion could sound decisions be made in planning for the future.[28]

Despite the general prosperity of the industry and the satisfactory connections he was able to establish with customers, Reed had to deal with a number of frustrating and never-ending business problems—problems that were endemic to the free enterprise system. Log prices, for instance, were kept as high as possible, which meant frequent disputes with purchasing mills, who naturally wanted to keep prices down. Reed's patience was sorely taxed by a series of such disputes with the Anacortes Box and Lumber Company, Simpson's main outlet for hemlock.

"The box market is very stagnant," E. C. Kaune of Anacortes reported in early 1922. He contended that he could run his plant only if the loggers were "willing to follow the market with us" and urged that the price be lowered from the prevailing thirteen dollars a thousand feet. Reed countered that he could get that price from other mills closer to home than Anacortes, "thereby bringing about less expense in the return of our [rafting] equipment." Even at thirteen dollars, there was "absolutely no money" in the selling of hemlock. By the spring of 1924, however, Reed had agreed to reduce the price of hemlock to ten dollars, noting that "it makes us stutter a little bit when we consider fixing such a price on our production."

But this was still not satisfactory to the Anacortes mill. "The box business has gone all to smash," Kaune informed Reed, adding that he could purchase hemlock from other sources at ten dollars delivered in Anacortes, while the cost of towage from Shelton brought the actual cost of Simpson hemlock to $11.35. Reed should therefore reduce his price to nine dollars to enable Anacortes to compete with other mills on Puget Sound and Grays Harbor. Reed agreed with Kaune that this was a difficult situation, as Anacortes could not compete at the old price and Simpson was already losing two dollars a thousand at that price. Reed hoped they could work something out, but "to make a $9.00 price now with no hope of reduction of cost, in fact with increasing cost due to broken weather, seems ruinous."

Reed managed to hold the price at the old level and to

increase it by a dollar in January 1925, planning to raise it to twelve dollars early in the year. Again Kaune balked at this prospect. "The market," he stated, "certainly does not justify that price at the present time" and those mills attempting to sell at that price were unable to do so. By spring he was urging restoration of the old ten dollar price. He asserted that hemlock was available for that price on the Columbia River and Grays Harbor. Mills in those locations were able to sell lumber for eighteen dollars per thousand feet, while Anacortes had to charge an uncompetitive twenty dollars.[29]

A similar procedure marked the two companies' negotiations over the price of cedar for the Anacortes shingle mill. In late 1922 Kaune informed Reed that British Columbia cedar could be purchased for twenty dollars a thousand, while that sum had to be paid at Shelton plus towing cost. Kaune asked for a reduction to equalize the actual cost, but Reed refused. Six months later, though, the latter agreed to a price of eighteen dollars. Kaune insisted that this was "all we can stand and if we get an even break we will be satisfied." As in the case of hemlock, the Anacortes Company was willing to pay a little more for Simpson cedar logs. "We do not like this B.C. Cedar as well as yours," Kaune explained, "and are willing to pay the difference in tow bill. We like your Cedar, because it cuts out."[30]

These continuous negotiations over prices were an ever-present aspect of the logging business. Reed strenuously opposed the efforts of the mills to drive log prices down. "It is all very well," he fumed, "for the sawmill man to say to the logger, you should cut off your timber and sell it at a price that will allow us to run our mill irrespective of the fact that the logger cannot replace the asset, which he has probably worked a lifetime to build up and pay for out of the proceeds from the logs that he is delivering to the mill." The mill owners did not have a comparable investment in their properties and if they "cannot see their way clear to bring about a condition . . . that will reflect at least the cost of production, then they should not expect someone else to keep them operating and pay the losses." Reed found that Simpson could not get a profitable price for its hemlock, and he was coming to the conclusion that the only way of doing so was to cut his own logs in his own mill.[31]

Maintenance of price in the face of mill pleas for reduction was the principal problem confronting Reed, but he also had to deal with a number of other matters. Although Simpson logs were recognized for their high quality, complaints were occasionally received at the Shelton office. "The logs have the appearance of having been down in the woods a long time," Kaune reported of one shipment received at Anacortes, "and I know you will be surprised when I tell you that these . . . Hemlock logs are absolutely no good for anything." They were completely rotten. Kaune requested a credit memorandum "for the full invoice price" plus towage.

Reed responded that the logs were from an area that had experienced a forest fire some years earlier. He had issued orders "not to haul any timber that showed evidence of having been killed long enough to damage it." It seemed, however, that "some of the fire killed timber got into these rafts, perhaps more of it than we think, and we have no doubt that it is to a great extent worthless." Reed suggested that many of the logs might still be usable, but agreed that "any of them that are all wrong or any that you will take a loss on, it is our loss."

Complaints also occasionally were received when quality lumber could not be manufactured from logs or when logs were lost in shipment. "The last raft," Herbert Clough of Clark-Nickerson informed Reed in one instance, "got stuck in the river on account of the dead heads and we had to get the Government snag boat to lift out eight or ten of them and put them on the bank of the river so that the raft could be towed on up the river." These complaints were generally handled in a manner satisfactory to both parties and, aside from the financial loss involved, were only a minor irritation. But they served to encourage a more careful handling of work in the camps and at the boom.[32]

The logger often had complaints about the mills as well. Reed was troubled by the slowness of mills in returning vital boom chains and other rafting equipment. Again, the Anacortes Box and Lumber Company was the main source of discontent, although in this instance the problem was exacerbated by the long haul from Shelton to Anacortes. At times Simpson could not promptly ship rafts to other customers because equipment had not been returned from Anacortes. For this reason, Reed preferred to sell as many logs as possible to Tacoma mills: "A raft is sold to a mill in Tacoma and when the tug comes for the second raft and brings with her the sticks from the first raft, thereby our equipment is kept constantly employed." At least in the Anacortes case complaints proved effective, as that company made a better effort to return equipment. Nevertheless, this remained a vexing problem.[33]

Reed was also occupied with a number of problems in the woods. The Simpson Logging Company continued to be an important purchaser of timberland as its operations gradually moved west. In late 1922, for example, Simpson acquired timberland from the Great Northern Railroad for $335,000 and other land from the western Washington timber operations of Representative Joseph W. Fordney of Michigan, chairman of the House Ways and Means Committee, for $72,000. Fordney, an old friend of Reed's wrote that he was "sorry I do not own more timber to sell to you, for our deals have always been so very pleasant, notwithstanding the fact that you have always bested me a trifle." Some timber was bought for purposes of preemption. When Reed heard that another party was negotiating for timber owned by the Milwaukee Railroad in an area adjacent to Simpson operations, he firmly reminded railroad officials that "we are to have the first right to purchase these lands. [They are] right in the heart of some of our very best timber."[34]

Simpson was becoming a large owner of land, a fact that caused considerable difficulty. The cost of logging was increasing year by year as logging operations moved onto rough ground far from water transport. In the mid-1920s, for example, Simpson had to build the fifth highest railroad bridge in the world in order to reach its timber. "The day forty years ago when you could take two or three yoke of oxen and pull logs in to the shores of Puget Sound or Grays Harbor and elsewhere, is . . . gone by," Alex Polson observed with a twinge of nostalgia. "Now it means railroads, donkey engines, logging cars, booms and tugs and everything else to deliver your logs to the market." As operations moved farther into the hills, however, increased use of modern technology, though initially expensive, became something of an economy device. "The more

of the heavy constructive work that can be done with power,"
Reed noted, "the cheaper the operation will be."[35]

Accident prevention was a major means of cutting costs. In
1921 nearly two thousand serious accidents occurred in the
state's logging industry, over a hundred of them fatal. Studies
indicated that only about a fourth of these accidents were pre-
ventable, but that would still represent a significant advance.
Virtually all accidents meant a disruption of work and a conse-
quent loss of money for both the company and the worker.
Most loggers, though, said Alex Polson, were "babes in reason"
when it came to recognizing this and taking steps to eliminate
safety hazards. "You can't maim or kill a man," Polson insisted,
"that it doesn't cost you as much as to put the automatic
couplers on a whole logging train, to say nothing of five or six
accidents a year." Simpson was an industry leader in promoting
safety through worker education and eliminating the most
egregious hazards to life and limb.[36]

Another problem that plagued loggers was the rapidly
increasing rate of forest fires. Nationally, the number of forest
fires more than doubled during the 1920s, and expenditures on
fire control increased from less than one million dollars in 1920
to over five million in 1930. Residents of the Pacific Northwest,
including lumbermen, had paid scant attention to the fire
menace prior to the twentieth century. Disastrous fires in 1902,
however, coupled with growing interest in conservation produced a new concern over the problem. The Washington state
legislature passed forest protection legislation in 1905. Three
years later, a group of private lumbermen, including Reed and
A. H. Anderson, formed the Washington Forest Fire Association in order to encourage fire prevention and meet the expense
of fighting fires.[37]

The Washington Forest Fire Association became involved, for
instance, in mid-1924, when Simpson timber near the Wynooche River was destroyed by a fire that Reed later contended
had originated in the works of the Donovan-Corkery Logging
Company to the west of the river. Simpson expended ten
thousand dollars in fighting the fire. When Reed approached
William Corkery of the offending company for compensation,
the latter denied any responsibility for the fire. Corkery claimed

that it could not have started in his operation because of precautions that had been taken by the logging crew. Reed was outraged and replied that he had visited the Donovan-Corkery camp and had never before seen such a fire hazard "due to unburned debris of years standing around a logging operation." He turned the whole affair over to the Forest Fire Association, which determined after investigation that Reed's charges were correct. Donovan-Corkery was assessed responsibility for the fire, and Simpson was reimbursed for half the cost of putting it out.[38]

Adding to the frustrations of these problems, the lumber market entered a prolonged priod of depressed conditions in 1924. "Many of the mills have been working two and three shifts," Kaune reported to Reed, "creating a heavy over production of lumber, with the result that the market is now entirely demoralized." The outlook for lumber and therefore the prospects for loggers, Reed noted, "is not very encouraging for the immediate future." This unfortunate prospect resulted, Reed determined after a visit to the East in the late spring of 1924, from "a general slowing down" in all lines of business, a condition that would no doubt prevail until after the fall presidential election. Log prices were reluctantly revised downward to an average of sixteen dollars for fir and ten dollars for hemlock.[39]

At the same time, Simpson's costs had risen. "Since the first of the year," Reed observed, "we have had the highest cost of production that we have had since 1920," due to increased wages and heavy construction expenses. Because these costs could not be reduced the logger could not afford further decreases in his prices. Most loggers reached the conclusion that the only sensible course was to reduce production, a course that seemed to require a significant degree of cooperation among the large number of operators to be successful. This was achieved for a time. Reed informed a trade publication in July 1924 that "from indications there will be a very small production, by the logging camps, during the months of July and August particularly" and that many camps hoped to remain closed down until fall. Mills in the Olympia area at least were "running under a 'slow bell' and it is safe to say that the lumber production for the next few months will be less than it has been over a like period for a number of years."[40]

By September both the cargo and the rail markets seemed to be strengthening. A. A. Scott of the Crown Lumber Company told Reed that mill owners were optimistic, "figuring that good logs were going to be scarce due to the fact that a number of operations were closing down or had been for some time." But as prices began to increase many mills began to run again, often on two or three shifts, to cut lumber for the California and Atlantic Coast markets. "The result," Scott observed in disgust, "is that prices have sagged and the demand is falling off." The market might not recover for some time.[41]

Reed had cut Simpson production in half by the beginning of 1925. "The only thing to do," fellow Mason County logger Thomas Bordeaux insisted, "is to stop logging and milling" until prices were forced up. But the problem, as Bordeaux pointed out, was "to get enough to shut down to do much good." In April the surplus of logs in the waters of the Sound increased by over thirty million feet, while a hundred million feet of lumber was sitting unsold on the California docks. Loggers and mill owners were unable to cope to any significant extent with the problem of overproduction and they continued to find it difficult to do so in the coming years. Reed looked, as 1925 drew to a close, to an extended stretch of bad weather, which would prevent logging, as the best solution: "It would be a blessing to the lumber business if some of the mills would have to shut down for a month or more, due to the lack of good logs." This remained the best hope, despite the strenuous efforts of Reed and others to bring some order to the industry.[42]

Timbermen had confronted most of these problems for years, and perhaps many refused to cope with them because they were part of the normal order of things. Still, a number of operators were coming to realize that loggers and millmen would have to bring about a more efficient operation of their concerns and their industry if they hoped to survive in the twentieth century. Looking to the future, some contemplated with trepidation a new problem that threatened the very survival of the industry itself: Was the natural resource limitless? Washington was supplying 20 percent of the nation's timber in the mid-1920s. "Despite the fact," one historian has written, "that the industry claimed it could supply half as much again if markets could be found to absorb the product, the big problems for the future seemed likely to come from questions of supply rather than demand."[43]

3

The most striking feature of the Northwest industry in the early years of the twentieth century, a lumbermen has recalled, was waste. "Timber was so plentiful! . . . Every lumberman you talked to felt the same. There wasn't one of them who could see the end of the timber." The forests had been pretty well decimated around the Great Lakes, but Northwest stands were so extensive that few could conceive of their exhaustion. "At the present rate of manufacture," a visitor to Washington calculated in 1900, "it would require five hundred years to go over the ground once." The Olympia *Washington Standard* noted that, even if production were greatly accelerated, "there is enough fir in Western Washington without any increase in the growth to last a long way into the 21st century and probably till its close." The future, in other words, would take care of itself, so there was no need to practice conservation.[44]

A new outlook began to prevail during the Progressive Era, with attention focusing on the control of natural resources by large business organizations and stressing the efficient handling of problems at all levels of society. Conservationists had previously concentrated on the preservation of nature unsullied by economic exploitation. Gifford Pinchot and other progressives argued, though, that natural resources should be carefully utilized. Controlled development was essential. Resources must not be depleted but must remain available for future utilization. Everyone stood to benefit from the efficient handling of the nation's heritage. Pinchot, concentrating on forestry, hoped to convince "practical men" in the lumber industry "that questions of forestry are no longer [to be] treated on hazy, sentimental grounds by those who are pushing the subject."[45]

Conservationist sentiment was slow to spread to the Northwest, which still possessed intact most of its vast stands of

timber. "I have not been able to give [the question of reforesta-
tion] much thought or time," George Long wrote Edwin G.
Ames in 1921, "and I question a little whether anybody else
has." The *Nation* commented that Westerners regarded the
Pinchot brand of conservation as "a fussy meddling with the
inalienable right of the West to burn its candle at both ends."
But many timbermen were concerned for the future of the
region, as they confronted three million logged-off acres in
Washington and predictions that the state's virgin timber could
last no more than sixty years. "The last great stand of timber
against the slaughter of the woodsman's axe," the *Mason County
Journal* noted, "is now being made in the Northwest, and in fewer
years than most of us now appreciate the logs that are left to
waste or wantonly burned will be prized as much here as now in
the barren sections."[46]

A great deal of this new outlook in the region reflected the
work of such foresters as David T. Mason and his associate Carl
Stevens, who argued with considerable skill for what Mason
called "the policy of managing . . . lands for permanent timber
production." Management would solve the problem of logged
off lands, and the future of the industry in the Northwest
would thereby be assured. Mark Reed was most receptive to
this approach. "I could see easily enough from my conversation
with you that you had the problem in your mind seriously for a
long time," Stevens, then with the federal government, wrote
Reed after visiting Shelton in 1922. "It is a crime that we in the
Northwest are cutting off this great resource as we are," Reed
believed, "and not bring anything back to this particular territory to replace this asset in a material way." He also noted that
the same thing had happened in other timber regions. "When
you deplete your assets by cutting the green tree and do not
receive a sufficient margin of profit in return, to build up
replacements with proper carrying charges considered, you are
not doing justice to yourself or to the country and people at
large." Lumbermen had so far failed "the trust which has been
reposed in us on behalf of others who are, directly and indirectly, interested in this very important resource of this section
of the country.[47]

But there was a great obstacle to action on these sentiments, one that made conservation of existing timber and reforestation, according to the San Francisco *Chronicle*, "a moot question." That obstacle was the system of taxation then in effect in the state of Washington. Tax levies on land had increased threefold between 1910 and 1920. And the property tax, which fell most heavily on large landowners and particularly on those holding valuable stands of timber, accounted for 70 percent of state revenue. As an example of the increasing burden, Reed described to a special U.S. Senate reforestation committee in 1923 three sections of virgin timber acquired by Simpson in 1906. "The taxes on that land per section in 1906 ran from $167 to $172 a section. In 1921, and it is more now, the tax ran from $3,740 a section to $4,100 a section."

One result of the tax system was that owners were encouraged to cut their timber in order to reduce the tax load. This added to the problem of overproduction and reduced the amount of timber left for future use. High taxation, Reed observed, "intensified a desire on the part of the owner to liquidate and get out from under the tax burden." Standing timber, the *West Coast Lumberman* insisted, was "being taxed to extinction." Conservation, a matter in which the state had a prime interest, was thus militated against by the policy of the state.[48]

Taxation also worked against reforestation, as many years were required for a new stand of trees to reach maturity, and owners would have to pay taxes on those trees all the while. "It is a simple mathematical demonstration," George Long pointed out in a 1909 interview, "that it will not pay the lumber corporation to pay taxes and wait for a new crop of trees on cutover lands." One Western publication remarked that this was a circumstance "Eastern Conservationists will do well to remember . . . whenever they feel inclined to treat all Western objections as the insincere mouthings of grabbers, speculators and monopolists." Lumbermen believed that the state constitution, with its requirement that property be taxed on an equal basis, prevented any serious reforestation efforts. Reed was forced to conclude: "The more I study the reforestation problem the more I am convinced that in the Douglas fir district particularly it is not an undertaking for the individual or private corporation. It is too stupendous a problem and the taxes, interest and fire patrol service would more than offset any compensation to be hoped for through the growth of the timber."⁴⁹

Although recognizing the considerable difficulties, Reed believed that the future of the industry was at stake. "All progressive lumbermen who hope to have a future before their operation," he told David Mason, "must give serious thought to this question" of conserving timber. He did not believe, however, that the prevailing practice of clear-cutting should be abandoned in favor of selective logging. The "high lead" system of logging, utilizing high-speed steam machinery and cables strung from spar trees, made selective logging impracticable. Rather, he was attracted to the theory of sustained yield, or the logging each year of only that amount of timber being replaced by natural regeneration. "Within the next two or three years, Reed wrote Mason in 1927, "we must make a detailed study of our operation with the thought in mind of bringing our production down to the point that would to a great extent carry out the theory and practice of a 'sustained yield.'" But before anything could be accomplished something would have to be done about taxation.⁵⁰

The logged-off land problem, according to state Land Commissioner Clark Savidge, was "the largest unsettled one that our state has before it today." The Simpson Logging Company owned nearly thirty thousand acres of cutover land in Mason and Grays Harbor counties, carrying a tax load described by Reed as "quite a burden." Since under prevailing conditions cutover land could not be held for reforestation, a popular solution was to turn such acreage into farms. An early scheme, developed by Secretary of War Franklin K. Lane during the closing days of the Wilson Administration, would have settled returning war veterans on the lands, a venture urged on Reed by one advocate as the solution to "the logged-off land problem for all time to come." But no soldiers became stump farmers on Simpson land, nor was the plan implemented elsewhere to any significant extent.⁵¹

A number of companies, including Simpson and Weyerhaeuser, attempted to sell land for agricultural purposes. Simpson made land available in forty-acre tracts at prices ranging from three to ten dollars an acre. "We are not offering these lands to promoters or speculators but to actual settlers," Reed informed one prospective buyer. "Some of these lands are very good for logged off lands but, as you know, any logged off land means a very considerable amount of good hard work to clear out the stumps." This factor no doubt largely accounted for the failure of these selling efforts. "We had hopes for selling much of our land," Long told Reed in explaining their mutual experience, "and yet I think we all realize that 75% of the land that is now being denuded will not be used or cannot be used economically for agricultural purposes." Some other solution, then, would have to be found.[52]

Rather than continue to pay taxes, many logging companies simply let their land revert to the county once the timber had been removed. One hundred thousand acres had been disposed of in this fashion in western Washington. But Simpson, Weyerhaeuser, and a number of other firms refused to take this easy route to disposing of their tax burden. George Drake, for many years Simpson's chief forester, speculated that "unconsciously . . . they had faith in the land." William G. Reed suggests that "they may have reasoned that if they let the land go for taxes, the company would have to make up for it in tax monies in some other way."

Mark Reed himself stated that "we have some pride in not seeing property standing in our name go delinquent." He told the Senate reforestation committee that "a man hates to see his property advertised for taxes, and he naturally strains every effort to carry it along, although it is a constantly increasing burden." Moreover, Reed had a genuine interest in the stability of Mason County and, as the largest property owner in the area, recognized the county's dependence on Simpson for revenue. "In a great many of the counties of Western Washington," he explained, "timber is the principal source of revenue for taxation purposes and if this source should be limited to any great extent . . . it would be rather troublesome to find the ways and means for carrying on government."[53]

The assessment and collection of this revenue, however, was a considerable source of irritation. The assessor in each county was responsible for property assessments upon which tax collections were based. Property valuations thus were subject to the whim of local officials, a situation that resulted in frequent complaints about varying rates of assessment from property to property and county to county. Favoritism was often charged. "Our present system of allowing the final say as to value of property to thirty-nine assessors in as many counties," Reed contended, "is, in my judgment, all wrong. Too much property is escaping taxation altogether, and too much is being listed far below the 50 per cent value fixed by law." Since timberland was the principal object of taxation in many western Washington counties, lumbermen were vitally concerned with assessment problems. A third of Mason County's revenue, for example, came from standing timber, and the portion in other counties was as high as 50 percent.[54]

Reed found little to complain about in Mason County. The Simpson Logging Company and its various affiliated concerns were the largest taxpayers in the county, providing in 1929 some $100,000 of the county's total tax levy of $450,000. As the most important citizen in the area, however, Reed was usually able to persuade the assessor to readjust assessments he felt were unfair. He would "just go in and make the best deal he could with the assessor," William G. Reed recalls. "I feel that our taxes have been more reasonable than they are in the other counties," the elder Reed said. When other timber owners urged him to support their protests to the assessor and the equalization board, he refused. He was also satisfied with the situation in Jefferson County to the north, where his politically powerful friend Ed Sims could be counted on to exercise his local influence on behalf of the company.[55]

But the situation in neighboring Grays Harbor County was, according to Reed, "simply . . . outrageous." He claimed that tax officials there "have a special spite against us, apparently because we are not delivering our logs into Grays Harbor." Reed engaged in a number of disputes with the county over taxes, some of which were settled in his favor by the state supreme court. Most of these arguments revolved around assessments made by longtime assessor R. A. Wiley. "He seems to be obsessed," Reed wrote of Wiley, "with the idea that about the most assured way of maintaining political prestige is to throw the burden of taxation on industry and allow the freeing of the smaller taxpayer from taxation to a great extent." The assessor's valuations, Reed further contended, were based upon inaccurate cruises. And he assessed logged-off lands at "from 25% to 100% more than can be obtained for them on the market."[56]

In a case filed in 1922, Grays Harbor County argued that a particular stand of Simpson timber was increasing in value. The company countered with the claim that the timber was "ripe, mature and no longer increasing in amount." Simpson won the case when Dean Hugo Winkenwerder of the University of Washington forestry school, Minot Davis of Weyerhaeuser, and four other expert witnesses testified to the validity of its claim.

Reed insisted on working through the courts in these matters, avoiding the paying of bribes that could mark such tax cases. In the 1922 dispute, for example, a Grays Harbor politician offered to help settle Simpson's assessment problems in return for support of his campaign for county prosecutor. Reed rejected this offer, but he did attempt to utilize political influence against Grays Harbor officials. "We are very much interested in having as many of your men vote as can," he informed camp foremen in the county, "who will vote right, and for our mutual interests." Employees should not be coerced into voting for the company's slate of approved candidates, but "we feel fully justified in saying that it is in the respective interests of ourselves as well as to our employees, that we give particular attention to these officers and centralize our vote as indicated." This particular effort appears to have succeeded, as an assessor more acceptable to the company was elected in place of Wiley in 1922.[57]

Reed and other independent loggers were confronted, then, with traditional logging problems, dwindling supplies of timber and increasing burdens of taxation. Their livelihood was dependent on forces over which they could exercise little influence. And, laboring under an archaic system of taxation, they were destroying their investments without gaining an acceptable return. In short, they could not control their situation, they could not rationalize their operations. These factors influenced Reed's decision to get into the production of lumber.

4

Mark Reed's plans to build a sawmill were motivated in particular by the increasing stands of hemlock encountered by the company as it worked its way inland from tidewater to the foothills of the Olympics. Hemlock had traditionally been considered, according to Chris Kreienbaum, who became manager of Reed's mill interests, a "weed tree" and "would just be burned up in the fires after logging." One observer noted that when milled, hemlock, which was little in demand, would be "used only in the manufacture of a coarse lumber." More often, though, it would simply be rejected by the mill if a logger attempted to ship some along with his Douglas fir. Reed explained to Secretary of Commerce Herbert Hoover in 1926 that "its name of hemlock acted to prejudice the prospective purchaser against it, due to the fact that it was thought to be the same as the eastern or Pennsylvania hemlock. It is a different wood entirely and a much better wood than the eastern hemlock."[58]

Operators found that 20 percent or more of their timber consisted of hemlock. But the Puget Sound market could not absorb the available hemlock logs at an acceptable price. "We were also leaving a considerable proportion of our hemlock timber in the woods," Reed noted. For several years, he told a Weyerhaeuser official in 1924, Simpson had been deliberating on how to handle the increasing output of hemlock. "Always to the forefront in the consideration was the possibility that a milling operation would be the only solution."

Alex Polson had pioneered in the development of a strictly hemlock mill with his operation on Grays Harbor. Now in 1924 Reed planned to build such a mill at Shelton, and Weyerhaeuser was building one at Everett. Reed hoped that these two mills would "have a stabilizing influence on the price of hemlock" on Puget Sound. "In any event," he said, "I am tired of having our hemlock production, which of course must be kept moving, forced to a point below cost of production every time there is an indication of a slackening of demand." If prices were low, the logs could still be cut and the new mill could simply "pile up a few million feet" until prices improved. Thus, by building a mill,

Reed could utilize more effectively a large portion of his timber and could influence the market to a significant extent.⁵⁹

He could also hope to make a considerable profit by shipping lumber to Japan. That country, where wood was the prime construction material and the native timber supply was largely exhausted, had become the principal export market for Northwest lumber after World War I. As early as 1918 it was, according to A. A. Baxter, general manager of the Douglas Fir Exploitation and Export Company, "impossible to supply the present [Japanese] demand . . . from Puget Sound mills." Reed was interested in exploiting this demand, as were many other lumbermen. "Every operator in this country," remarked Everett Griggs of the St. Paul and Tacoma Lumber Company, "is interested in the development of the lumber market in Japan." Reed planned to ship across the Pacific much of the lumber cut in his mill.⁶⁰

The community of Shelton would also benefit from a mill. A Forest Service study of western Washington indicated that those towns totally dependent on logging could not prosper over a long period of time. Newspaper publisher Grant Angle pointed out that Shelton had never suffered severe economic dislocation, but also "never gets very high when things are flourishing elsewhere, becuase it only gets one 'crack' at the logs which shoot through to the extent of millions of feet every year." On the other hand, if a mill was established in the town, "the local payroll would be increased several times and the town and its people [would] reach 'high C' occasionally instead of being just normal 'when the logs come down.'"⁶¹

Mark Reed had chosen to remain in Shelton even though Simpson maintained an office in Seattle, preferring the security and pace of small town life. "The small town," he believed, "offers a more diversified life, a more diversified experience. The person who ridicules a small town simply stamps himself as small." As we have seen, Reed viewed the town and its inhabitants with a paternalistic eye. He had, one associate has noted, "a lot of dedication to the community in which he lived." The elegant colonial mansion built by Reed in 1920 reflected the permanence of his attachment to Shelton.⁶²

Irene Reed did not share her husband's affection for the

town. She had been active socially in Seattle prior to her marriage and had reached an understanding with Mark in 1901 that they would remain in Shelton only until the company was liquidated, and then reside permanently in Seattle. This understanding collapsed when her husband decided to make Simpson a permanent operation. Irene had a difficult time adjusting to life in the small town. "She became rather withdrawn," her youngest son notes, and "she was not active socially, which was a difficult sort of thing for her." She did not wear fashionable clothing in Shelton for fear of arousing the jealousy of the townspeople. Irene compensated for the relative loneliness of her life by keeping a number of local girls about the house as maids and by close supervision of the activities of her sons. She also found an outlet in educational activities, serving for many years as chairman of the local school board, a postion that reflected her standing in the community. "It was the kind of feeling that if anybody voted against her in the school election," her son comments, "why he'd just be tarred and feathered." In 1922 Reed recognized his wife's interest in education by donating the land and building for a new town high school, with the proviso that it be named the Irene S. Reed High School.[63]

Reed's plans also took into consideration the future of his sons. Sol, Frank, and Will were all sent to the Culver Military Academy in Indiana, their father recalling his own influential exposure to military discipline, and then to the University of Washington. Reed regarded his sons with affection and hoped to turn over a successful operation to them upon his retirement. "They are young, enthusiastic and at times too quick on the trigger," he wrote of the three boys, adding that he was "trying to iron out these shortcomings, if they are shortcomings, and as time goes on, I have hopes that they will fully rise to their responsibilities." The destiny of the Reed family seemed to be closely linked with that of Shelton.[64]

"It is worth while," Reed later wrote, "to look back over the past and feel that you have really accomplished something constructive for your community." He told another correspondent that he had worked to develop Shelton "slowly and effectively, paving our way as we went along." The people of Shelton, in turn, regarded Reed with respect and affection. It is "a rather rare and very fine thing," Clark Savidge commented, "to find a community that appreciates a fellow citizen as your community does you." The *Mason County Journal* observed that "Shelton has been good to Mark Reed and conversely Mark Reed has been good to Shelton." Despite his business and political success, he had "never grown 'too big' for the little town which has been the family home and the center of his successes, nor has he lost pride in making his surroundings better for himself and the people around him."[65]

Reed's concerns were subsumed in a general desire to bring a greater efficiency to the company's operations, a desire that reflected a general trend in American life during the first decades of the twentieth century. Everywhere the tendency was toward larger and more coherent, centralized organization. Reed's own search for order was meant to perfect a rational handling of the Simpson Logging Company and its affiliates and to bring about a more stable market structure. This did not mean that Reed was a theorist, or that he was influenced by advocates of scientific management. Instead, he made decisions on the basis of what he called "common sense" observations. "He was a seat-of-the-pants operator," William G. Reed remembers. "He didn't use time studies, professional consultants, and such." The elder Reed "ran the company by knowing it thoroughly and making decisions on the ground, rather than as a result of studying written reports." This approach, though, was sufficient to bring about a major development in the history of Simpson and of Shelton.[66]

On 25 April 1924 the *Mason County Journal* announced in a banner headline that "Two Big Mills" were going to be erected on the south side of Shelton harbor. The plans, which had been three years in the making, had "been conceived and worked out in detail almost entirely by Mark E. Reed." The Reed Mill would have a daily capacity of 150,000 feet of hemlock lumber. Adjoining this structure, Henry McCleary, owner of the door plant and company town of McCleary to the west of Shelton in Grays Harbor County, was going to construct a sawmill with a capacity of three hundred thousand feet of Douglas-fir lumber a day. An electric plant, owned jointly by the Reed and McCleary companies, would supply power for both mills and be fueled by their waste material. (The plant would also provide current for distribution to area residents by the West Coast Power Company.)

An estimated one million dollars was to be expended on construction of the mills and the dredging and filling of the mudflats in front of the town, where they were to be built. "Each of the mills," the *Journal* reported, "will be modern in every respect, with labor saving machinery all electrically equipped, and besides being model plants will be planned for future extension and convenience of handling the output by both rail and water." Construction of a second Reed Mill to handle cedar was anticipated, and Reed hoped to add a pulp mill to the complex as well.[67]

When asked if he intended to refine his mill product Reed answered that he did not plan to do so. "We will cut this lumber," he observed, "and ship it with as little expense after it leaves the saw as possible." If the lumber was refined the Reed Mill might be forced into direct competition with such giants as Weyerhaeuser and Long-Bell and require considerable expenditure. In such a situation the mill would find it "very difficult . . . to make a satisfactory showing." Reed did not wish to make such an attempt. His primary goal was efficiency in his overall operations, not competition with the large lumber companies.[68]

Reed also succeeded in acquiring railroad connections for Shelton when the Northern Pacific announced in June 1924 that it would extend its tracks to the town. Negotiations with a number of roads had been going on for some time, but the best that had previously been obtained was terminal rates at Olympia. With the coming of the Northern Pacific tracks, though, the new mill would be able to ship lumber direct to the Midwest. "Hampered in its progress in the past by being out of the line of transportation," Grant Angle exulted, "Shelton now has the last flaw to its otherwise faultless location removed, and the last doubt of its most promising future."[69]

One element in Reed's plan remained to be implemented: establishment of a pulp mill alongside the Reed and McCleary plants. U.S. paper consumption doubled between 1914 and 1925, and the manufacture of paper from wood pulp became a major industry in western Washington. "I feel confident," Reed observed, "that the pulpwood industry is going to be a very important factor in the development of the Northwest in years to come." A pulp mill would allow for a maximum utilization of material by the use of wood chips from the Reed and McCleary operations. "If this industry could be successfully operated on the waste material from our lumbering operations," Reed pointed out, we would be "bringing about real conservation."[70]

In January 1926 the Reed Mill contracted with the Washington Pulp and Paper Company of Port Angeles to supply that mill with chips. This concern was managed by Edward M. Mills of San Francisco on behalf of the Zellerbach interests. After chipping at the sawmill, the wood was loaded on lighters and towed to Port Angeles. "This arrangement," Reed wrote, "is somewhat of an innovation in the paper industry of the Northwest, but it is the thot [sic] of all that it is a workable plan and if it is, it is our thot that other similar installations will be made for the handling of this waste material." But this was just an interim arrangement.[71]

The *Mason County Journal* announced in late May 1926, again in a banner headline, that a sulphite pulp mill would be built in Shelton by Mills and the Zellerbachs. Named the Rainier Pulp and Paper Company, the mill would turn out pulp for use in the manufacture of writing and book paper. The *Journal* informed its readers that the announcement "marks another step in the plans conceived by Mark E. Reed some years ago and worked toward until the many obstacles were overcome." Again, this venture represented a breakthrough in the industry. "All attempts made so far to use a large percentage of sawmill waste in the manufacture of sulphite," Mills reminded Reed, "have been failures and have been abandoned." But the combination of new technology and increasing demand would make the Rainier mill a success.[72]

Reed and his associates owned over a hundred thousand dollars worth of stock in the pulp mill, a sound investment because of the mill's impact on Simpson's overall operations. "Practically all the entire waste product," Reed informed a Forest Service official, "that is suitable either for pulp or for generating electrical energy and steam will be utilized from all of these mills." And the pulp mill would send crews onto

Simpson timberlands to cut cordwood from trees that previously had been excluded from logging. The mill complex, moreover, provided a prime example of the benefits of practical conservation. "The power and value of what the nation is wasting," Grant Angle commented, "cannot be better illustrated than in the events under way in Shelton in which a mammoth industry to cost ultimately several million dollars, is to be founded solely on material which for a generation has drifted [through] this single community to the sea and been swallowed up in waste."[73]

All components of the Shelton mill complex were in operation by mid-1927. The Reed Mill had already been running for over a year and had, remarked Reed, achieved a degree of efficiency "equalled by but very few mills in the Northwest." Efficiency was further increased when the Rainier Mill began to operate. "The beauty [sic] part of it is," Reed noted, "that we are utilizing every inch of sound wood that comes into the mill and we are taking at least 20% more material off the ground than we were before we had the pulp mill." (Forest Service studies indicated that 30 to 40 percent of each tree was left in the woods and wasted by standard logging methods.) Selling chips to Rainier, moreover, helped "very materially to bring about an even break of the sawmill operation." "Taking it all and all," he was convinced, "it makes a very satisfactory operation."[74]

The mills also brought a new degree of stability to Shelton, assuring the future of the town at a time when other communities totally dependent on logging were slowly falling apart. A thousand men worked for the Reed, McCleary and Rainier mills, an addition to the work force that helped increase the town's population to nearly four thousand. During the 1920s, while Washington's population increased by fifteen per cent, Mason County's doubled, representing the second highest increase among the state's counties.[75]

Reed had brought a good deal of order out of the traditional chaos of the logging industry. By mid-decade, he had provided company-owned mill facilities for Simpson logs that could not be sold profitably on the market. Thereby, he could expect to secure a better rate of return for the logging company. And he could expect, as well, a more rational and forward-looking utilization of Simpson's timber holdings. Additionally, he had furthered the advantages of Shelton as a worthwhile place to live and work.

Reed looked to the future with optimism, believing that his Shelton industrial complex would bring a new prosperity to the company and the community, especially as Calvin Coolidge, the prophet of business advancement, was firmly ensconced in the White House. Reed was not alone in his optimism. "The situation in the country," Supreme Court Chief Justice William Howard Taft wrote to his friend Sam Perkins of Tacoma, "seems to be as good as we could expect it to be. . . . Business on the whole is good and the people are fortunate in having a man at the helm who is not disposed to interfere in any way with the even flow of events, and is striving to let the people work out for themselves the prosperity they deserve."[76] The industrial East lunged onward and upward for several years more before collapsing into the Great Depression. But in the mills and forests of the Northwest, the optimistic outlook proved to be short-lived. Mark Reed, far from standing on the threshold of new and greater success, was about to enter a time of troubles, both in politics and in business.

CHAPTER 3

The Man Who Would Not
Be Governor

The Republican party dominated Washington politics during the four decades following the achievement of statehood in 1889. "This is a republican state," the *Mason County Journal* proudly proclaimed.[1] In what amounted to a one-party state, political conflict took place within the sometimes fractious confines of the Grand Old Party. Tacoma and Seattle Republicans fought for control of the state party organization, while rural and urban Republicans battled over the right to direct policy in Olympia. Mark Reed, with his reputation for integrity, his stance as a conservative reformer, his business and personal ties in both Seattle and Tacoma, and his popularity in rural areas west of the Cascades, was the one party figure able to unite the Republican factions behind his leadership. During the early 1920s, he was the dominant figure in state politics and the most influential person in state government. Had he wished to run for governor, he would have been elected to the office with ease.

1

Olympia had changed considerably since Reed's birth there in 1866. Then, legislators had met in a cramped and drafty wooden building. By the 1920s they had held sessions for many years in an ornate Victorian structure that had previously been the Thurston County courthouse, and the massive marble edifice that would take its place was beginning to rise on the hill overlooking the town. But politics was no longer Olympia's sole reason for being. "Time was when sessions were the principal local topic of discussion," one long-time capital observer noted. "We lived on them, and just existed between the gatherings."

Now, the periodic arrival of the legislators meant the disruption of the normal course of business and made it impossible for out-of town visitors to secure hotel accommodations. "We rather dread the coming of the legislature," the disenchanted commentator continued, "and welcome their departure."[2]

As the principal figure in the state house of representatives and the strongest backer of Governor Louis F. Hart, Mark Reed dominated the Olympia political scene in the first half of the twenties. A Tacoma attorney and fervent joiner of fraternal organizations, Hart had become lieutenant governor in 1912 in his first venture into elective politics. He succeeded to the governorship upon the death of Ernest Lister in 1919 and won election to the office in 1920. Hart suffered from diabetes, a condition that helped induce a rather lethargic personality. His political success owed more to good fortune, especially the death of his predecessor, than to any great ambition or ability. Hart was a competent administrator, but lacked a thorough grounding in the issues of importance to the state and was rather unsure of himself. As a result, he tended to defer to stronger and more experienced men like Reed. The Shelton lumberman was seen both by supporters and by opponents of the Hart Administration as the power behind the governor, the principal source of advice on issues and patronage. Reed thus added substantially to the political influence he had already amassed as the spokesman for business and the dominant figure in the house committee system.

Along with Senators P. H. Carlyon of Olympia and Edward L. French of Vancouver and state Land Commissioner Clark Savidge, Reed ran the state Republican party in the name of Governor Hart. Tacoma Republicans, led by Hart, had allied themselves with rural Republicans in the southwestern and eastern sections of the state in what was known as the "cow county" alliance, controlling the state party machinery to the exclusion of Seattle and King County. Seattle had long since surpassed Tacoma in terms of population and economic power, and Seattle's Republicans felt they deserved the leading voice in state politics. Seattle's efforts to wrest party control from Tacoma, a quest that often deteriorated to petty squabbles over the proper name for Mt. Rainier or the correct point of embar-

kation for President Warren G. Harding on his 1923 trip to
Alaska, lay behind much of the Olympian struggle of the
period.[3]

Although Reed has often been linked with the Hart-cow
county machine, he was actually not of it, standing instead as
the major figure of unity in the party. He liked to spend summer
weekends riding horseback on the prairies near Tacoma with
such friends as banker Sam Jackson and had many important
connections in the city on Commencement Bay. But he was not
unpopular in Seattle, where most of his financial interests were
located, and where he spent a good deal of time looking after
business and visiting his sons at the University of Washington.
"He was more a Seattle man than he ever was a Tacoma man,"
one associate has recalled. Reed always avoided the appearance
of taking sides in the struggle between Tacoma and Seattle, and
was the one political leader acceptable to both sides.[4]

His position as a party unifier was enhanced by his success in
avoiding public involvement in the debate over prohibition, the
most emotional issue dividing urban and rural Washingtonians.
Reed maintained a cache of whiskey in his Shelton home and
delighted in swapping stories with friends over bourbon and
water. Moreover, he viewed the "noble experiment" with some
trepidation. Liquor could still be obtained by even the margin-
ally resourceful, but its acquisition required a panoply of
rumrunners, speakeasies, and corrupt police officers and public
officials. "No one that I know of," Reed wrote privately, "is in
favor of the return to the old saloon days but in some partic-
ulars, the present situation is even much worse." Prohibition,
he argued, was "the greatest disturbing factor that we have in
our civil life today. It is responsible to a great extent for our
orgy of crime and the almost universal sentiment of disrespect
for law." Despite such personal sentiments, however, Reed
refused to come out publicly against prohibition, recognizing
the damage that this would do to his political standing.[5]

Within the legislature, Reed's influence was aided by his
reputation for fairness and integrity. "There are legislators in
whom most of the members have confidence," political writer
J. H. Brown noted of Reed. "If he supports a bill they will follow
his lead blindly and usually they are right." Reed was one of the

few members to inspire such confidence. He "wins his following," explained a fellow legislator, Maude Sweetman of Seattle,
"by the qualities of his personality, drawing men and women in
their weakness to the protection of his strength." Reed relied on
his personal standing and on his control of the committee
system to dominate the course of business. The Seattle *Argus*
commented in 1921 that the legislature might as well appoint
Reed and two other members "a committee of three to fix up
some new laws, and then go home. Give them a week and then
come back and ratify what they have done." His standing was
such that he rarely had to resort to pressure tactics to get his
way.[6]

Little pressure would be required in the legislature that
convened in January 1921, considering the usual huge Republican majorities. The senate and house each contained only one
Democrat, while two members of the Farmer-Labor party sat in
the latter and one in the former. Moreover, a strong consensus
existed on the principal problem to be dealt with: the state's
rapidly increasing rate of taxation. State tax levies had nearly
tripled since 1910. Taxes levied for all purposes—state, county,
and municipal—had increased from $43 million in 1917 to $72
million in 1920. "The limit to the public purse may not yet have
been reached," the *Seattle Times* contended, "but it is certain that
the limit speedily will be reached unless all appropriating bodies
favor the closest economy consistent with efficiency and faith-
fully practice this policy."[7]

The state's property owners, Reed believed, could no longer
afford to carry the burden. Taxes were discouraging business
and preventing proper management of Washington's timberland. The people had to curb their desire for ever increasing
government services so that expenditures could be reduced and
the tax load lessened. Only by doing so could a healthy economic future for the state be assured. Reed's concern with taxes
motivated much of his political activity in the 1920s.

He wrote lumberman J. H. Bloedel that the tax problem
resulted from the fact that "during the war our natural ten-
dency toward what might be termed unnecessary expenditures
was greatly accelerated, and since that war period we do not
seem to be able to get over the idea that we must have every

facility for the advancement of our particular pet ideas." Some
called for new taxes, usually an income tax, to meet the rising
cost of government and relieve the burden on property. But this
would not reduce expenditures and would place an additional
load on business. "The more sources of revenue you have,"
Reed argued, "the more money our disbursing officers will
spend." What was needed was to bring government under
control, to force it to operate in a more efficient manner. This
policy would lead to achievement of a goal which was simply, as
Alex Polson put it, "to quit spending so much money."[8]

State agencies could be created at will by the legislature and
once established were rarely abolished, regardless of whether or
not they performed useful work. Several agencies might
perform the same task, or some might perform no task at all.
Various interest groups usually had a stake in particular offices
and would fight for their preservation. Legislators were also
alive to the political possibilities that went with the creation of
offices and the expenditure of funds. Too many members, Reed
pointed out, were determined to "spend as much money as they
can in their districts so that they can go back to their constituents and say, 'See what I have brought home in my basket for
you.'" The state bureaucracy was the obvious target of
economizers.[9]

Governor Hart, following the lead of several other states,
had appointed a committee to study the reorganization of state
government. Early in the 1921 session he presented the committee's recommendations to the legislature. The plan called for
the gathering of state agencies into ten departments, whose
heads would be appointed by the governor. In this fashion
duplication would be eliminated, the governor would exercise
direct control over the bureaucracy and, as a hoped-for result,
expenses would be cut and the tax burden lightened. "The great
economy," Hart informed a fellow governor, "is in the greater
efficiency and businesslike method of transacting public
business as one would handle his private affairs." According to
the *Seattle Post-Intelligencer*, "no more progressive and promising
piece of legislation has ever been proposed for the State of
Washington."[10]

Reed was given the responsibility of securing passage of the proposed administrative code in the house, serving as chairman of a special panel of all committee chairmen. The state was "the largest and most intricate business we have" and should be managed accordingly, he argued. Exercising tight control over the measure, Reed allowed only one amendment, a clause he introduced upgrading the role of the state fisheries board. (The politically influential Ed Sims, Reed's long-time friend, and other leaders of the fishing industry feared the subservience of the fisheries board to the code's fisheries and game director. As a result of the amendment the fisheries board, chaired by Sims, became one of the most powerful bodies in state government.)

The code passed the house 89-5 with little debate as a result of Reed's management. "I was to some extent responsible for the passing of the bill," he later recalled. It passed the senate with the addition of amendments exempting the state's colleges from executive control over salaries and capital expenditures. Once in effect, the code achieved a more efficient handling of state money. By 1925 the state had a general fund surplus of over four million dollars, compared to a one million dollar deficit in 1921, and state tax levies had been reduced significantly.[11]

The code provisions dealing with the state's industrial insurance system were of particular interest to Reed. Most lumbermen accepted workmen's compensation and the other labor legislation of the previous decade, but many were dissatisfied with the performance of the various commissions and with the presence of labor representatives on these boards. They charged that administration was lax, that improper payments were made to injured workmen, and that unqualified doctors were relied upon for medical diagnoses. "It is very manifest," Everett banker and lumberman William C. Butler wrote Edwin G. Ames, "that under political administration, the Act is being prostituted and overburdened with claims of doubtful propriety."[12]

Reed noted that he had kept the Industrial Insurance Department "largely in mind while giving consideration to this proposed [administrative reform] legislation." He hoped to bring about a more efficient administration of the department, thereby reducing the contributions of employers, and to head off a movement to junk workmen's compensation entirely. J. J.

Donovan informed Reed that the Bloedel-Donovan Lumber Mills had paid forty thousand dollars into the insurance and medical funds in 1920, payments that "made us sit up and take notice and wonder whether in insurance we had better not permit old line casualty companies to come back."[13]

Despite the opposition of the State Federation of Labor, the code centralized administration of the labor laws in the Department of Labor and Industries and eliminated labor representation. Under Hart's appointed director, Edward Clifford, the department won the approbation of lumbermen. One wrote that the department was "in the hands of a thoroly [sic] competent man." Another commended "a more businesslike administration, more efficiency in management, and, what is more to the point, a determination to reduce as much as possible the heretofore increasing cost of Industrial Insurance and its allied branches." Reed argued that this increased efficiency was "due to the fact that the dual management has been done away with under the administrative code." Labor complained, but Reed had again demonstrated his concept of balanced interests. The abuses in the system had been corrected, he believed, employers were given fairer treatment, and injured workers retained the benefits of the state's compensation and insurance monopoly.[14]

One other measure in the 1921 session was designed to relieve the tax load on property owners. The poll tax, an annual levy of five dollars on all persons between the ages of 21 and 50, was instituted by the legislature at Reed's instigation. The money obtained would go into the soldiers' bonus fund approved by the voters in 1920 and into the general fund as well. The burden of supporting the government, argued advocates of the tax, would be extended to those previously avoiding taxes. Reed claimed that he was "a firm believer in the theory that every person over 21 years of age receiving the protection of our laws should contribute something towards the cost of government." The revenue obtained, Governor Hart declared, would allow the state to relieve those who paid property taxes, thereby encouraging the ownership of homes. "A lack of home and home environment," he contended, "has more to do with the encouraging of the spirit of Bolshevism in the country than any other one thing."[15]

The tax was highly controversial, despite the governor's assertion that only the person "who stands around on the street corner and cusses the Government" was foolish enough to attack the tax. The measure was regressive, collection was erratic and, more importantly, its unpopularity could well redound against the G.O.P. in the 1922 elections. Reed changed his mind as a result of the tax's reception and urged Republicans to support its repeal. The tax had only been an emergency measure, he informed party leaders, so the voters should simply be informed "that [the] emergency has passed." The electorate needed no urging and the poll tax was repealed by a three-to-one margin at the polls in 1922. The difficulty of altering the tax structure was, not for the first and certainly not for the last time, demonstrated by the episode.[16]

The one major issue of the 1921 session that did not involve taxes showed Reed to be more realistic than most of his colleagues and demonstrated that he could not always get his way. The postwar years had witnessed a resurgence of anti-Orientalism on the West Coast, focusing on the Japanese—this despite the fact that only about 1 percent of the residents of Washington were Japanese. The American Legion and other self styled patriotic groups railed against what they believed to be "the menace of Japanese colonization." Ultimately this sorry display of bigotry and ignorance led to introduction of a measure prohibiting ownership or control of land by aliens not intending to become American citizens. (Asians were barred from naturalization by federal law.) Lands owned by such persons were to be taken over by the state, which in turn would presumably sell them to acceptable white purchasers.[17]

Reed led the fight to dispose of the alien land bill. Planning to enter the Japanese lumber market, he feared the bill's impact on trade with Japan, as did most trade-oriented businessmen. Recognizing the popularity of the measure, as well as the futility of speaking out against prejudice, Reed urged that its consideration be indefinitely postponed in the national interest. "I hold no brief for the Japanese," he claimed, "and I do not believe in the free and unlimited admission of Orientals to this country, nor do I believe that they should be permitted to hold real estate here." Nevertheless, a new Republican administration would soon be in office, and President-elect Warren Harding was said to be giving the land ownership problem "his most serious consideration." Therefore, Reed concluded, the legislature should await action from the nation's capital.[18]

This strategy failed, and the house passed the alien land bill 71-19, with Reed voting in the negative. The Seattle *Argus* crowed that the passage had come "in spite of the efforts of Mark Reed, who has seemed to feel as though he had that body in such shape that he could do all kinds of stunts with it." The supposedly sophisticated Seattle publication continued that if the Japanese did not care for the law, "they know what they can do about it." The *Argus*, moreover, denied that the bill would harm Puget Sound exports. "We can get along without them a great deal better then they can get along without us." The bill was passed by the senate and enthusiastically approved by Governor Hart, who showed that he was not always subservient to Reed.[19]

Following the session most observers assumed that Reed would be chosen speaker of the house in 1923. (Reed held the speakership only once, since that position was rotated from session to session.) Reed professed reluctance to run for another term in the legislature, apparently wishing to appear to be drafted for the speakership. Legislators from throughout the state pledged their support for his candidacy for speaker if he would agree to run again. In late November 1922 he announced in Seattle that he would run for the speakership, pledging a "square deal for all members and for lower state taxes." He had the support of sixty-eight to seventy of the eighty-five Republican members, he told reporters, and had ceased to "count noses" in the race.[20]

A brief revolt flared when the legislators assembled in Olympia in early January 1923. Representative Thomas Murphine of Seattle, backed by a coalition of progressive Republicans and the three Farmer-Laborites, indicated that he would challenge Reed in an effort to win a greater role for the newer members. Reed agreed to rule that a majority of the members could place a bill on the calendar for floor action, apparently decreasing the power of the rules committee, and could force any committee to discharge a bill after twenty days. These concessions, which really were of little substance, caused Murphine to drop out and Reed was elected by a unanimous vote. He was the first native-born Washingtonian to hold the office of speaker, the same position his father had occupied in the territorial legislature six decades earlier.[21]

Although granting some apparent concessions to the progressives, Reed refused to surrender his power to appoint committees. Despite the fact that over half the members had been elected for the first time in 1922, he retained as many former committee chairmen as possible, meaning a continuation of the traditional old guard control. "Better work can be accomplished in this way," he contended, because of the experience of the chairmen. Reed did institute a departure in the handling of the state budget, one designed to prevent increased expenditures from being approved in the hectic closing days of the session. The general appropriations bill containing money for existing state institutions was to be disposed of within the first five weeks of the session. Fund requests for new programs would then be brought to the floor, "forced to stand on their own merits." This, Reed pointed out, would "cause most of them to drop out of sight." The Washington Tax Limit League and other advocates of reduced taxation were elated over this procedure.[22]

The delight of the organized tax reduction forces, however, turned to disappointment when Reed engineered the defeat of their pet measure, the so-called forty mill bill. Pushed by the Tax Limit League and the real estate lobby, the bill would have fixed real and personal property taxes at forty mills, a reduction from the sixty-eight to seventy mills then in effect throughout the state. The measure would force the state to reduce expenditures, its supporters contended. The bill also provided for a state income tax to make up for much of the lost revenue, a factor that aroused opposition to the bill among some businessmen. Nevertheless, many lumbermen were among its supporters.[23]

Reed, however, was vehemently opposed to a tax on income. He told Tax Limit League members that while they would have to "offer something definite with which to raise the revenue needed for government," individual and business income must remain sacrosanct. He also informed them that there were practical obstacles to enactment of the forty-mill limit. A slight reduction in millage rates might be possible, but interest on state bonds and the increasing expenditures demanded by the people made a drastic reduction impossible. A mandated forty-mill limit would wreck the state, because it would not provide adequate revenues.[24]

The bill's opponents concentrated their fire on the income tax provision and the disruption the measure would cause. Their contention was that the state's school system could not survive a massive cut in property tax revenue. The bill's defeat was regarded by Reed as the most important work of the session. He contended that the income tax section was "one of the most vicious measures ever presented" to the legislature. He denied that his opposition was based on self-interest, even though he had the highest income in the legislature. Rather, the measure "was so unscientifically constructed that it would have worked a great hardship, in my judgment, on the business interests of this state."[25]

The defeat of the bill revealed a split between advocates of tax reduction. Supporters of the forty-mill limit desired an income tax, which would shift much of their tax responsibility to other shoulders. Reed and other opponents of the bill, while equally desirous of reduced property taxes, opposed the creation of alternative revenue sources, or at least those that they would have to provide. Rather, Reed wished to retain the property tax system, but with reduced collections and a special break for owners of timberland. Under the prevailing county-centered system, he could exert maximum political pressure, be it the informal discussions that worked so well in Mason County or the more overt exercise of political muscle he and Alex Polson often attempted in Grays Harbor. The reduction of taxes, not their proliferation, was his desired goal.[26]

While concentrating on taxes, Reed did not abandon his interest in labor reform. By 1923 benefits paid under the state's workmen's compensation system were among the lowest in the nation and had been further depleted by the postwar inflation. As a result, the state Federation of Labor introduced legislation to increase payments by one-third. This move, predictably, outraged many conservatives. J. J. Donovan argued that increased benefits would make it "quite an incentive for a certain class of men to get hurt, and when injured to stay incapacitated on paper as long as possible." On the other hand, an establishment spokesman like the *Seattle Times* conjured up different versions. "A palpable injustice to injured workmen or to their widows and orphaned children," the paper intoned, "should not longer be continued." Haggling over "miserable dollars" that measured the "bread and butter and shoes and stockings for orphaned children and widowed mothers" did not present "an inspiring spectacle."[27]

Joined by Polson, a former state senator who retained considerable influence in Olympia, Reed favored a substantial increase. Opposed to him were the forces of the state Federation of Industries, which decried the need for an increase and instead sponsored a bill that would authorize an optional insurance system. (Employers would be allowed to purchase insurance for their workers from private companies, dropping out of the state system.) Reed believed that the main force behind this effort was the insurance industry, which hoped to destroy the state insurance structure and gain for itself the resultant business. Passage of the Federation of Industries bill would "in all probabilities destroy the act in that the private corporations would undoubtedly take out from under the act the most desirable risks." This would be a disaster for workers and employers alike.[28]

In a departure from normal procedure, Reed left the speaker's chair to argue on the floor of the house for a 25 percent increase in benefits, winning out over the die-hard conservatives. "With Reed taking the floor on behalf of increased compensation," the *Seattle Post-Intelligencer* reported, "opposition vanished." He won the plaudits of organized labor for his efforts. "Despite the entreaties of a vicious minority of employers," William Short of the state Federation of Labor commended, "Mark Reed has risen like a great mountain of righteousness above their narrow, sordid selfishness." Reed had once again demonstrated that reform was not solely the province of traditional reformers and that, for him, the interests of workers complemented the interests of their employers.[29]

Many of the people who commended Reed's efforts in the area of workmen's compensation regarded with suspicion his attitude toward public power, the 1923 session's most dramatic issue. By World War I both Seattle and Tacoma had developed publicly-owned electric utilities. The goal of public power advocates—urban reformers, the state Grange, and the Farmer-Labor party—was to extend such service across the state, destroying in the process the corporate utilities, many of which were owned by the Stone and Webster interests of Boston.[30] In order to further public ownership they backed legislation introduced by Farmer-Labor Representative Homer T. Bone of Tacoma which would allow municipal utilities to sell power outside city limits. Low cost power, made available to all the small towns and their outlying areas, would supposedly undermine and destroy the private power companies.

At the close of a legislative hearing on the Bone bill in late January Reed, to the surprise of those who viewed him as a reactionary on public power, stated his position on the measure. He claimed to support the principle behind the Bone bill, noting that the city of Tacoma, in its Lake Cushman power project, was removing some three hundred thousand dollars of taxable property from the Mason County rolls "and by reason of the law the people of that small county are not permitted to buy one kilowat [sic] of power." It was clearly not right that the inhabitants of a county could not take advantage of a development within its borders. The transmission lines would pass by homes and businesses that were forbidden to tap into them.

But the great issue raised by the Bone bill was not that of municipal ownership at all, Reed insisted. The real issue was whether public utilities could take property off the tax rolls, thereby increasing the burden on owners of the remaining property, and not give something back to the county as compensation. Not to do so would be to "make a priveleged class of the people of Tacoma." Reed questioned a situation in which the citizens of the state were being "required to feed the people of Tacoma electric power on a silver spoon." The solution was to assess a 5 percent tax on the gross earnings of public power plants. The Tacoma plant, he pointed out, had a gross income of over one million dollars in 1922 and a net profit of eight hundred thousand dollars. "Show me any private business in the state," Reed asked, "regardless of its nature that shows any such earnings as that." Indicating that the Bone bill as presently written could not pass the legislature, Reed stated in conclusion that he would introduce a substitute measure containing the gross earnings tax, which would be paid to the state. (Reed felt that a third bill that would have the tax paid directly to the counties was unconstitutional.)³¹

Reaction to Reed's presentation by the state's urban press depended upon ideological point-of-view. Public power advocates questioned his integrity, suggesting that he was a tool of the private power companies. Reed's proposed tax on the gross earnings of municipal power, the *Seattle Post-Intelligencer* insisted, represented "a direct smash in the face of public ownership." The *Seattle Union Record* charged that Reed was interested only in reducing taxation on his own property: "If Mark Reed's . . . dictates are followed by the legislature, Reed will be making a rare investment with his $600 salary as a state legislator." At the other end of the ideological spectrum, the *Seattle Times*, which violently opposed the principle of municipal ownership, cried that "it is time to call a halt on this monstrous folly!" The paper asserted that the years of Seattle City Light's operation had "been a period of costly experiment and humiliating failure!"³²

But Reed had raised a serious question, one of particular importance for rural counties forced to subsist on a small tax base. The legislature, argued the *Mason County Journal*, would be "recreant in its duty to all the people of the state if it does not find the way to return to such counties as Mason and Skagit, where muncipalities are reaching for power and developing great plants without the necessity of paying taxes to the counties, something to make good their loss in assessment values and tax moneys." When large holdings of land were taken off the rolls, taxes on other landholders increased and private development of the site, development that would pay taxes, was precluded. "Instead of being able to reduce levies in response to popular demand," editor Grant Angle noted, "they must be maintained and even raised in spots to raise the funds needed to carry on county government." The debate over the Bone bill, then, involved much more than public power; the issues involved were a matter of concern for everyone in the state.[33]

A week after the hearing the house public utility committee voted 7-6 against recommending passage of the Bone bill, reporting instead the Reed bill (which was, in effect, the Bone bill with the tax amendment tacked on). On the floor, Homer Bone led the fight for his original measure, contending that the 5 percent tax was unfair in comparison to the average tax of 2 percent paid by private utilities. Moreover, the tax could pyramid from 10 to 15 to 20 percent as power was bought and resold. Reed replied that he would amend his bill to prevent pyramiding. The house subsequently voted 57-39 to indefinitely postpone the Bone bill, with most rural legislators voting for postponement and urban members against.

House debate on the Reed bill found the original public power backers now in opposition. The *Post-Intelligencer* insisted that supporters of the public interest would "reject the power tax proposal with such emphasis as will permanently discourage further attempts to throttle the development of public power service." Backers of the Reed bill were accused of being "recreant to the interests of the state." Nevertheless, the bill, containing a referendum clause, passed the house 57-38. Supporters of the Bone bill began to plan an initiative campaign for their measure.[34]

In the senate the private power companies—Reed insisted that they had not backed his bill in the house—exercised considerably more influence, and the house bill was set aside. Instead, the senate approved a measure that set the tax at 6 percent and put publicly owned utilities under the regulation of the state department of public works, a move that was expected to stifle any chances of expansion of existing operations. Deadlock ensued in the conference as Reed, under considerable personal strain from the illness of two of his sons at Culver Military Academy, refused to accept the senate version. "You will make this conference power bill conform to the house bill," he told senate conferees, "or I promise you that this session will end with no power legislation." If that happened, "you will wake up the morning after the next November election and find that the Bone power bill has been crammed down your throat." The

senate caved in on the last day of the session, and Reed's
measure was passed on to consideration by the voters in 1924.35

Reed's sincerity in this whole episode was questioned by
many people at the time and has been the subject of much
misunderstanding. One correspondent, referring to Stone and
Webster, informed Senator Wesley Jones that "Reed, as you
know, is their man." The power trust supposedly intended to
use the nearly two-year delay before the 1924 election to buy up
all the small town power plants "so that if the Bone bill should
be passed . . . the electric people would have no place to dispose
of their surplus juice." Reed had struck a corrupt bargain with
the trust to gain its support in future campaigns for higher
office. "Stone and Webster," this writer concluded, had "nur-
tured Reed's political ambitions." Others felt certain that Reed
intended to run for governor and wished to create the impression that he supported public power while at the same time
gaining conservative backing for having, in actuality, stymied
the movement. The *Post-Intelligencer* commented that Reed had
arrayed himself "on the side of selfish privilege."36

These commentators, though, were far off the mark, as
Reed's position was sincere. He was not the "tool" of Stone and
Webster. The power trust had not supported his bill and he felt
that its legislative course was entirely mistaken. "I have not
been able to wholly agree with the political policies adopted [by
Stone and Webster]," Reed noted. Moreover, while philosophically he might have objections to public power, he recognized
that "the public, in considerable proportion, . . . is in favor of
municipal development." The problem was to accept this fact
and devise the fairest possible system. He objected only to "the
making of a preferred citizenship for the residents of the cities
of this state at the expense of those on the outside." He told
Homer Bone several years later that he had never been "at all
averse to this program in its finality." In the end the voters
would decide between the Reed and the Bone approaches, or
perhaps reject both.37

As the session came to a close, Reed regarded the results with
some satisfaction. Scheduling early consideration of the budget
had helped keep new expenditures to a minimum. And the
legislature had demonstrated its good sense in rejecting the tax

limit bill and in accepting sensible power and compensation measures. "In the final analysis," Reed concluded, "sanity and the interests of good government generally" prevailed. Still, he was disappointed that tax reduction had not been achieved, a fact that rankled some observers. "While much time has been spent in hunting up new sources of taxation," the *Argus* grumbled, "little has been expended in hunting up places where money was being wasted and attempting to plug the holes."[38]

During these early years of the 1920s Mark Reed was the dominant figure in state government. He had steered through the administrative code, bringing the governmental apparatus into the twentieth century. He had presided over a strengthening of the workmen's compensation system, advocating the increase of benefits while ameliorating much of the employer criticism. And he had been a central actor in the dramatic debate over public power. By the end of 1923 he was at the peak of his political power and influence.

2

Mark Reed was boomed as the leading contender for the Republican gubernatorial nomination in 1924. Much of the initial speculation over his candidacy resulted from an accolade delivered by Homer Bone at the close of the 1923 legislative session. Despite their differences over public power, Bone applauded the speaker's fairness toward the minority group. "If the people of Washington . . . should choose our Speaker governor two years hence," Bone stated, "the same ability and fair play could be expected of him then as he has exhibited while presiding over the House." Reporters reflected on the unlikely possibility that Bone and his followers would decamp from the Farmer-Labor party and support Reed in 1924.

Though few believed that would ever occur, many of Reed's friends urged him to put his business affairs in order in preparation for the race. Some had called on him to run in 1916 and again in 1920, but now their calls had particular force. "Mr. Reed," the *Mason County Journal* informed its readers, "is spoken of as the outstanding figure for the next Republican gubernatorial candidacy." Following Bone's pronouncement, Reed denied that he was a candidate, but eager reporters played up his refusal to rule out a race for the governorship. "His friends say he would not spurn the job," one journalist reported.[39]

Privately, Reed expressed reservations. The governorship was a full-time job, he pointed out to his friend Stephen B. L. Penrose, president of Whitman College. But he was responsible for an extensive group of business interests. "For something like twenty years the organization has been maintained largely as a personal one, and it would be very difficult to turn over the organization to another—within the next year or so especially." (The plans for the Shelton mills were approaching their final development at this point.) Most of the stock in the Simpson Logging Company, moreover, was owned by the widows of Sol Simpson and A. H. Anderson, who had for years trusted Reed "fully in the management of their property. I owe them a very lasting obligation and, aside from my personal loss were I to turn over the management of our business to another, I feel that theirs is the first call upon me." Nevertheless, he had "given some consideration" to the idea of running, finding it an attractive proposition. Still, he concluded that he could not "see my way clear to encouraging my friends greatly."[40]

Talk about the governorship with respect to Reed died out during the summer, particularly as Governor Hart had not indicated whether he would run for reelection. There was little likelihood that Reed would run against Hart, splitting the organization vote and electing an outsider like Roland H. Hartley of Everett, who had finished second in both 1916 and 1920 Republican primaries and was planning a third race for the governorship. But the situation changed in mid-November when Hart, pleading poor health, announced that he would not run in 1924.[41]

The attention of political observers again focused on Reed as the successor to Hart. The *Seattle Post-Intelligencer* said that the governor's withdrawal would force Reed into the race, as he was the logical candidate of the state organization. Guy Kelly, Republican national committeeman, argued that the state needed "a good business man in the governor's office" and, in what was taken as an endorsement, pointed out that Reed was a businessman of "proven ability." The *Tacoma News Tribune* contended that Reed possessed the "character and business ability and experience sufficient to run the affairs of as great and complicated a corporation as the state has become." That paper also noted the great financial obstacles in the way of a Reed candidacy. Privately, the *News Tribune's* editor, Charles Welch, wrote Reed: "For the sake of the state, business and the Republican party it is my belief that you should make the sacrafice [sic] necessary and become a candidate." Welch was confident that Reed would be elected.[42]

Alex Polson told Reed that he was the logical successor to Hart, a view that even many of those less friendly to Reed assumed. The *Seattle Union Record*, which had lost much of its earlier admiration for Reed during the power fight, ran his picture on the front page and told readers it was "a safe bet that you will have many chances to see the same face staring at you from a thousand telephone poles before the campaign is over." The labor paper recalled that Reed had stated he would not be a candidate, a disclaimer that would make little difference when the time arrived.[43]

Some opposition to a Reed race was expressed. The *Seattle Star* stated that Reed could not win because public power supporters would oppose him. The Spokane *Spokesman-Review* conceded that he was "a leader of wide-spread personal popularity and high party standing," but reiterated its support for Roland Hartley.[44]

Hartley himself responded with characteristic pungency. "The people are tired of this ring-around-the-rosey business," Hartley said of the Hart announcement and build-up for Reed. "This whole situation is a systematically worked out plan of Mark Reed's" and would have no impact on his own decision to run. Hartley contended that the people wanted "a housecleaning in Olympia." This sentiment had produced Hart's withdrawal, but the people would not be satisfied "by passing over to Reed." Everyone, Hartley concluded, "knows that Reed has been the power behind the administration for years. Having him come into the open now doesn't alter conditions as they have existed at Olympia for years." Agreeing with Hartley, the *Spokesman-Review* reported the "prevailing impression" of state politicians that Hart had "stepped aside" for Reed.[45]

In the days following the governor's statement Reed spent a

good deal of time on the telephone with political leaders around the state. For a time he seemed to be succumbing to the pressure from his supporters. "The party should find some man who has not such large and dominating interests as I have," Reed stated, continuing that "I do not know whether I can get loose from them or not." But he also said that he was "making right now a careful survey of them to see what might happen if I did put them aside." Those observers familiar with Reed's habitual professed reluctance to run for public office were sure that he would accede to the pressure and become a candidate.[46]

They were disappointed when on 1 December Reed announced, after conferences with business associates, state party chairman Charles Hebbard of Spokane and Land Commissioner Clark Savidge, that he would not enter the race. "The business enterprises of which I am the active head," he stated, "are passing through a period of development which calls for the closest attention." His partners were not actively involved in the running of Simpson and related enterprises, and his sons were not yet ready to assume an active role in the business. "The energy and ability necessary to properly administer the office [of governor]," Reed pointed out, "cannot, in justice to the state, be divided by other activities." He had concluded that "my first duty is to my family and to those who have trusted me" and therefore "with sincere regret" he removed his hat from the gubernatorial ring.[47]

Reed informed his brother Tom in Alaska that he had received offers of support from every county in the state and from 90 percent of Washington's Republican newspapers. This support had made it "pretty hard to turn down a offer of this kind," he noted, "coming as it was without any effort on my part, but I believe I am doing the right thing." Had the opportunity arisen "a few years later I would be very glad . . . to get into a real fight, but now I feel I have other duties which come first." This was the deciding factor. Reed could not afford to relinquish direct control over Simpson and the development of his mill plans. His decision was undoubtedly reinforced by the fact he would have to actively campaign in a statewide primary. Reed abhorred publicity, and he had never had to do more than put his name on the ballot to win election in Mason County.

And the prospect of free-wheeling attacks by Roland Hartley must have been extremely distasteful to Reed.[48]

One lumberman wrote to Reed, expressing approval of his withdrawl from the race: "50% of your efficiency would be wasted, as it takes only an ordinary business man to be a good governor." The *Tacoma News Tribune* lamented the unfortunate fact that "too small a percentage of those who have made outstanding successes in business and professional life" could be persuaded to run for public office. Reed had displayed in his declination "the high sense of obligation to his associates, with which he would have acted for the taxpayers if elected" to the governorship. "It is doubtless all for the best," sighed the *Mason County Journal*.[49]

His decision was not at all in the best interests of the state party organization, however. Reed insisted that he did not care who secured the party's nomination as long as that person was "safe and sane and will give us a good business administration." But following Reed's refusal, Clark Savidge, the other potentially strong candidate of the Hart coalition, also announced that he would not run. The organization was forced to fall back on Edward French, a much weaker candidate. This, combined with the collapse of the "cow county" alliance, meant the nomination by a narrow margin of Hartley in 1924. Reed eventually learned that he should have cared more about the potentiality of such an outcome.[50]

Although he had declined to become a candidate for governor, Reed did play an active political role in 1924 as temporary manager of President Calvin Coolidge's election campaign in the state.

Reed had hailed the election of Warren Harding in 1920 as signaling the electorate's preference for a safe conservative administration in the mold of William McKinley. The Harding administration, as far as Reed was concerned, infused a new spirit into the nation's capital. "It evidently needed some new blood instilled into the veins in order to drop off the old conks who had attached themselves to the trunk of the tree during our Democratic regime and possibly before." Reed was particularly gratified that Colonel Charles Forbes, Harding's campaign manager in Washington state, had become one of "the real live wires of the organization" as head of the Veterans' Bureau. (Forbes later was exposed as one of the most infamous figures involved in the Harding scandals, going to prison for his thievery.) In July 1923 Reed and other state leaders had accompanied the president on his train trip from Portland to Tacoma, where Harding took ship for a tour of Alaska. Reed asserted that Harding was "a splendid fellow."[51]

Harding's death following his return from the north put Vice-President Coolidge in the White House. And it was followed by revelation of the Teapot Dome and other scandals of the Harding administration. (Reed owned stock in the Wyoming Teapot Oil Company, a Tacoma concern formed to drill for oil on the Teapot Dome.) "This 'Tempest in a Teapot' in Washington," Reed told Alex Polson, "is going to upset business very materially." This fear seems to have been an important factor in Reed's decision to organize the state for Coolidge. "As long as we have such a muddled situation politically," he noted, "we cannot expect men with money to invest to be seeking opportunities for increased 'Big Business Activity.'" Reed accepted the post of campaign manager for Coolidge in early 1924 and immediately set about organizing statewide Coolidge machinery.[52]

The appointment of Reed to head the president's campaign was a good one according to most observers. The Seattle *Argus*, which had often been critical of Reed's political course, applauded the selection. The Shelton lumberman was "not only an astute politician, but he is something that is rare in a politician—a businessman as well. Moreover, Mr. Reed has the confidence of everybody who knows him." Some political leaders, though, distrusted his motives. Informants told Senator Wesley Jones that Reed was using the Coolidge campaign as a cover to set up his own organization in anticipation of an effort to unseat Jones in the 1926 primary.[53]

Reed played no role on behalf of the president, once Coolidge had secured the nomination, aside from keeping tabs on efforts to get out the vote in November. A high turnout would assure victory over the divided opposition forces of the redoubtable Progressive Robert M. LaFollette and John W. Davis, unlikely candidate of the dispirited Democrats. "I am convinced that there are 200,000 votes for Coolidge in the state," Reed pointed out. "Our task is to get them out." The president's backers seem to have succeeded, as Coolidge received 220,000 votes in the state to 151,000 for LaFollette and 43,000 for the sorry Davis. "A great deal of the credit is due you," one politician wrote Reed, "for the manner in which you handled the pre-convention campaign for President Coolidge."[54]

The 1924 election also presented the voters both with the Reed power bill (and its gross earnings tax) and with the Bone bill, which had reached the ballot as an initiative. Reed realized that his position was not popular, "but it does seem to me that a majority of the people of the state would not approve of the municipal ownership program if they really realized what was happening." In an effort to justify his position Reed made a number of addresses on the power issue during 1923 and 1924. His bill, he told the State Bankers Association convention, "merely proposes to prevent the grave injustice of permitting further withdrawals of taxable property from the tax rolls." He argued that there was nothing to be gained in extension of municipal ownership "to serve a part of the people at the expense of all the people, when those not served can derive no benefit thereby."[55]

In the final outcome the voters rejected both measures, the Bone bill by 217,000 to 139,000 and the Reed bill by 209,000 to 99,000. (Mason County voters voted down the former 1,033 to 455 but approved the latter 867-625, the only county in the state to do so.) Reflecting on the results, Reed denied that the electorate had declared itself against public power. "The friends of the Bone bill voted against the Reed bill and the friends of the Reed bill voted against the Bone bill," he explained. "If you add the affirmative votes cast for the two bills, you find a majority of 40,000 in favor of allowing cities to sell power outside." Reed continued to support the concept of public power, always with the inclusion, however, of some form of taxation. But the 1924 vote took much of the steam out of the public power move-ment, which did not revive for several years.[56]

Calvin Coolidge won a full term in 1924 and the rejection of the Reed bill was balanced by the defeat of the Bone bill.

Considerable satisfaction could be derived from these developments, but Reed must have felt some trepidation at the thought of the unpredictable Roland Hartley in the governor's chair beginning in January. The Everett Republican narrowly defeated Senator French 58,700 to 56,900 in a field of seven in the G.O.P primary (French outpolled Hartley by a five-to-one margin in Mason County) and then easily bested the token Democratic challenger. Reed could have prevented this outcome, which brought to the fore a major threat to his political predominance in Olympia, by running for governor, as he probably could have defeated Hartley.[57] He had been in a strong position to bridge the gap between the party factions. But he had not done so, as his sense of obligation to his family and business associates outweighed what ambition he had to be governor. Instead, he had hoped someone else could provide a safe, sane, and businesslike administration of state affairs. That hope was to be sorely tested in the coming years.

CHAPTER 4

The Politics of Vilification

Political predominance in Washington passed from Mark Reed to Governor Roland H. Hartley in the mid-1920s, although not without a dramatic struggle. Hartley had been born in Canada in 1864 and had moved with his family to Minnesota fourteen years later. In 1885 he became secretary to David Clough, a prominent lumberman and political figure who became governor of Minnesota, later marrying Clough's daughter. Taking part in the great exodus of Midwest lumbermen to the Pacific Northwest, Hartley followed Clough to Everett in 1902. There the Clough and Hartley families dominated the logging and lumber business of the area, and Hartley became the town's mayor. In 1914 he was elected to the state legislature, serving with another freshman member named Reed. Hartley ran for governor in 1916 and again in 1920, and was finally elected to the office in 1924, bringing to an end what he called "this long period of waiting."[1]

The careers of both Reed and Hartley had followed a similar course. They were important figures in the state's lumber industry. They had advanced themselves by marrying the daughters of prominent men. They had both served as mayor of their home towns: Reed in Shelton, and Hartley in Everett. And they had entered state politics in the same year.

The two men also shared the view that the reforms of the progressive era had gone too far and that taxation must be reduced. The "American people today suffer from too much government," Hartley contended. "We are striking at the very vitals of the Republic by robbing the individual of his independence, his self-reliance, his will to work, and his zeal to achieve, thereby reducing him to the status of a ward of the government." Hartley, though would reduce the role of the government to a much lower level than that desired by Reed, who had sponsored major labor reform legislation. While Reed was an enlightened conservative, recognizing that businessmen and conservatives had an interest in reform, Hartley was an out-and-out reactionary. He had been one of the most vitriolic opponents of concessions to labor during the wartime Wobbly scare, and in the 1920s he stood for a return to the laissez faire of the Gilded Age. The nation's citizens, Hartley cried, had to be freed "from the damnable practice of regulation, domination, dictation, and interference by governmental bureaus, boards, commissions and inspectors."[2]

Reed and Hartley also had quite different personalities. Reed eschewed conflict and publicity. Hartley, on the other hand, saw himself as a sort of populist Teddy Roosevelt in Social Darwinist garb, commanded to stand at Armageddon and battle for the Lord. Hartley wrote that he delighted in fighting for what was right, even though "it meant the alienating of a large and powerful group of voters." All he needed was to be "quite sure that I am doing the right thing and doing it well. . . . My only worriment is as to whether or not I shall really recognize my full duty." Hartley brooked no opposition to his plans. "He is a man who in power dominates and controls," a supporter remarked. "He whips from his way men whose minds do not run along with his or who would attempt to modify his purposes." An enemy agreed, noting that "anyone holding a different idea from him can never be right."[3]

The contrasting personalities of Reed and Hartley were reflected in differing approaches to politics. Reed was the classic insider, the master of legislative committees and a practiced lobbyist. In contrast, Hartley was an outsider who served only one term in the legislature, finding little satisfaction in the drudgery of house business. He made effective use in his campaign for governor of the fact that he was not part of the Olympia establishment. Mark Reed was the leading symbol of that establishment, the man who could have defeated Hartley in 1924 and might run against him in 1928. Thus, it was inevitable that Reed would become the principal target of the new governor in the latter's effort to secure political dominance in Olympia.

1

Reed, back in his accustomed position of house majority leader, and the governor seemed to work in perfect harmony at the outset of the new administration in January 1925. Hartley proposed that the legislature act only on items of immediate necessity, then go home and return for a special session in the fall. In the meantime, Hartley promised, he would make a thorough study of state government and prepare a program for the legislators' consideration. Reed believed that this was "a good constructive recommendation." The *Seattle Times*, an enthusiastic supporter of Hartley, observed that "the idea of having a broad, comprehensive plan for guidance in legislating for the state" made a great deal of sense.[4]

Acceptance of the governor's proposal left only two controversial matters for disposition. Reed steered repeal of the one-and-a-half mill highway levy on general property through the house, replacing the lost revenue, as Hartley had recommended, with money from the motor vehicle fund. Counties would still receive the same amount of money for highway construction, Reed argued, defending the $300,000 in property tax relief the change would grant to railroads in the state, including his own logging road. "The railroads are still our most important methods of transportation," he pointed out, "and they are entitled to the same consideration from the standpoint of right and wrong as is the smallest taxpayer."[5]

Though succeeding on this issue, Reed failed in his effort to sustain the governor's veto of a measure appropriating $400,000 for loans to eastern Washington farmers for purchase of seed wheat. He contended that supporters of the bill were "voting against the principles of good government." It was simply bad policy for the state to extend credit to private interests. The house, however, voted 77-20 to override the veto, although the senate eventually voted to sustain. In these actions, observers noted, Reed was the spokesman of the Hartley Administration, continuing the role he had customarily played.[6]

The *Seattle Times* was ecstatic in its approval of Hartley's first months in office. The governor, the *Times* asserted, had "impressed the state with his sincerity, his force of character and his determination to follow what he considers to be the path of duty." If, in the nearly four years remaining in his term, Hartley "should maintain a record of achievement as good as that of the last thirty-three days," the paper concluded, "he would be acclaimed as one of Washington's greatest governors." The *Times*, along with many others, soon found reason to discard such commendations.[7]

Hartley's study of the functioning of Washington's government turned out to be more haphazard than thorough. He engaged in a series of disputes with supporters of education, reclamation, and child welfare and angered most other holders of statewide office, initiating a feud that disrupted state government for years. Reporting for the *Argus* from "Under the Capitol Dome," J. H. Brown observed that if Hartley had not exactly earned the enmity of other elective state officials, he had managed to lose their support. The governor seemed "to intrude the fixed belief that he is the supreme power, the source of all knowledge, forgetting that he got less votes than any other state official."[8]

Still, most observers anticipated executive-legislative harmony in the special session. Hartley himself informed legislators that he had "no desire other than to cooperate with the members of the legislature, . . . for the best interests of all the people of our state." He assured them that his proposals would "be submitted in this spirit." Reed, though, seemed to have a premonition of bad things to come, expressing a real reluctance to set aside his business concerns. "Sometimes I wonder at our willingness to make the sacrifice that we are called upon to make," he told Lieutenant Governor Lon Johnson, "in endeavoring to do what we can to advance the cause of good government as we see it."[9]

Hartley's hour-long speech opening the session on 10 November 1925 amazed the legislators. Everyone, Hartley pointed out, realized that state government had to be made more efficient so that expenditures could be reduced. But the only means of doing so was to make changes in those institutions spending most of the tax dollars. Education was the best place to start. "Education is the biggest business in the State of Washington," he contended, "and the most neglected in so far as business thought, business planning and business management are concerned." Not only that, but the University of Washington, in particular, was always on the scene in Olympia, lobbying for yet higher appropriations. Hartley proposed to tame the education money monster by replacing the separate university, state college and normal school boards of regents with a single education board appointed by the governor. This board would also assume jurisdiction over the common schools, and the elective office of superintendent of public instruction would be abolished.

Education was by no means the sole target of Hartley's economizing wrath. The state's highway system should be overhauled, with expenditures sharply curtailed. As currently managed, the highway program was motivated by "the wheeze and gurgle of the bang of the old familiar pork barrel, rather than the voice of economic necessity." The state's reclamation policy, moreover, was "a dismal failure" and the reclamation laws should forthwith be repealed. Hartley concluded his diatribe with attacks on a number of other state programs, ranging from the state library to the pension system. The legislature should apply the knife to state government, cutting back and eliminating those activities not consistent with the governor's philosophy.[10]

A number of commentators openly criticized the governor's stance. The *Seattle Post-Intelligencer* suggested that, in formulating his educational proposals, Hartley hoped to secure control of the state's schools "as an adjunct to a political machine." The people of the state were demanding economy in government, the *Argus* observed, and the governor had pledged himself to satisfy that demand. But, the Seattle weekly continued, economy did not call "for a man having a hundred-mile trip before him to shoot his horse in order to save the feed bill, and walk." Likewise, economy did not require the throwing of "a handful of monkey wrenches into the various pieces of state machinery which are functioning perfectly."[11]

On the other hand, the Olympia *Morning Olympian*, published by veteran political figure Sam Perkins of Tacoma, commended Hartley for performing "the valuable service of creating issues and stimulating discussion." The message had given the voters an opportunity to judge how their legislators stood on important state problems. Most of the press, however, adopted a wait-and-see attitude. The *Seattle Times* commented that Hartley had presented "enough startling proposals to satisfy any reasonable demand for sensations," but these proposals did approach "big problems in a broad and comprehensive way." Mark Reed's hometown paper, the *Mason County Journal*, contended that talk about tax cuts was "a chimera," then applauded the governor's "sincerity and his desire to find ways of reducing taxes."[12]

Reed told reporters that Hartley had delivered "a courageous message" but expressed disapproval of the criticisms of the state university. Privately, he wrote Hartley's nephew, Herbert Clough, that the governor "has delivered the most destructive message that was ever presented to any Legislature during the history of this commonwealth. Fortunately it is not likely that his recommendations will be enacted into law." Reed recognized that Hartley's strikes at education, reclamation, and other state programs, would, in addition to damaging the state, lead to the governor's domination of the machinery of state government, a domination until now exercised by Reed and his friends in the bureaucracy. He had supported centralization of power in the governor's hands when Hart was in office, but such powers could not be entrusted to Hartley. Following the address Reed began to lay plans to exercise his control of the house in order to defeat the governor.[13]

Reed was, of course, aware that supporters of programs threatened by the governor had a common interest in the defense of their respective causes. Together, for instance, advocates of reclamation and education could stymie Hartley's designs. Reed recognized the importance for the state of reclamation of arid lands east of the mountains, as well as the issue's importance in maintaining the unity of the Republican party. Indeed, he had sponsored the state's first reclamation program in 1919. As for education, Reed was commended by the University of Washington alumni association as "a steadfast friend of education." Resistance to the governor, then, reflected Reed's long commitment to the welfare of the state, in addition to his own political self-interest.[14]

Ten days after Hartley's message, the house undertook consideration of a measure introduced by Representative E. F. Banker of Okanogan. The proposal would remove irrigation and reclamation from the jurisdiction of the director of conservation, an appointee of the governor, and place them under the elective state land commissioner. The bill also required the state to cooperate with federal reclamation policy. By removing the reclamation program from the governor's control, the Banker bill would prevent its destruction. For this reason, Hartley and his supporters launched an assault on the bill. At the reclamation committee's hearing the governor's secretary, A. R. Gardner, charged that the bill's support "is not so much due to the merits of what the governor said about reclamation as to what he said about timber and taxation." (Hartley had briefly attacked the state's timber policy in his message.) Hartley's opponents, Gardner contended, were not really interested in reclamation and education. Rather, they hoped to stir up controversy to overshadow the governor's call for reform; they were motivated by "other interests and selfish desires."[15]

Reed denounced the governor the next day in a speech that made headlines throughout the state and said that he would fight to preserve the reclamation program. Hartley's spokesman, Reed pointed out, had unfairly impugned the motives of house members. The governor's proposals had been considered solely on their merits, he insisted, and thus the criticism was not warranted. Proponents of the Banker bill hoped only to preserve the state's involvement in reclamation. Education, moreover, was the principal function of the state and, like reclamation, had to be saved from the governor. Reed, for one, did not believe that education should be made into "a football of politics and used as an instrumentality by politicians in carrying out their selfish ends."[16]

The anti-Hartley press supported Reed's stand against the governor. The *Tacoma News Tribune*, commenting on "Another Hartley Blunder," pointed out that it was a sorry state of affairs when sincere opponents of the governor were accused of not having the public interest at heart. There were the tactics of Mussolini "and other rulers who would crush all those who dare to disagree with them." Reed, the newspaper maintained, had taken "proper exception to this attitude." Even the Spokane *Spokesman-Review*, while arguing that Hartley was right in fighting the Banker bill, observed that he had failed to exercise "intelligent discrimination" in impugning the motives of reclamation supporters.[17]

The Banker bill was passed by both houses by substantial margins, but was vetoed by the governor. The house failed to muster the two-thirds majority needed to override, revealing a political configuration that marked the rest of the session. Led by Reed, the house majority could pass the measures of its choice. But the pro-Hartley minority made up just over one-third of the body and could thereby prevent the majority from prevailing over a veto. In this situation neither side could govern.[18]

Reed's old friend Ed Sims, having returned to the legislature, led the Hartley supporters. Sims was one of the most experienced politicians in the state and an important figure in the fisheries industry. The two men had been close for years, both in the legislature and in private business affairs. Sims was a much more ruthless leader than Reed. He "whips his human factors into the structure of his politics," Representative Maude Sweetman observed, "by promise, cajolery, bluff, threat, and every effective means that the shrewd mind can devise."

Sims seemed almost totally preoccupied with these manipulations, ignoring issues and eschewing any real devotion to Roland Hartley. "He is in politics for the love of the game," J. H. Brown commented. "He dotes on a fight and is having the time of his life." Even the governor's most devoted followers could not down their distrust of Sims. "No matter how much his fighting may aid a cause which is filled with solid merit," the *Morning Olympian* contended, "it becomes increasingly apparent that his fights are for Ed Sims—most of the time." Whatever his motives, he made a formidable opponent.[19]

Following the demise of the Banker bill the sixty-two members who had voted to override the governor's veto met to put together a formal organization. An executive committee, chaired by Reed, was chosen to draw up a program and work for a resolution of the dispute with the minority. The subsequent thirteen point report called for preservation of the reclamation and highway programs and defended the state's educational system. Presenting the program to the full house, Reed denied that the majority was attempting to dictate to either the governor or the legislature. Rather, the hope was to provide a framework within which legislative harmony could be secured and the government conducted.[20]

The door of the majority caucus, Reed pointed out, "stands ajar for any member who believes in the general principles laid down in our report." He held out the possibility of compromise over the specifics, contending that "no member of the caucus is tied hand and foot to the details of the program." Two Republican factions were in existence in the house. Furthermore, these factions were not limited to Republicans, as Banker, a Democrat, was a member of the majority executive committee. "National politics," observed one member, "make practically no difference in the Legislature." What mattered was where one stood on the program and personality of Roland Hartley.[21]

Reed and the other caucus leaders met with Sims to begin work on a compromise reclamation measure. Until an agreement was reached, Representative W. B. Price of Ellensburg reported to his friend Austin Mires, "mighty little Legislation is going to be done on other matters." The conferees finally agreed on legislation funding reclamation in Kittitas County. The *Seattle Times* commented that passage of the bill and its acceptance by Hartley was regarded by political observers as ending the tension between the governor and the legislature. Reed could "see no reason why we should not get along nicely from now on."[22]

Governor Hartley chose this moment to appear before a joint legislative session and launch a bitter attack on state timber sales. He had mentioned the subject only briefly in his opening message, but now concentrated on it as a means of discrediting Reed, one of the state's major lumbermen, in the public eye. Hartley insisted that the state was not getting full value for its timber and thus the "little red school house on the hill" was suffering, since revenue from timber sales supported the common schools. He called for legislation making logging railroads common carriers, thereby increasing competition and the bids for state timber. (Owners of railroads in a given area were able to control adjacent timber, as other prospective purchasers would have no means of shipping timber out.) The legislature should also mandate that state timber cruises, upon which sale prices were based, be made public. "I want a law," Hartley cried, "that will tear the mask of secrecy off this timber business."[23]

The speech was viewed by most observers as a direct attack on Land Commissioner Clark Savidge and an indirect assault on Reed. When queried by reporters for his response, however, Reed described the speech as "the best message I have ever heard Governor Hartley deliver. There is a lot of meat in what he says." Reed was well acquainted with the practices of the land commission, having been its secretary in the 1890s as well as an occasional purchaser of state timber over the years. Hartley's timber proposals, he believed, were not without merit. If some workable method of making timber cruises public could be found, this might lessen public suspicion of the land commission. Reed's own logging railroad, moreover, was already a common carrier, a fact which had not caused any problems for Simpson.

But by no means did Reed accept Hartley's implications of corruption and incompetence. These had to be countered, as did the suggestion that Reed himself was involved in improper activities. Moreover, Hartley was attacking the traditional system by which private lumbermen obtained timber from the holdings of the state. Reed arranged a rebuttal appearance by Savidge before a joint session of the legislature. The Land Commissioner argued that the state, in its timber sales, made a comparable amount to private sales.[24]

Reed also helped push through a joint resolution commending Savidge's conduct of his office and establishing a special committee to investigate the points raised by Hartley. When then governor's timber bills came up for consideration, Reed manipulated parliamentary rules to forestall consideration. The bills, he claimed, were too hastily drawn and legislative action should at least await the report of the special committee. His position, he insisted, resulted only from considerations of the public interest. His logging railroad was already a common carrier, Reed reminded his colleagues, and only two small tracts of state timber would come under his influence in the foreseeable future. With his personal integrity under attack, Reed was more determined than ever to best Hartley.[25]

Political commentators strived to explain the ultimate reason for the quarrel, the one that would render coherent the strange doings in Olympia. The *Mason County Journal* suggested that Reed and Savidge "were logical candidates" for the governorship and that this accounted for Hartley's assault. The governor was attempting to destroy his two strongest rivals for leadership in the Republican party, men who might run against him in 1928. The *Journal* also brought up Hartley's combative and erratic personality. Hartley, the paper argued, was "crazy for power and hopes to reign the monarch of all he surveys in Washington."[26]

Hartley supporters, on the other hand, found the governor to be the innocent victim of his vindictive enemies in the Republic party. The *Morning Olympian* charged that Reed had meant to control the governor. This, it claimed, "had been the condition during the previous administration." When Hartley refused to knuckle under, the house leader determined to destroy him. "This opposition sprang from the failure of the governor to accept Reed domination." The *Argus* asserted that some legislators had come to Olympia "looking for an opportunity to stick a knife into the governor and turn it around." Hartley had been elected without the aid of the old state organization, noted the *Argus*. "In fact, he was elected in spite of the active opposition of that organization." By disdaining diplomacy in his opening message and subsequent actions, Hartley had presented his opponents with "the opening for which they were looking." Other Hartley backers also contended that Reed and the other "lumber barons" were out to crush the governor because he had dared to raise the timber issue.[27]

One commentator ventured into the realm of folklore to explain the situation. Writing in the *Seattle Union Record*, Mark Shields said of Reed, Hartley, and Sims that the "three Paul Bunyans have transferred their quarrel from the lumber camp to the capital, and the capital isn't big enough to hold them all." Because none of the three was capable of recognizing a master, because they needed to dominate other men, they would tear each other to pieces before accepting compromise. "They are dominating, ruthless, ambitious," Shields contended. "No lumber camp would be large enough to accomodate [sic] the three, and the legislative halls are too small to give them elbow room." This argument, however, ignored the long friendship between Reed and Sims and the fact that Reed and Hartley were in general agreement on many issues.[28]

Some observers discerned a gigantic power struggle for control of the Olympic Peninsula behind the Reed-Hartley imbroglio. The four million acres of the peninsula, most of it administered by the federal or state government, contained the nation's largest stand of timber yet to be exploited. The future prosperity of the area's loggers depended on the opening up of the peninsula. At its southern end, Mark Reed's Peninsular Railroad drove westward from the Sound into the foothills of the Olympics. "We have expended a considerable sum of money," he pointed out, "in developing our railroad facilities so that we could handle this Forest Reserve timber to good advantage." To the west, Reed's friend Alex Polson was in a position to haul logs out of the Olympics to Grays Harbor.

Reed and Polson anticipated considerable profit when the region was opened to logging. Reed's railroad was a common carrier, and all other loggers in the southern part of the peninsula would have to use it to ship their cut to the Sound. "Mark Reed," noted J. H. Brown, "stands to make much money from the state's timber in the peninsula whether he purchases from the state or whether someone else does." Operators along the Strait of Juan de Fuca to the north hoped to open up the peninsula from Port Angeles and Port Townsend. Roland Hartley's business associate Joseph Irving was one of those operators. By adding to this competition the fact that the state's timber was under the jurisdiction of Clark Savidge, conspiracy-minded persons conjured up the behind-the-scenes machinations that often determine public events. Unfortunately, there is no evidence with which to document the extent and impact of these maneuverings. Moreover, the real competition was between the northern operators and Polson, as Reed's control of the timber in the southeastern part of the Olympics went unchallenged. Still, struggle for control of the Olympic Peninsula was viewed as the great hidden issue in state politics during these years.[29]

The situation on Olympia continued to deteriorate, focusing in the end on appropriations. Education supporters determined to hold the general appropriations bill hostage, hoping to force the governor to sign measures appropriating funds for constructing at the five state colleges and providing a fixed millage for higher education. In doing so, Reed outwitted H. F. Goldsworthy, chairman of the house appropriations committee and a Hartley supporter. He promised Goldsworthy that the measures would be placed on the calendar on the same day. (They had previously passed the senate.) Thus, he reassured the minority members, who were aware of the majority's strategy. Suspending the rules, the house passed the education bills but then failed to suspend the rules in order to advance the general appropriations measure to third reading. The strategy to get the education measures out of the house and onto the governor's desk and to keep the appropriations bill tied up in the rules committee had succeeded.

Goldsworthy charged that he had been tricked by Reed. With a fight threatening to break out on the floor, Reed denied that he was guilty of a double-cross. He had merely promised that the bills would be on the calendar, not on what action would be taken. "If I ever made an agreement in my life," he contended, "I carried it through yesterday as I agreed to do." Reed had outsmarted the opposition, but the governor refused to give in. The two education bills were vetoed. The house, with the minority again on its toes, failed to override the veto. As the old year passed into 1926, the deadlock remained unbroken and tension mounted in Olympia.[30]

Governor Hartley appeared again before a joint session of the legislature in the first week of January. He stated that he had vetoed the education bills because of the devious means by which they had been passed. "From the very beginning of this session," he insisted, "the majority organization has employed ruthless and ruinous tactics, unparalleled in the history of this state." He would find some means of financing the colleges, he continued, daring the legislators to go home "and take with you the responsibility for failure . . . to even provide for the necessary functions of the state government." Hartley said that much of the conflict which had marked the session resulted from "the fact that the executive had the audacity to attack the system by which the state's timber lands are sold, a system which has lost to the state millions of dollars, and which, if continued, will result in the loss of many more millions."

The governor then launched a personal attack on Reed. Referring to the setting aside of the timber bills, Hartley stated: "One significant fact is that the chairman of the House majority, who is one of the state's largest and wealthiest timber operators, is the man who administered the anaesthetic. This same House leader, when in my office, agrees with me that I am right, but down here he moves in just the opposite direction." Hartley then concluded his remarks by sarcastically noting that "no matter how many millions may be lost to the state in timber deals, the majority organization may rest secure in the knowledge that the Rhododendron has been protected." (Reed had introduced legislation protecting the rhododendron, which was widely grown in Mason County.)[31]

Reed was on his feet even before Hartley finished, demanding the floor. He started to respond to the governor's charges, but was interrupted by Lieutenant Governor Johnson, the presiding officer, who said that Hartley should be excused. "I thought he would like to stay and hear what I have to say," Reed retorted. Nevertheless, the governor, exchanging glares with Reed, was escorted from the chamber. Many members jeered and only a few stood in the traditional gesture of respect.

Reed took the floor to respond to what he called the governor's "special and most extraordinary" message. With respect to the timber bills, he asserted that Ed Sims had agreed with the idea of setting the measure aside. The majority faction, he claimed, had at all times attempted to be fair. "We have not attempted to steam-roll, to trade, or brow-beat or to do anything in connection with the passage of the program except well out in the open." And the majority would follow the same course in attempting to overcome Hartley's vetoes. The majority would "carry on by a straight-forward action and not by subterfuge." When Reed concluded his remarks, the joint session was officially adjourned and the legislators retired to reflect on the governor's outburst.[32]

Meeting the following day, the house debated a resolution censuring the governor. The resolution declared that Hartley was guilty of "an abuse of his constitutional privilege and an invasion of the rights of the legislative branch." Ed Sims attempted to halt the debate, but was shouted down. Reed stated that Hartley's charges "were downright lies." He again reviewed his disinterest in state timber, going so far as to declare that "not one stick of state timber will be bought by any of my companies" in the coming years. With a few of Hartley's previous supporters abandoning him, the house voted 60-32 to censure the governor.

Having vented its spleen, the majority then moved to reconsider the vetoes. He had never taken a more reluctant step, Reed observed. "Yet the fundamental principle governing this legislation is that a majority is always in control." He pointed out that the rules provided that votes, including those on vetoes, could be reconsidered. Over the protests of die-hard Hartley supporters, who questioned the legality of the move, the vetoes were overridden. Hartley's outburst, by alienating many of his own supporters, had given his opponents the opening they needed to secure victory.[33]

Reed's mastery of the legislature had enabled him to thwart Hartley's designs. But the governor refused to admit defeat, continuing his fight against the house majority and its leader. Reed was not without his defenders, however. The *Tacoma News Tribune* declared that his only offense had been to oppose the program of Roland Hartley, "who imagines himself a divinely appointed czar, whose word is omnipotent on every subject." Reed the paper noted, was a highly respected business and political figure, not only in the state but across the nation as well. "For the governor to permit his temper to get the better of him to the point of hurling mud at a man like Mark Reed . . . is a performance disgusting and unworthy [of] the high office of governor." The *Mason County Journal* reprimanded Hartley for charging Reed and others "with being 'crooks,' in substance at least, merely because his personal aims have been thwarted." Shelton service organizations passed a resolution condemning the governor for having "overstepped the bounds of decency" in attacking Reed.[34]

Governor Hartley also had his defenders. The *Morning Olympian* had become the principal spokesman for Hartley. It conceded that the governor might have been guilty of indiscretion, but contended that his behavior during the session had been distinguished by "honesty, . . . manifest sincerity, an outstanding willingness to state his position fully, clearly and firmly, coupled with judgment that is sound more often than it is in error." The Spokane *Spokesman-Review* commented that Hartley had delivered "a severe indictment of the legislature," an indictment that was well deserved. The "onus" for the session's failure, the *Spokesman-Review* declared, rested "on the majority and the majority house leader, Mark Reed." The "Reed-timber interest majority" had engaged in behind-the-scenes chicanery "to put to sleep what they could not knock out in committee."[35]

Other observers underplayed the seriousness of the controversy. "The public has no special interest in parliamentary battles," noted the *Seattle Times*, still unable to make a complete break with Hartley. The *Seattle Star* wondered "what difference does it make? Peanuts in politics are still peanuts, aren't they?" The *Star*, however, soon came out for the governor. Hartley had "fearlessly and aggressively attacked almost every practice that usually is 'soft-pedalled' by aspiring politicians." He was "sincerely trying to better the community according to his judgment."[36]

The special session had truly been a most extraordinary one. A day had not passed during its course, J. H. Brown observed at its close, "that I have not heard in detail stories of deliberate broken promises and double-crossing." And the turmoil was not likely to end with the departure of the drained legislators from Olympia. The Republican party was divided as the 1926 election campaigns got underway, particularly as Hartley was determined to continue the attacks against his opponents. "The Taft-Roosevelt split," Brown predicted, "will be a pink tea in comparison."[37]

In late January the house majority issued a lengthy statement of its position. Hartley's views, Reed and his associates argued, "were based upon inaccurate information, false economy, and a reactionary and destructive political philosophy which would undo a half century of progress in the functions of state government." The document's timber section decried any objection to the governor's common carrier bill or to the idea of selling state capitol commission timber at auction rather than by sealed bid. (Distinct from the state land commission, the capitol commission—made up of the governor, land commissioner, and auditor—had jurisdiction over state timber set aside to finance construction of state buildings.)

But the majority opposed making public the results of state timber cruises. Timber cruises were only estimates, they pointed out. "Both sides must depend on their own judgment as to the amount of timber on the ground." If the state released its cruise figures, it would leave itself open to litigation. Private companies kept the results of their cruises to themselves, allowing the purchaser to determine the fairness of the price in order "to avoid any controversy after the timber is cut." A better course might be for the state to adopt the federal government's policy of scaling the timber as it was cut. But this would mean that payment would not be made until the timber was cut and the state would also lose the taxes that were paid on its timber by purchasers. In spite of its weakness, then, the prevailing system remained the most satisfactory.[38]

Appearing before the Shelton Kiwanis Club, Reed stated that he had distrusted Hartley's education proposals from the first. By placing the state's schools under the thumb of the governor, Hartley's program would have created a vast political machine and wrecked education in the state. When Hartley realized that his plan was unpopular, he had raised the timber issue as a "smoke cloud" to cover his attack on education. The legislative majority, Reed concluded, had not set out to thwart the governor. Rather, it was merely asserting its rights as a co-equal branch of government and was defending the public interest as well.[39]

Meanwhile, Hartley began his own offensive in a series of speeches around the state and in newspaper columns. The *Seattle Star* gave him front-page space to air his views. "If the corrupt special interests and the selfish politicians, who bossed the

Mark E. Reed, ca. 1930 (*courtesy of William G. Reed*)

Mark E. Reed in the mid-1890s (*courtesy of the Photography Collection, Suzzallo Library, University of Washington*)

Thomas M. Reed (*courtesy of William G. Reed*)

Sol Simpson (*courtesy of Simpson Timber Co.*)

Irene Reed (*courtesy of William G. Reed*)

Mark Reed's home in Shelton (*courtesy of William G. Reed*)

Sol and Mary Simpson with their grandsons, Frank and Sol Reed (*courtesy of William G. Reed*)

Loggers relaxing in the bunkhouse (*courtesy of the Photography Collection, Suzzallo Library, University of Washington*)

Mark Reed standing at butt end of log, ca. 1910 (*courtesy of William G. Reed*)

Primitive logging camp in Mason County (*courtesy of the Photography Collection, Suzzallo Library, University of Washington*)

Above: Mark E. Reed, ca. 1920 (courtesy of the Photography Collection, Suzzallo Library, University of Washington). Right: George S. Long (courtesy of Weyerhaeuser Company Archives)

Left: R. D. Merrill; right: Alex Polson (courtesy of the Photography Collection, Suzzallo Library, University of Washington)

Clockwise from top left: Louis F. Hart, Ed Sims, Roland H. Hartley, and Henry Suzzallo (*courtesy of the Photography Collection, Suzzallo Library, University of Washington*)

special session and prevented any reform laws from being enacted, or even honestly considered," he declared, "think I am going to lie down, then they are greatly mistaken." His legislative program, Hartley contended, had been designed with no thought of politics, as he had believed the legislators to be intelligent and independent and desirous of acting in the interests of the state. But, as things had turned out, no legislature in the history of Washington had been "more boss-controlled and lobby-ridden than this one."

The "powerful timber crowd" and other special interests had banded together to defeat the program, an action, the governor asserted, that "completely astonished me." And it was the raising of the timber question that explained this development: the "forces of special privilege have been led or driven into action by the timber crowd." Hartley had lost this time, but he intended to fight on, using his knowledge of the timber industry to try to convince the people of the state that they had been swindled through "the antiquated, inefficient, graft-encouraging system of sales now in use." (The governor claimed that he had "never bought a stick of state timber in my life.") His ultimate goal remained the reduction of taxes, but this could not be accomplished until the "politicians, special interests and cinch seekers" had been driven from public life.[40]

Attention focused on the special legislative committee appointed to investigate Hartley's charges, which was scheduled to hold hearings in late March. The governor refused to appear before the committee or to cooperate with its investigation. He charged that the panel had been handpicked by "the leader of the house majority and likewise a leader in the powerful timber group." Its sole purpose was to whitewash the existing situation. "The timber group named the committee to investigate the timber group," the *Spokesman-Review* charged, and the *Olympian* sarcastically described a situation wherein Reed and his associates were conducting an investigation of "the relations of the state to their own personal business."[41]

There was some truth to these assertions. The committee chairman was Senator Richard Condon, manager of the Charles McCormick Lumber Company and a long-time political associate of Reed's. Its conclusions could be expected to reflect the views of the state's lumbermen, especially as Reed himself gave the most important testimony in the three days of hearings in Olympia. Reed stopped off to testify on his way to Seattle to board a ship for a business trip to Japan. If purchasers cut more timber than was indicated by the state's cruise, he argued, this was simply because of improved logging methods rather than any deliberate underestimate of the timber by the land commission.

Reed also made a series of recommendations. He supported Hartley's proposal that logging railroads be made common carriers. And in a significant alteration of his previously expressed views, he advised that cruises should be limited to small tracts of timber, with the results made public provided the state was absolved of liability for accuracy. Large tracts should be scaled when cut instead of cruised. In its report, issued at the conclusion of the final day of hearings, the committee concluded that the transactions investigated had been "conducted in a regular manner" with the state receiving "a fair price" for its timber. It also urged that Reed's recommendations on scaling be adopted by the land commission.[42]

Hartley supporters chortled over Reed's testimony and the committee report, which seemingly endorsed the governor's position. Hartley himself told the Young Men's Republican Club of Seattle that the lumbermen had been "licked to a frazzle." Reed, he charged, had written the committee's report and then departed for Japan in order to avoid public embarrassment. "Mark Reed seems to have led his followers out to a desert island," J. H. Brown observed, "and gone back to the mainland alone in the only boat." In changing his mind about Hartley's timber proposals, Brown continued, Reed must have been reflecting "what he hears with his ear to the ground."[43]

When he returned from his trip to the Orient in late May, Reed delivered a rebuttal at the Young Men's Republican Club, which had asked him to reply to the governor's address. He began by denying any great interest in state timber. Less than 2 percent of his timber purchases had been from the state, Reed noted, and only about two thousand acres of state timber would come under the influence of Simpson in the next fifteen years. Thus, he claimed, his position on the timber question was not motivated by selfish designs on the state's natural resources. Timber had been only a minor point in the governor's original program, Reed reminded his listeners. "But as the antagonism and the lack of faith in his other recommendations developed," Hartley had created "a smoke-screen out of timber to cover up his recommendations on these other disputed points." Reed claimed that he had been on the verge of working out an education compromise when Hartley "delivered that vitriolic, unnecessary, abusive and uncalled for speech known as his last message . . . that was such a message that no man with any self-respect could sit there and take without a feeling of resentment."

As for the rumors about conspiracies to defraud the state of its Olympic Peninsula timber, Reed pointed out that the "Irving-Hartley operation" was "more directly available to this timber than any other operator in the Northwest" as a result of Irving's logging activities in the northern part of the peninsula. He was also supposed to have written the timber committee report and then fled to the Orient, "afraid," Reed said, "to face the music." This was complete nonsense. Reed insisted that he had not seen the report until he read a newspaper account while in Yokohama and "I hope I will not get so old and decrepit that I will want to run away under conditions like that."

Turning to timber values, Reed told his audience that there was an "operation down here known as the Everett Logging Company, on the Tulalip Indian Reservation," an operation in which Governor Hartley owned a one-third interest. The reservation timber was costing Hartley and his associates $3.50 per thousand feet, "with all the favorable conditions surrounding the contract, including short haul, short tow to market, no taxes and no interest." And yet the governor insisted that something was crooked if the state did not get $5.00 per thousand for Olympic timber "isolated way up on the mountain, fifty-three miles from tidewater." Hartley's charge that timber owners were "robbing the red schoolhouse and the children of this state" was simply incredible. Reed concluded that the governor was "passing out ill-advised information to the people of this state." All state officials, he contended, had a duty "to lead us along in a harmonious and proper way, giving to all a square deal." And the time had come for the governor to realize this paramount fact.[44]

But the situation in the Republican party was far from harmonious, as each side in the dispute geared up to destroy the other in the primary campaigns. The governor continued to make use of the timber issue in his effort to discredit Reed. At a meeting in Aberdeen in late August, Hartley charged that new cruises initiated by his office varied significantly from the original cruises upon which the state had sold timber. He stated that in 1920 Reed purchased a three-quarter section cruised at sixteen million feet; a recent survey of the stamps, however, indicated that the cut had exceeded the cruise by ten million feet. And in 1924, the Simpson Logging Company, applying for a half section, admitted that it had inadvertently logged a hundred acres of timber in that tract twenty-five years before. "It took them a long time to find that trespass," Hartley sneered. "They found it after we started talking about timber."[45]

Responding to these charges of dishonesty, Reed opened his company's books to anyone wishing to investigate the transactions in question. The anti-Hartley forces also mounted a counterattack, releasing 1910-12 correspondence in which Hartley refused to purchase a tract of state timber because the asking price was too high. Not only did this disprove his claims about land commission prices, the governor's opponents pointed out, but it also compromised his assertion that he had never been interested in state timber. The *Mason County Journal* said that the governor was responsible for "a good deal of hot air and smoke going around the state about timber sales."[46]

As the campaigns were drawing to a close, they were overshadowed by the dismissal of Henry Suzzallo as president of the University of Washington. In the decade he served in that post, Suzzallo worked to strengthen the academic standing of the Seattle institution. But he also alienated many people by his arrogance and his forays into politics, which especially irritated supporters of the then Washington State College, a frequent loser in the Olympia appropriations battles. And he earned the ire of Roland Hartley as well, first by his efforts to improve working conditions in the lumber industry during the war and then by his opposition—along with the university's alumni association—to the governor's education proposals. Representative Maude Sweetman of Seattle, a supporter of Hartley, said that Suzzallo was "a petty, intriguing, self-seeking politician." Hartley was determined to destroy the educator.[47]

The problem facing Hartley was that Suzzallo was an appointee of the university board of regents and enjoyed its backing. Hartley made a start by filling two vacancies on the board with his supporters in March 1926, then by dismissing two other members for disobeying his order not to expend money appropriated by the legislature's controversial education bills. By dropping a third regent in August the governor enjoyed a 5-2 margin on the board. In early October the regents called on Suzzallo to resign. "I told them I would not quit my job," Suzzallo described the confrontation in a private letter. "It really was funny. They found it difficult to know just the next step. I could laugh at them—they were such small and unintelligent souls." Summoning their courage, the Hartley regents fired Suzzallo.[48]

This step brought howls of outrage from the anti-Hartley camp. Suzzallo, the *Mason County Journal* observed, "is merely another of the really big men of Washington who are marked for victims of a petty jealousy which listens to neither reason nor compromise but would rule or it must ruin." The *Seattle Times* undertook sponsorship of a campaign to recall the governor. That paper, which had long refused to criticize Hartley, now found that he was "the most despised man in the State." Suzzallo was confident of his vindication, telling a friend that Hartley was sure to be recalled.[49]

The backers of Suzzallo had to secure enough signatures to validate their recall petition before an election could be held. Hartley set up a strong committee, including such lumbermen as Everett Griggs and E. S. Grammer, to defend his conduct. (Some commentators claimed that these men wished to halt all state timer sales so that their own timberland would increase in value.) The recall forces, on the other hand, failed to establish an effective organization or to take advantage of the momentary indignation over Suzzallo's dismissal. The influence of the *Times* was no match for hostility east of the mountains and Suzzallo's unpopularity with his own faculty.

Reed and the other leaders of the house majority did not take part in the recall campaign. At least one Hartley supporter, however, imagined that he had discovered the influence of Reed behind the whole affair. Agnes Anderson, the widow of A. H. Anderson, had donated the forestry building to the University of Washington. Noting Mrs. Anderson's signature on a recall petition, Edward E. Flood detected "the countenance of one Mark E. Reed, as it was her husband who made responsible the operation of the Simpson Logging Company and later on the possibility of Mark Reed's success." Anderson Hall, moreover, "will cost the State many thousands of dollars a year to operate." But Reed steered clear of the campaign, recognizing its futility. In addition, the recall process was one of the progressive innovations disliked by Reed as a wrongful intrusion into the correct operations of government. The recall effort was indeed futile and the backers finally gave up in early 1927.[50]

Meanwhile, the legislative elections ended with neither side able to claim victory. Over a third of the members in the new house were freshmen, but the relative strength of the pro- and anti-Hartley forces remained unchanged. The first two years of Roland Hartley's administration had been an incredible period. The governor vilified his opponents and would not recognize that opposition could be based on sound motives. And those opponents, recoiling from his blows, determined to resist the governor's effort to win control of state government. With a new legislature, still controlled by the old majority, due to convene in January 1927, most observers looked forward to more bitterness and division. The legislators moved into a new capitol building in 1927, but they took with them the old emotions. "The Republican party in this state," Lieutenant Governor Lon Johnson lamented, "is becoming disorganized for lack of efficient leadership . . . . The result probably will be the loss of this state by our party."[51]

2

During the 1929 legislative session an unknown wit slipped into the house chamber one night and removed the members' nameplates, replacing them with signs upon which appropriate nicknames had been inscribed. At Reed's desk was the name "Question Mark." This jibe indicated the difficulties encountered by observers, and historians as well, in understanding Reed's behavior during his final two sessions in the legislature. The continued battles predicted after the 1926 elections never materialized between Reed and Hartley, for Reed more often than not sided with Hartley.

Soon after the legislature convened in January 1927 it became apparent that the situation had changed drastically. A pro-Hartley faction, led by Ed Sims, still confronted an anti-Hartley faction. But occupying the middle ground between the two was a third or "neutral" group led by Reed, which stressed compromise in an effort to avoid further disruption.

Acting in conjunction with Sims, and surprising his colleagues, Reed moved to strike the rule permitting reconsideration of vetoes. This rule had made possible the final pasage of the educational appropriation measures and was being counted on by the majority as a major weapon in the continuing fight against Hartley. Reed argued that the rule had been adopted in an emergency, an emergency that no longer existed. Opponents contended that dropping the rule would be an admission that the house "hadn't the nerve to stay with what we did a year ago." The refusal to adopt the rule was interpreted as a major victory for the governor. As for Reed, some observers suggested that he was afraid to continue the conflict with Hartley.[52]

Reed and Hartley apparently agreed to suspend their dispute for the duration of the session. Continuation of the wrangling of the previous year was not in the public interest. Hartley feared, moreover, that continued disharmony would endanger his chances for reelection in 1928. For his part, Reed detested public conflict and lacked the full-time commitment to politics necessary to carry on the fight. "There is no more harrowing or nerve racking work," he had earlier noted, "that a human being can be engaged in" than service in the legislature. Remarking on

Reed's seeming diffidence, Representative Maude Sweetman observed that "he enthuses and in the midst of your own enthusiasm, he cools." In addition, the cessation of Hartley's personality attacks meant that the essential agreement between the two men on the issues of timber and taxation could again come to the fore.[53]

Reed and Sims fought together against the session's major piece of legislation, a tax classification amendment to the state constitution. Sponsored by the Tax Limit League as its latest solution to the taxation problem, the amendment authorized the legislature to reclassify property for tax purposes. It was opposed by most lumbermen, who feared that they would be forced to bear an even greater burden if the tax structure was placed at the mercy of a farmer-dominated legislature.[54]

Reed and Sims countered the Tax Limit League measure with a substitute constitutional amendment that would classify intangible personal property. With these classifications imbedded in the constitution the legislature would have no role to play. Reed argued that under the original bill the legislature could change classification at will, benefitting whatever interest group was able to exert sufficient pressure. The legislature could, he said, "do anything except murder." The substitute, however, was handily defeated, and the tax classification amendment was approved 73-20 and sent on to the electorate in 1928. "The combination of the State Grange, the organized real estate men, school organizations, and the anti-Hartley fight got away with us," Reed later recalled. Observers could not recall any other time when Reed and Sims working together had been defeated.[55]

Reed temporarily resumed leadership of the anti-Hartley faction in an effort to set up an independent highway commission which would prevent the governor from gaining control of state highways. The state patrol and parks would also be a part of the new agency. Reed said that he had been the model of conciliation. But the new department would increase efficiency by uniting all matters relating to highways. He hoped that Hartley, "when he studies the effect of the bill," would see its merits and give it his approval. Hartley, however, wanted to assert his control and was able to mobilize enough support to have the measure indefinitely postponed.[56]

This opposition to the governor was only temporary; Reed concluded the session by fighting for a timber program he had worked out in conjunction with Sims and Hartley. Their program would replace the land and capitol commissions with a new state land board, increase the governor's role in timber sales, provide for more accurate cruises, implement Hartley's common carrier proposals, and limit individual timber sales to 160 acres. The bill was approved by the house but died in the senate. Reflecting on Reed's sponsorship of this measure, observers were as mystified by his behavior as they had been when he failed to resume the fight with Hartley in January.[57]

The rapprochement between the governor and his most prominent enemy did not last long, indicating that it was only a temporary political expedient. Hartley was soon attacking Reed again, charging in a July radio broadcast that the house leader had succeeded in getting the state to pave the main street of Shelton, "thereby relieving his property, of which he owns much, of local improvements." The *Mason County Journal*, speaking for Reed, answered that the street was part of the Olympic Highway, which had, of necessity, been routed through Shelton. Hartley's charges, the paper noted, "illustrate the brand of political buncombe which is being peddled to credulous people over the state who don't know any better." The antagonism would not die out. Reed, despite his circumspect behavior during the session, did not intend to let Roland Hartley win a second term.[58]

"My single purpose in this next campaign," Reed wrote privately in mid-1927, "will be to defeat Hartley for reelection, first in the primary, if it can be done, and secondly in the general election with the Democratic nominee, whoever he may be." He had nothing personal against the governor, he claimed. They had differed on many occasions, but this would not ordinarily lead him to support removal of a Republican incumbent. The problem was that "this constant turmoil" caused by Hartley was "very injurious to our state and there does not seem to be any way to stop it except with a change." Despite this disclaimer of personal animus, Reed was also motivated by a desire to wreak vengeance on Hartley for his defamations. An election campaign in which money, organization, and hard work were key factors might well produce victory over the governor.[50]

The problem was to find the right candidate to take on the man Yakima publisher W. W. Robertson called "the pest now in office." Initially, Reed encouraged the gubernatorial ambitions of Lieutenant Governor Lon Johnson. The Eastern Washington Republican believed that Hartley could not be reelected because of the party split. He charged that the governor had "misled and deceived the people so successfully that many of them believe that he is the Savior of the State." Johnson could not recall a similar situation in the state's history.[60]

But Johnson was not the only Republican planning to run against Hartley. Senator Edward L. French of Vancouver, who had been the Hart organization's candidate in the 1924 primary, planned to run again. Johnson informed Reed that French could not win the nomination. French had enjoyed strong support east of the mountains in 1924, but Johnson had yet to find "the slightest indications of support for him" now. Therefore, Johnson asked Reed and Alex Polson to visit French, inform him of the facts, and urge him to withdraw. The anti-Hartley forces must not be divided. "I cannot win it with any handicap," Johnson pointed out. "It will take a real battle to displace the present crowd."

Reed answered that Polson would call on French. The Grays Harbour logger stated that if French insisted on making the race he would "not waste his time or effort in the primary but will promptly announce to the public and his friends in particular that he is not interested in the Republican ticket and is supporting the Democratic." Reed also passed along the news that Ed Sims might tender his considerable influence on behalf of Johnson. Hartley had dropped Sims from his cherished position on the state fisheries board and the disgruntled Sims desired revenge. "I have great hopes that he will be with us during the coming campaign," Reed reported.[61]

The Johnson movement, however, fizzled out by late July 1927. French refused to drop out of the race and little enthusiasm had developed for either man. "Our friends seem to be apathetic," Reed informed Johnson, "and too generally it is taken for granted that Hartley will be the primary nominee." You should run, Reed continued, only if you "have a reasonably clear field and have at the start what would seem to be a reasonable chance for success." This was no longer the case, and Reed was prepared to concede the primary to the governor: "I do not want to and will not waste my energy and funds in an primary campaign that seems hopeless."[62]

French was left as the sole candidate of the anti-Hartley Republicans. Although French was reported to be gaining strength, Reed rejected entreaties that he support the Senator. Wenatchee businessman John A. Gellatly, who was running for lieutenant governor, wrote that the governor's opponents "are in a deal of a plight." Hartley was "a comedian on the platform and can make white out of black . . . . Nothing but brimstone will hold him down." But, Gellatly lamented, "God knows where to find the brimstone . . . and we will just have to sit by, I presume, and let nature take its course."[63]

For a time Reed considered running himself. His mill plans had been implemented and the business could now get along without his direct supervision. But Reed shied away from running against Hartley. "While you could have had the place four years ago by simply saying so," J. J. Donovan wrote, "just now the psychology of the situation is wrong." The *Mason County Journal*, reflecting Reed's position, suggested that Clark Savidge run instead. French, though, remained the only alternative to Hartley, and the governor easily won nomination for a second term.[64]

After President Coolidge announced in the summer of 1927 that he would not run for reelection, Reed took a leading role in the presidential campaign of Herbert Hoover. Reed respected Hoover's ability, particularly his business sense, and was one of his early supporters in the state. National committeeman Richard Condon was nominal head of the Washington Hoover campaign, but Sims and Reed wound up shouldering most of the financial and organization load. "You and I are holding up [the] Hoover campaign," Sims grumbled.[65]

Reed also played an important part in the fight against the tax classification amendment, which had been referred to the electorate by the legislature. It was, George Long of the Weyerhaeuser Timber Company argued, "the most dangerous proposal which has been presented during the past decade." Legislative classification of property meant that "if one class secures a favorable rate another must secure an unfavorable one," Long continued, noting that "business has been subjected to the heaviest rates of taxation" in those states where the approach had been adopted. Reed joined with Long and a small group of businessmen to raise fifty thousand dollars to finance newspaper ads and radio commercials against the amendment. "This is probably," Reed believed, "the most serious taxation problem that we have had for a great many years."[66]

Reed's main difficulty, as the general election campaign got underway in late September, was to decide what to do about Roland Hartley. The Seattle *Argus* had urged the defeat of the governor in the primary, declaring that it was "not so much interested in who will be the next governor of this state as in who will not." Now, however, the *Argus* determined that "after all, Governor Hartley has not been so bad" and called for his reelection. Other anti-Hartley Republicans, though, found themselves, as the *Mason County Journal* observed, "between 'the Devil and the deep sea' and must choose what to them will seem the lesser of two evils."[67]

Reed indicated privately that he would support the Democratic candidate if Hartley was renominated. And this he did, by providing money and support in southwestern Washington for A. Scott Bullitt, the socially prominent Seattle attorney nominated by the Democrats. Many other Republic businessmen and editors did likewise. "The welfare of the state and its people," one of those editors, Grant Angle, contended, "is more vital to every citizen than merely to elect a Republican name to the office of Governor with the assurance of continued discord." Bullitt ran a vigorous campaign, but lost to Hartley by 214,000 to 282,000 votes (he won nearly 60 percent of the vote in Shelton), a much better showing than Democrataic candidates usually made in these years of Republican domination. This was no doubt the result of his support among Republicans. "I appreciate very much what you did in my behalf," Bullitt wrote Reed.[68]

The reelection of Hartley had been anticipated philosophically by Reed. "If a majority of the people," he noted, "feel that a change should not be made, it is all right with me." Still, he did not look forward to spending four more years as a target of the governor. The latter's reelection was a major factor in Reed's decision to retire from politics. But he could take some satisfaction in the victory of Hoover and the defeat of the tax classification amendment, both by two-to-one margins. "It certainly is gratifying to all of us." he wrote of the defeat of the amendment.[69]

There was some talk following the election that Reed would be offered the position of secretary of the interior in Hoover's cabinet. "President [-elect] Hoover is a western man," the *Mason County Journal* pointed out, "and he also knows that it was the West which gave him the first big boost for the high office he has gained." Yet the region had failed to receive much recognition in the nation's capital "since Richard Ballinger was secretary of the interior under President Taft." These were just rumors, however, and no offer was made. Besides, Reed wanted to give up politics and planned to do so after the 1929 legislative session. His service in Olympia had been "too long and not worthwhile," he concluded. "At times I have enjoyed it but one cannot go down there for sixty days and give his own affairs anything but hit-and-miss attention." And once a session was over it took "about thirty days to bring your nervous system back to normal." Eight terms was clearly enough.[70]

The last of these eight was a humdrum affair in comparison with earlier gatherings. Reed and Sims joined together to exercise nominal leadership of the house, but both, noted the *Seattle Times*, were "quietly slipping into the background." Despite his opposition to Hartley's reelection, Reed became once again the principal house spokesman for the administration, ending his career in a position he had occupied many times before. Those who remembered the battles of previous years witnessed Reed supporting legislation to place the proposed new highway department under the jurisdiction of the governor and to repeal the millage levy for higher eduction. Little was accomplished during the desultory two months in Olympia, and many members blamed Reed and Sims for the failure. Political commentators stated that the two would have to fight to retain their leadership positions when the legislature next met.[71]

Reed also sided with the governor in a curious dispute that developed in 1930. When William Butler, the very conservative Everett banker and lumberman and brother of Columbia University president Nicholas Murray Butler, asked Clark Savidge to extend the time required for removal of state timber he had purchased in 1920, Savidge refused. (Whatever timber was not cut during the period of a contract—usually ten years—reverted to the state, although the land commissioner could grant an extension.) Savidge said that if Butler could persuade Governor Hartley, Butler's frequent business associate, to be more amenable toward the land commission, he would reconsider. The governor had refused to attend meetings of the state capitol committee, preventing it from operating, and had recently been attacking Savidge again.

Butler, asking Reed to intervene, fumed at what he termed "a real, hard-shelled holdup; the purse, instead of the usual shakedown, being the control of the Governor in the conduct of his office." While conceding that such an arrangement was theoretically possible, Butler refused to accept Savidge's proposal. In a "very personal" letter to Savidge, Reed admitted that the land commissioner had a just grievance. However, Savidge was not being fair in attempting to cause Butler to suffer because of this "malice," as Hartley had no investment in the involved timber. And should the public become aware of the affair, as it certainly would, the reaction would be "that you have allowed your political differences with the Governor and his friends to so unbalance your judgment that you have brought politics into the administration of the business of your department." Savidge, under more prodding from Reed, eventually relented and granted the extension. The episode indicated the extent of feelings in Olympia and demonstrated Reed's concern with maintaining harmony in the party as well as his own distaste for continuation of the squabble.[72]

After returning from the 1929 session, Reed announced that he would not run for reelection. "The public effort we have been putting forth," he remarked privately, "can probably be carried on better by younger and more active citizenship." Reed's statement, Grant Angle observed, was received with regret by residents of Mason County. If there was a "better informed or broaderguaged man in state affairs his name is not now recalled." Without another citizen of Reed's prestige, Mason County was sure to lose its representation in Olympia when the people voted to redistrict the state in 1930 and the county was merged into a district with other more populous counties. Some associates tried to talk Reed out of quitting the legislature. "There has been some unfavorable reaction towards my decision," Reed informed one correspondent, "but I am thoroughly convinced that I am right and the decision will stand." He was tired of the style of politics practiced by Roland Hartley. Nobody, a friend wrote, could blame you for placing yourself "beyond the further reach of ... censure, innuendo, criticism and vituperation."[73]

Mark Reed was sixty-three years old when he retired from elective office. He had been the most respected person in state politics, at least until he became the target of Roland Hartley's abuse. Even then, few doubted his essential integrity and ability. His had been the politics of issues and reason, a politics that pursued private interest while stressing the interest of the community and often managing to serve both. In contrast, the new politics of the Hartley style was the politics of mass persuasion, utilizing whatever tactic, no matter how gross or misrepresentative of the truth, would gain public support, recognizing no ethics but those of the tally sheet. Mark Reed served in politics again by directing lobbying efforts and managing Herbert Hoover's state reelection campaign in 1932. However, Reed did not again serve in public office, nor was he again in the public eye.

CHAPTER 5

Markets and Mills

With the implementation of Mark Reed's mill plans, the Shelton waterfront came alive with industrial activity. The Reed and McCleary sawmills turned out over three hundred thousand feet of hemlock and fir per day. The Rainier pulp mill began operations in May 1927, building toward a daily capacity of one hundred tons. Eastward along the bayshore from the main complex the Reed Mill Company's cedar mill cut one hundred thousand shingles a day. As a result, the Simpson Logging Company was able to do a more thorough job in the woods, hauling out logs that would not previously have been cut for the market. "We are conserving our timber," Reed observed, "and what we are losing in the cost in logging, we are more than making up in the larger cut of timber from the lands." This meant that the Shelton mills were operating on low quality logs. "I realize, of course," Reed noted, "that the quality of the product we are delivering to the mill is not such as we would be compelled to offer if we were selling our logs in the open market, but that is what we built the mill for." The mills, then, improved management of the logging company, but they also had potentialities of their own.[1]

1

The Northwest lumber industry had always been Pacific-oriented, selling its output not only in California but also across the ocean in Hawaii, China, and Australia. This remained so even after the coming of the transcontinental railroads at the end of the nineteenth century provided access to domestic markets in the East, as lumbermen were prevented by high freight rates from competing on the Atlantic Coast. Foreign shipments, most of them within the Pacific basin, doubled in the first decade of the new century and continued to grow apace

132

afterward, remaining a vital ingredient in the prosperity of the industry. By the end of World War I the island empire of Japan had become of particular importance to the mill owners of Washington and Oregon.[2]

Japan, a nation of eighty million people, was, Reed noted, "peculiarly a wood consuming country." Wood was "the all-dominating material in construction." Only the more substantial business and governmental buildings were constructed of other materials. The nation consumed four billion feet of lumber a year, two-thirds of which came from rapidly diminishing native forests and from the island of Sakhalin, which had been captured in the Russo-Japanese War. An increasing portion had to be imported, especially after the great Tokyo earthquake of 1923. The Northwest supplied six hundred million feet a year by the mid-1920s (5 percent of total Pacific Coast lumber production) and was expected to increase this to over a billion feet by 1930. The public, observed the *Mason County Journal*, "has little idea of the magnitude to which the demand from Japan has grown in the past few years."[3]

Most of the wood shipped to Japan was in the form of so-called "Jap Squares," lumber that would be further refined in Japanese mills. This grade was described by the principal Northwest exporter as "sound, strong lumber free from shakes, and large knots, loose knots or rotten knots, and defects that materially impair its strength, well manufactured and suitable for good, substantial, construction purposes, also suitable for remanufacturing into smaller sizes without unreasonable loss from defects." The Japanese demanded quality lumber and Reed meant to meet that demand. "The better it is the better [the] price," one agent commented. "We produce a better lumber than they do almost anywhere else in the state," Alex Polson boasted of his and Reed's mills, "and the Japanese want it."[4]

Although large amounts of lumber were shipped to Japan, conditions did not appear altogether auspicious as the Reed Mill geared up to begin operation in mid-1925. This was largely due to the glutting of the market by shippers eager to cash in on the Japanese bonanza. "We are having some depression in the market here now," one observer wrote in the spring, due to speculation among Northwest exporters. Prices were lower than they had been for several years. But by the fall, with Reed loading his first shipment at Tacoma, conditions had improved. "There are no stocks to speak of and our own yard is entirely cleaned out," Polson's agent reported. With economic conditions in Japan improving and available supplies low, the year 1925 seemed after all to be a good time to be entering the market.[5]

The Reed Mill was invited to affiliate with the Douglas Fir Exploitation and Export Company, an association of exporting sawmills that included such firms as Long-Bell and the St. Paul and Tacoma Lumber Company. This organization controlled 40 percent of the lumber exported to Japan and desired to control even more. Turning down the invitation, Reed remarked that his mill, operating strictly on hemlock, must depend solely on itself in the exploitation of markets. "We must," he said, "have orders on hand at all times to keep our mill operating efficiently." Reed disliked the idea of losing his independence; indeed, he had worked hard to decrease his dependence on others. "Our identity would be lost in that of the Douglas Fir," Chris Kreinenbaum, who had been hired to handle sales for the new mill, pointed out. "The possibility of building a trade on merit and quality and for future years would be lost." The mill, moreover, would lose control over decisions, being "subject to ideas and policies from units in other districts that might be absolutely at variance with the object of our operation."

The DFE and E, as it was commonly known within the industry, pressed Reed to reconsider, sending representatives to Shelton to urge him to join the organization for the good of the industry. Polson was also subjected to this pressure, and likewise refused, noting that the company was selling lumber below the cost of production even though this was not necessary. "There is something," he told Reed, "infinitely wrong with the salesmanship under the Douglas Fir." Agents of the company had confronted Polson in his Hoquiam office, telling him that they would stay there "till Hell freezes over, to get me in. That doesn't frighten me," Polson observed. "I can skate on Hell if it freezes over, just as well as I can skate on ice." Reed and Polson agreed that it was to their advantage to remain independent.[6]

The Reed and Polson mills entered into an alliance for the

handling of Japanese sales. As agent for his shipments, Reed hired Robert S. Fox, who was already handling the business for Polson's Eureka Lumber Company. An experienced lumberman, Fox worked with the Nakagawa Company of Osaka to market imports from the Northwest. He received a dollar for each thousand feet sold and, for his part, put up a $50,000 bond and a $50,000 life insurance policy. Precautions were necessary, Reed felt. "Mr. Fox is entirely honorable and in a business way is perfectly reliable," he told Polson, "but he is doing business in a country that is far away and where business standards are entirely different from those we are accustomed to in this country." Therefore, Reed concluded, we must "protect our agreement with Mr. Fox, either in life or death."[7]

The first Reed Mill lumber for Japan was shipped from Tacoma in September 1925. From then on one steamer a month called at Olympia, receiving there a load of two million feet brought by lighter from Shelton, and then proceeded to Grays Harbor for a load of equal size from the Polson Mill. These sailings meant prosperity for the Shelton area and were given prominent notice in the *Mason County Journal*. "While Japanese orders are being handled by a number of the mills of the Northwest," the paper informed its readers, "the local mill has some advantages for this trade and is expected to have its share of orders."[8]

In early 1926 Reed journeyed to Japan with his wife and J. C. Shaw of the Eureka Lumber Company. (This was the trip supposedly taken by Reed to run away from the political fight with Roland Hartley and was also the only time in his life Reed went abroad.) Along with Shaw, Reed spent two weeks getting acquainted with Japan's lumbermen and market. "At one banquet," he later recalled, "we had present over four hundred lumbermen dressed in garb all the way from a breech cloth to dinner dress." Reed was impressed by the energy and ability of the Japanese and by their efficiency as well. "If our people displayed the same energy and activity as is evidenced in your country," he told his host, "we would doubtless far out-distance the results we are now obtaining."

Reed also found the future prospect for imports from Northwest mills to be highly promising. "It is estimated," he

pointed out, "that five years will practically see the cesession
[sic] of cutting of all timber in any quantity from their local
grounds." This would mean that the demand for American
lumber "will increase if we properly care for the market." All
that was needed was for exporters to stabilize their prices and
provide better quality lumber. "Much lumber," he observed,
"has been shipped over there which has tended to give our
product, in general, a damaging reputation." This unfortunate
tendency would have to be corrected. As Reed returned to the
United States then, the future looked bright for the export of
lumber to Japan.⁹

But the Japanese market was unable to keep pace with the
surplus, failing to do so by a large margin. Shipments from
Washington and Oregon in 1926 increased by 50 percent over
the previous year, to nine hundred million feet. At the same
time demand was falling off. Much of the earthquake damage,
which had been largely responsible for the flourishing demand
for American lumber, had been repaired, and the death of the
emperor in the summer further dampened business conditions.
"The market at Osaka," Fox reported in late 1926, "is now only
taking 50%, or even less, of the amount of lumber used here in
1924-1925."

Fox had considerable difficulty when customers canceled
contracts taken out during better times. He informed Reed that
prices would have to be cut. In a situation where everyone was
scrambling to dispose of inventory at whatever price could be
obtained there was no chance of maintaining stable prices. "It is
hard to blame these folks," Fox wrote, "when they resort to all
kinds of tricks to get out of taking lumber at high prices after
the market drops two or three dollars per M [thousand feet] as
they have no protection at all." Reed reassured Fox, telling him
that "you have done better with the sale of your product than
has any other operator in that district." Even in bad times, he
continued, one could not complain "when we are doing better
than our competitors."¹⁰

Reed placed much of the blame for the chaotic conditions in
Japan on the Douglas Fir Export Company. That organization
had decided to increase its share of the Japanese trade to 60
percent and had adopted a policy, Reed commented, "of selling

on the market and getting the business irrespective of price." This decision resulted from pressure by member mills to move their stock, particularly from Long-Bell. "They have such a tremendous production," Reed pointed out, "that they are compelled to sell." He believed that Long-Bell had threatened to drop out of the DFE and E unless its lumber was sold. "To prevent it they will have a fixed policy of taking all business offered at the best prices they can get." As a result, prices in Japan fell to new lows.[11]

Reed considered A. A. Baxter, general manager of Douglas Fir, to be a particularly disturbing factor in the Japanese market. "Mr. Baxter is so filled with animosity toward anything outside of his organization," Chris Kreienbaum wrote, "that his mind has become perverted with the idea of destroying every independent producer to satisfy that animus feeling." The animosity toward Baxter was so intense that members of the DFE and E would not allow him to attend meetings designed to lead to cooperation with the outside mills. Reed counseled patience, observing that Baxter's "ruinous" policy would in the end lead to his own destruction. "It is rather difficult," Reed noted, "to drive any normal human being who has a spark of independence, especially where he is in such a position that he cannot be ruined financially."[12]

Japan was a bitter disappointment for Reed. By 1929 exports to the island nation had dropped to half the level of 1926 and they continued to fall. "Our Japanese market is dormant," Kreienbaum observed. Credit was being restricted there and the rate of construction was falling off. A new source of lumber was being developed in Siberia, where extensive stands of high quality timber awaited exploitation. And, most important, the Japanese government instituted a tariff on imports of lumber from America. "The [Japanese] lumbermen generally are against it," Reed told Everett Griggs of the St. Paul and Tacoma Lumber Company, "but it seems as if the Government is being urged strongly to adopt this policy not only from the standpoint of revenue but from the economic standpoint of more employment for their own people." There no longer appeared to be a profitable future in the Japanese market.[13]

Northwest lumbermen had expected to make great amounts

of money exporting lumber to Japan. The only thing that could prevent this, Polson had claimed, was "an earthquake that will move the Japanese current a thousand or more miles off the coast." But the lumbermen had demonstrated their proclivity for attempting to make too much of a good thing, dumping more material than the market could bear and driving prices down to a point that mocked the hopes for profit. With the Japanese bonanza collapsing, they would have to fall back on other markets.[14]

2

The construction of the Northern Pacific and Great Northern railroads made it physically possible for Washington and Oregon lumbermen to sell their product in the East. But the rates for rail shipment and the problem of obtaining enough cars made it difficult to compete with Southern and Midwestern operators, particularly in the great urban markets on the Atlantic Coast. The opening of the Panama Canal, however, cut the water mileage between Puget Sound and New York in half and meant that lumber could be shipped by water. Northwest lumbermen, though, fumed over President Woodrow Wilson's refusal to accept the idea that American ships should be allowed to use the canal without paying tolls. Requiring that all shippers pay the same rate allowed British Columbia operators to compete with their fellows south of the border for the Atlantic trade. Wilson's action, complained Edwin G. Ames, was "one of the worst things we have been up against for a long time." Still, Northwest mill owners were no longer shut out of the East—there was a new cargo trade to be exploited.[15]

As his business affairs expanded to include trade with the Atlantic Coast, Reed began to delegate decision-making responsibilities to subordinates. Since the death of A. H. Anderson in 1914 Simpson had been a one-man operation. Reed "simply made all the decisions," his son recalls. He was given complete control over the company by the widows of Anderson and Sol Simpson. Reed, with long-time vice president Arthur Govey, made up the entire membership of the board of directors. When meetings of the directors were required, Reed "simply dictated the minutes," according to his son, "and then had them signed by the people concerned." No one regarded this as an unusual or dictatorial practice.[16]

Reed's sons began to take over some of their father's duties as they reached manhood in the middle and late 1920s. The eldest son, Sol, became Reed's principal assistant and gradually assumed supervision of logging operations. Frank had to spend a good deal of time in Arizona because of poor health, but was being counted on as manager of marketing for Simpson. Will, the youngest, was completing studies at the University of Washington in preparation for a career in commercial banking. Reed was especially close to Sol, who impressed friends and associates with his sense of responsibility and desire for hard work. Sol was seriously injured in an automobile accident in 1924, and the young woman companion who administered first aid, Dorothy Scarbrough, later received a sizeable bequest in Reed's will, indicating the latter's fondness for his son.[17]

Chris Kreienbaum, the young businessman hired to handle sales for the Reed Mill, also earned Reed's trust. Kreienbaum so impressed Reed that he soon was made manager of the mill company, which he operated with only minimal supervision. "He'd come over to the door of my office," Kreienbaum recalled of Reed, "stick his head in, and say, 'Chris, are you too busy to have a chat?' Well, I never was too busy to have a chat with a man like that." George Drake, who became an important company official in the early 1930s, remembered that Reed "would talk over with me what my plans were for the week. . . . He gave me quite a bit of rope which I think was his approach— you are responsible and you pay the consequences." As his business grew in new directions, then, Reed gathered about him talented younger men who could take some of the load off his shoulders.[18]

Reed planned to ship most of his lumber to the Atlantic Coast. He believed, with the nation's economy in full prosperous swing in 1925, that this would mean a good return for the mill. Building permits for the first ten months of the year exceeded the number issued in all of 1924. "From all reports," Kreienbaum noted, "we are just entering an area [sic] of prosperity which will extend a great distance in the future."

Demand in the East was high, lumber shipments from the Pacific Coast having increased eight times between 1921 and 1925. Reed and Kreienbaum were "very optimistic" about the future.[19]

One associate of Reed's, C. H. Springer, observed that the marketing of a mill's product "is a very vital and difficult problem." Several methods were in use in the intercoastal lumber trade. Some mills sold their product to local wholesalers who in turn sold it to their Eastern counterparts. A few of the large companies, such as Weyerhaeuser and Long-Bell, maintained their own yards in Atlantic Coast cities. Others stationed agents in those cities to handle wholesale transactions. Still others, like the St. Paul and Tacoma Lumber Company, maintained large forces of salesmen to take orders directly from retailers. A final method involved the sale of lumber by the mill to such firms as Dant and Russell of Portland, which controlled large amounts of steamship space.

Individually, these established methods involved either too much cost or too little control over disposition of product, so the Reed Mill adopted a combination of several. The mill sent its lumber on consignment to Atlantic Coast wholesalers. Two million feet a month went to the Duquesne Lumber Company, an experienced organization which sold lumber in the Mid-Atlantic states "as far back as the railroad rate will allow competition." The rest of the mill's output, five hundred thousand feet a month, was consigned to the Hold-Meredith Lumber Corporation of New York. By adopting various methods of marketing, Kreienbaum and Reed hoped to successfully establish Reed Mill lumber as a quality product.[20]

In doing so they overcame the traditional antipathy toward hemlock. As we have seen, that grade had long been regarded as inferior and was not in much demand. With increasing amounts of hemlock being encountered, however, a market was gradually developed. This required aggressive salesmanship. Kreienbaum recalled that in the beginning "it had been a question of choking the hemlock down the customer's throat." By the time the Reed Mill began shipping lumber to the Atlantic Coast, hemlock had gone far toward supplanting Southern pine as the principal common lumber used in that region.[21]

Washington mills shipped over a billion feet of lumber through the Panama Canal to Eastern ports in 1926, twice the combined total of British Columbia and Oregon. Once again prices slumped under the impact of these shipments. The average sales price of hemlock fell 10 percent by the end of the year. But Reed, typically, was concerned more with establishing a steady market for his mill than with immediate prices. "Steadily and surely," Kreienbaum reported after a tour of the East, "we are intrenching ourselves with our grade and with our service to such an extent that in the future . . . we will have developed a trade which will be of great value to us." Already the mill's product was preferred when its price matched that of competing operations.[22]

The problem, though, was meeting the competition, as many mill owners were more interested in short-term return than in long-range development of stable markets with stable prices. Great quantities of exports had undermined the market in Japan, and equally large domestic shipments were doing the same on the Atlantic Coast. "It is appalling," Reed commented, "that the lumbermen who are supposed to be men of reasonable intelligence will allow their business to drift into such an unsatisfactory situation." The old methods of free-wheeling independence, of letting the future take care of itself, had to be abandoned in favor of sensible cooperation among mill owners. The obstacles preventing this development had to be overcome if the industry was to survive. "Let us stop riding our industry around in a horse and buggy," Kreienbaum argued. "Let us modernize and give it an automobile."[23]

The Atlantic Coast was regarded as a dumping ground by many operators. Much lumber was shipped unsold and then unloaded for whatever price could be obtained. These "transit shipments," noted the *Mason County Journal*, "have been largely responsible for the demoralization of eastern markets." Writing from New York, Kreienbaum informed Reed of one retailer who had ordered lumber "and on the same vessel was 1,500,000 feet of transits which his competitors were able to buy for less, so why should he order when he can fill his stock from transit shipment?" Apparently the wholesalers were mainly responsible, as they had to fill their steamer space whether or not the lumber had been sold. But all producers occasionally found it necessary to ship transits. Charter rates were too high for ships to be dispatched only partially loaded. The result was a highly sensitive market for Northwest lumber.[24]

These conditions worsened during 1928 and 1929. The amount of lumber shipped to the Atlantic Coast remained the same but demand fell off, further depressing prices. "During the war we were all called upon to expand our industry and increase our production," Reed pointed out after a trip to the East in early 1928, "and this has been going on ever since, with the result that in every line of industry there has been an overproduction." The economy was noticeably "slowing down." By the summer of 1929, credit was being restricted and building permits in the great cities of the East were down by 40 percent. "On the Atlantic Coast," Kreienbaum commented, "we have a condition today which is probably worse than any we have ever seen in that market." Northwest mills, he predicted, could expect to dispose of only two-thirds of the normal amount of lumber there in the coming years.[25]

During these years Reed's hemlock mill shipped some lumber to Europe, and the shingle mill shipped by rail to the Midwest. But the Atlantic Coast was the principal market. Its decline, following the collapse of the Japanese trade, meant difficult times for the lumber industry. The trend presaged the kinds of economic problems that would confront all of American business during the Great Depression years. Reed was confronted with serious problems in Shelton as well.[26]

3

The great expansion of the pulp and paper industry during the 1920s was welcomed by Reed. "The construction of pulp mills is proceeding at a rapid rate," the *Tacoma Ledger* reported. The number of pulp mills in Washington tripled between 1923 and 1928, and the state ranked fourth in the nation in wood pulp production. While the nation's pulp mill output decreased slightly in 1927, Washington's increased by over one-third. The pulp mill's utilization of what had been waste wood made for greater conservation in logging and in the sawmills and also promised considerable financial rewards.[27]

With the pulp industry prospering, the Zellerbach interests laid plans to expand their operations in the Northwest, including building a paper plant alongside the Rainier mill. The problem was to secure a dependable supply of wood. Reed suggested to E. M. Mills in October 1928 that the Rainier organization "take over the Reed hemlock mill and the power house, entering into a long-time contract with the Simpson Logging Company to take our hemlock logs at the ruling market price." In return for his mill interests Reed asked for $1.5 million in Rainier stock.

Mills agreed that the deal would secure a wood supply for the pulp mill but rejected Reed's offer. "None of our large stock-holders," Mills told Reed, "would look with favor upon any plan that meant any one stockholder, even yourself, increase his investment in the Rainier Pulp & Paper Company." This was the crux of the matter as Reed was interested in securing the major voice in the larger operation that would include both the pulp mill and his own sawmill. He would thus exercise greater control over an increasingly integrated manufacturing plant in Shelton. Although his offer was rejected, he intended to keep it alive for possible future consideration. The prospects of Rainier, however, were soon deflated.[28]

Oyster cultivation had always been an important industry in the Shelton area, and Reed himself had a sizeable investment in the beds. Local oystermen considered the establishment of the Rainier mill, which would dump acidic waste into the bay, with some trepidation. The *Mason County Journal* reassured them, noting that the plant, "being of the safer class and planned to have every modern feature and safeguard to public health and welfare," would pose no threat. Besides, while the oystermen had a right to seek information about the impact of the pulp mill, they had no right to question its establishment. "The communities need the pay rolls," editor Grant Angle pointed out.[29]

Output from the oyster beds declined after the mill began using Shelton bay for waste liquor disposal in 1927, an occurrence that was far more than a coincidence to the oystermen. The state brought in scientists from the University of Washington to study the problem, but proof of a connection could not be found. "It has not been demonstrated to me (that is, satisfactorily)," Reed told one oyster grower, "that the pulp mill is responsible for the lack of a seed catch on the oyster beds." He claimed that his interest in the mill was "very nominal and does nót compare in amount to my investment in the oyster beds." The Shelton *Journal* asserted that there was no way of pinning down responsibility for the decline in production. While the *Journal* did not wish to see the end of the oyster industry, neither did it wish to "see any unnecessary burden placed on the new industry upon which the future prosperity of Shelton largely depends."

In October 1929 the oystermen met with Governor Hartley in Olympia to learn the results of the state study. The state reported that the waste discharge was not harmful to oysters or other marine life, but promised to keep an eye on further developments. The report was enough for Reed. "I do not think it is fair," he observed, "to charge this condition wholly up to the pulp mill activity, when we don't know what the trouble is and all reports thus far of the scientists tend to disprove that the discharge of waste from the pulp mill is responsible." The oystermen, though, faced with ruin, did not find the report satisfactory and made plans to press the case against the mill.[30]

A study undertaken by the federal government in early 1930 indicated that pulp mill waste was to blame for the declining oyster production. "Apparently," the *Journal* observed, "the oyster industry, so far as this bay is concerned, is extinct." Eighteen suits asking over a million dollars in damages were brought by the oyster growers against the Rainier Company in federal court. "If I felt that we were really responsible for serious damage to the oyster beds in question," Mills informed Reed, "I would not have waited for suits to have been brought but would have endeavored to compensate the people reasonably and in a friendly way."[31]

Rainier contended that studies made under its auspices proved that it was not responsible for the damage to the oyster culture. "Yet," Mills warned Reed, "the mere bringing of these suits and the expense involved in them, and the possibility of other suits, has caused us seriously to consider whether the Shelton plant should not be shut down, probably dismantled, as an economic proposition, the machinery and equipment transferred to Port Angeles." The mill had been located in Shelton because of the proximity of raw materials and water supply, and the addition of new facilities had been planned. These plans, apparently, "must . . . now be abandoned." Moreover, the "continual harassment" from the oystermen had depreciated "the market price of the company stock" and immediate action was necessary to protect the stockholders.

Removal of the plant would be a serious blow to Reed's mill complex and would result in reduction of the market for chips from the Reed Mill. In addition, the troubles of Rainier were causing some personal embarrassment. "Through the use of my name and through my direct influence," Reed reminded Mills, "quite a considerable amount of financing of the [Zellerbach] plants at Shelton, Grays Harbor and Port Angeles has been carried out." His friends, faced with the damage to their investments, were clamoring for explanations. "It is rather startling how confidence can be shaken," Reed observed.[32]

The *Mason County Journal* informed its readers in mid-December that the future of the mill and its monthly payroll "is in jeapordy." This was no longer simply a dispute between the mill and the oystermen. Rather, the citizens of Shelton must reflect on "what the loss of the big pulp industry with its otherwise promising future means to all." Oystermen countered with the assertion that those "local interests who were responsible for bringing the plant to Shelton, with full knowledge of the fatal results . . . are now attempting to play on public sympathy and picture the oystermen as an octopus not interested in public welfare." Waste from the mill, they charged, "has made a regular cesspool of the bays."[33]

On 22 December two thousand people attended a meeting called by the Shelton-Mason County Commercial Club to discuss the situation. As the main speaker, Reed explained the relationship of the mill to the town's prosperity. Rainier allowed the sawmills to operate even in bad times to produce wood for the manufacture of pulp. He noted that management had no objection to meeting legitimate claims for damage but felt that most of the complaints were unwarranted and that the townspeople were failing to support its position. "I hope someone has a solution for a situation which seems preposterous," he concluded, "but it does exist and I see no remedy." The meeting ended with the appointment of a committee of local businessmen to see a solution. "Your statement . . . put the whole matter in a different light," one told Reed, "and I am now able to support any measure to retain the mill here with intelligence and conviction."[34]

Reed informed Mills that he had never seen "a community that is more alive to the situation than are the people of Shelton since the facts have been laid before them." He had made it perfectly clear that "it is time now for the community at large to stop this pernicious persecution or they all stand to lose materially." Reed was confident that, with the public behind the mill, a satisfactory conclusion of the dispute could be attained. To facilitate this development he arranged for the committee of businessmen to visit San Francisco for personal consultations with Mills.[35]

The committee reported to the Commercial Club in March 1931 that the oystermen had agreed to drop their suits in return for $166,000 to be raised by the townspeople. Reed pledged $50,000 to this fund and passed along a promise that Rainier would, if the money was raised, expand and modernize the mill, including installation of a waste disposal plant. The fund was complete by mid-April, and the suits were dropped. "Shelton citizens, led by Mark Reed," the *Tacoma News Tribune* applauded, "met the impending calamity with resource and courage." The future of Rainier seemed secure.[36]

Oystermen not parties to the agreement, however, continued to bring suit against the mill. Reed insisted that these claims be vigorously fought in the courts. He had told the oyster growers, he commented, that he "could not see any justice in the claims at all, and did not feel that the pulp mill was responsible for any damage.' He told one associate that the mill "seems to be looked upon as a source of easy money by many who are in financial difficulty." These suits continued to be a nuisance, endangering the mill until it was finally closed in the late 1950s.[37]

From the perspective of today Reed's position in this affair seems to be that of the polluting industrialist, opposed to the public interest. However, little was known about the effects of pollution at the time, and responsible people could, with reason, conclude that the economic benefits of a pulp mill more than compensated for the dangers of pollution, which were largely theoretical at that time. Shelton residents, as the authors of the W.P.A. Washington Guide later noted, welcomed the pollution, "for it signifies jobs for workers and jingling cash registers in business establishments."[38] The closing of the Rainier mill, moreover, would have meant a severe loss to Reed, both as a stockholder and as the operator of logging and milling operations that benefitted from the mill. Reed could hardly have been expected to take a position other than the one he did.

4

The lumber industry had enjoyed a few prosperous years in the early part of the 1920s, but then it entered a period of decline. West Coast production continued at a high rate, far in excess of demand, which had fallen off considerably. "The lumber industry of the Pacific Northwest," Reed reported to Secretary of Commerce Herbert Hoover in late 1926, "is now passing through one of the most disastrous periods it has experienced since before the war." Reed forecast a depressed market for the coming years and observed that "a leveling process" would have to be endured "in order to bring our production within the limitations of the demand." Hard times had been experienced before and if patience and restraint were exercised most operators should "weather the storm with our flag still well towards the top of the mast."[39]

All would be well, Reed noted, if production could be controlled so as to correspond to demand. Like most simple solutions, however, this one confronted some serious obstacles. Most loggers and mill owners would have to restrict their output if there was to be any real curtailment. But many lumbermen found it to their advantage not to cut back, negating the efforts of those who did. "It would be folly on our part," one mill owner informed Reed, "to close down for any great length of time when it would do so little good to the market when all the others ran during that period." Pressure from the mills made it difficult for loggers to reduce their output, as this would harm their customers. "Selfishness seems to be the predominating sentiment in our industry," Reed observed. "Too many of us are inclined to think that we can produce an excessive portion of the output and are expecting the other fellow to curtail to allow us to carry on such a production."[40]

Too many producing units existed in the industry to make voluntary cutbacks a viable solution. "Lumbermen go out and slash prices, cut each other's throats and raise hell generally," Reed grumbled, "with no seeming objective in view." Cooperation among operators to enforce curtailment, moreover, risked violation of the antitrust laws. Even suggesting such a step, Reed noted, "may be indictable under the anti-trust laws of our country but present conditions are so deplorable in our industry that it possibly would be no greater disgrace to be indicted for trying to do something that would be helpful to the entire community than to go to the poor-house and become a charge on the community." The most feasible solution remained prolonged bad weather, which would prevent logging. It was "rather a discrediting admission on the part of those engaged in the industry," Reed pointed out, "that we must depend upon an active God to save us from the result of our own folly."[41]

Some effort was made to stimulate demand with formation of the West Coast Lumber Trade Extension Bureau in 1926. Supported by Reed, the bureau propagandized for Douglas fir and other woods of the region. "There must be something radically wrong," George S. Long contended, when population and building permits had increased during the early 1920s and yet the value of lumber had gone down. Substitutes for lumber had been gaining in popularity, particularly as many urban areas were restricting the use of wood in construction because of the fire danger. The new agency would also combat this development, striving to increase lumber's share of the construction market. Its work, however, seems to have had little impact on the deteriorating situation in the industry.[42]

Conditions continued to worsen as a result of the slump in construction. Consumption of lumber would be reduced further, Reed predicted, "rather than maintained at the past few years' volume." Excess production mounted, "brought about," Reed observed, "by the building of new operating units of large capacity." At the same time, older mills were adding shifts and prices were responding to the pressure of the softening market. We "are taking the stand," a mill operator noted, "that we will make whatever price is necessary in order to secure our percentage of the business." The West Coast Lumbermen's Association reported that member mills averaged a loss of $ .74 per thousand feet of lumber sold in 1927.[43]

The idea of effective curtailment began to receive wider acceptance in 1927. "A reduction in lumber production is essential to every division of the industry," argued the *Timberman*, "and to the people who earn their living in or from it." Most of the major loggers, including Simpson, shut down for two weeks in the spring in an effort to reduce the surplus of logs in the water. These efforts, however, had little impact as most mills continued to operate and were able to find the logs with which to do so. By the end of the year Reed hoped that the operators of these mills would come to their senses and "realize that they are operating on a basis that eventually means ruination." If they could only "see the light we would accomplish results." But this remained a tall order.[44]

The following year, 1928, was, Reed observed, "the most unsatisfactory business year that our organization has had in the last eight." Even so, he added a second shift to the mill's operation. While increasing production, this move also increased the plant's efficiency. The cost of production, Reed believed, could be reduced and the pulp mill would be able to operate more economically by securing its entire supply of wood from the Reed Mill. Reed pointed out that the industry was passing through a critical period and "only the most efficient and low cost operations will probably survive the readjustment."[45]

He had few doubts that Simpson fit this category. The Shelton mills allowed the company to get the maximum return from its timber resources. Moreover, Reed's conservative financial policies had kept Simpson free of debt. He had experienced some difficulty in paying off the loan from the Dexter Horton Bank that had financed purchase of the outside stock in Simpson in 1906, and he had determined never to borrow money again. William G. Reed recalls that his father gave him little business advice, but did recommend that he avoid debts. "It can cramp your style, and you take a risk of going broke." As a result of efficiency and avoidance of debt, Simpson was able to earn a profit in years when most other companies were losing heavily. Simpson was "probably the most profitable company of anything like its size in the Pacific Northwest," the younger Reed observed.[46]

Reed looked forward to better times in 1929, as a result of the "wonderful boom in the stock market and business activity that we have throughout the country." The logging and mill companies had not been suffering badly anyway, at least as far as Reed could see. "We don't need very much money in this world for our own personal requirements," he claimed, "but it is a pleasure to be successful in your operation." He had often thought that "the game [mattered] more than . . . the gain."[47]

While the stock market boom was given some of the credit for this optimism, most was due to the increased curtailment of production. The Simpson Logging Company reduced its output of logs by one-fourth. The Reed Mill kept running two shifts, but reduced each by one day a week. By fall the second shift was dropped, and Reed was planning to cut production by half during the winter months in order to avoid "piling up a surplus of stock." These efforts were matched by many other operators. "Practically all the mills in the state are either cutting one shift or reducing a day," the *Mason County Journal* reported, "and some plan to close for a period to avoid a great overproduction of lumber." Reed observed that "about a 20% reduction in the volume of production" had been achieved. The total of logs in the water was some "fifty million feet below the amount in the water a year ago at this time" and prices were stable. Better times seemed ahead.[48]

Optimism was temporarily dampened in early 1929 when the federal government planned to open the forest reserve on the western slope of the Olympic range to logging. This set off a scramble for access to the timber. Bloedel-Donovan and the Irving-Hartley interests planned to extend their railroads from the north to exploit the government's decision. The Northern Pacific intended to build north from Grays Harbor to meet this threat, and Alex Polson was being forced to extend his road as well.

We are "much disturbed by the fact that a large amount of timber will be thrown upon a market already burdened with an oversupply," R. D. Merrill wrote to Reed. "It is a crime which the government should be ashamed of," Polson expostulated. Reed agreed that it would be a terrible mistake to offer the timber for sale. Overproduction had already "brought about such a demoralization in price and returns to the state for its natural resource that we are facing the situation of cutting off this the greatest asset the State of Washington has at the present time and bringing back nothing to replace it." Adding the Olympic timber to the current market would only aggravate this deplorable condition. It should be "held back," Merrill argued, "until it is absolutely needed." If not, observed Representative Albert Johnson, "we will all go to a pauper's funeral at about the same time."[49]

The villain, in the minds of opponents of the government plan, was J. H. Bloedel, the economically powerful and politically influential Bellingham lumberman. "If he is so concerned about a supply of logs from this district for his mill," Merrill commented, "it would be advisable for him to curtail his logging somewhat and not put so many logs on to the open market." It was absolutely necessary to thwart Bloedel, as this would end the clamor from others interested in beating him to the timber. "Even the prospect of the building of a railroad" into the western slope, Merrill pointed out, "has had ill effect on the lumber market."[50]

Reed called on Forest Service officials in Portland and had Senator Wesley Jones and Representative Johnson do the same in the nation's capital. He also urged restraint upon the Northern Pacific, while Merrill and Polson combined to buy control of the old Spruce Production Division logging railroad from Irving, eliminating one claimant for the timber. Reed learned in Portland that the government had decided not to sell the timber. The problem, he told Albert Johnson, "had been pretty well disposed of for the present." No action would be taken by the government until a common carrier railroad had been built north from Grays Harbor. By the time that had been done the market would, Reed hoped, be in a position to absorb the influx of timber. Merrill said that this was a "reasonable" solution. Even though the threat had been removed, however, the lumber market failed to revive as anticipated.[51]

To carry out an adequate curtailment program was impossible. "Approximately 50% of the industry is carrying the entire burden of curtailment," Chris Kreienbaum exclaimed. Reed believed that the effort could not be carried further. "The mills that have been honestly and religiously living up to this curtailment program," he claimed, "have been eating into their surplus funds to such an extent that they must open up and go ahead on a basis of reducing their cost." Reed's patience with the failure of lumbermen to act in concert for a common goal was at an end. He concluded that the only real curtailment possible would be that brought about by "the survival of the most fit and most efficient" after a period of wide-open production. The ruination of marginal producers would leave the industry in the hands of fewer operators, who could then exercise more effective leadership.[52]

Attempts at voluntary cooperation had been negated by the large number of competing units in the industry and by their conflicting interests. "We do not seem to be able to maintain a solid front," Reed observed. "It is just hopeless for a few organizations to talk and practice curtailment . . . what we reduce the other fellow will probably produce." The traditional methods of free-wheeling independence could not be overcome by those seeking to manage their affairs on a long-range basis. Many lumbermen were coming to believe that the only effective approach was to find some means of forcing the necessary policies upon the industry by substituting coercion for voluntarism.[53]

5

The development of trade associations was a popular and widespread movement in the early twentieth century, one encouraged by such disparate prophets of up-to-date economic wisdom as Herbert Hoover and Franklin D. Roosevelt. Formation of the new West Coast Lumbermen's Association in 1928 was a manifestation of this development. Headed by Colonel William B. Greeley, the association took over the functions of the Trade Extension Bureau and encouraged cooperation within the industry. It would undoubtedly, Reed believed, "bring about more efficient results."

Still, Reed balked at joining the organization. He had supported the efforts of the Trade Extension Bureau, but other major operators had not done so. His business interests had "helped to carry on this activity while many have remained on the outside who were more interested than ourselves, being larger producers, and felt that they should not bear their proportion of the cost." He was not inclined to carry the burdens of others again. George Long, who was actively supporting the new association, urged Reed to change his mind. Greeley argued that the organization could succeed only if supported by "individual men of influence and standing in the industry," thus Reed's participation was essential.[54]

Reed recognized that his position was "rather untenable," as he believed in the contemplated program and realized that his refusal to join would discourage others from becoming members. In the end he agreed to support the association, although his support was never vey enthusiastic. While providing a useful source of information for the industry, the association could not combat the economic decline. It made available production figures for member mills and encouraged cooperation, but these efforts were not enough. Some more effective solution was needed.[55]

At a meeting of lumbermen in Tacoma in the fall of 1929, J. D. Tennant of Long-Bell proposed making Colonel Greeley czar of the lumber industry. "There was not a voice raised against it except by the writer," Reed informed an associate. Reed told the lumbermen that the scheme would not work. It would have to be extended to the loggers and there were "too many cutting units of our industry to hope for anything like a unanimous sentiment" for the plan. As soon as prices began to increase, moreover, "dissatisfaction would grow up with the operators when the dictator attempted to restrict their operations." "Naturally," Reed commented, "we were looked upon as an obstructionist by some of the more enthusiastic idealists." The points raised, however, were sufficient to prevent any serious effort to establish a lumber czar.[56]

During these years a number of lumbermen considered the possibility of working out a large-scale merger in the Northwest. In 1927 Reed attended a meeting at the Tacoma office of the St. Paul and Tacoma Lumber Company with Everett Griggs of that company, Polson, William Butler, and representatives of Eastern financial interests. The participants discussed merging their respective mills, but failed to reach agreement beyond a willingness to keep the concept in mind. Merger promised greater control over the fortunes of the industry and could go far toward overcoming the obstacles to voluntary cooperative efforts. It was an approach that became increasingly attractive as the industry encountered growing difficulties.[57]

Reed was already accustomed to the idea of mergers as a result of his banking interests. The Anderson estate was a major stockholder in Seattle's Dexter Horton National Bank, the largest in the state, and Reed had served as a director for years. In 1929 Dexter Horton merged with the Seattle National and the First National banks, forming the First Seattle Dexter Horton National Bank. Remarking on banking in particular and business in general, Reed noted that economic tendencies seemed "strongly to be for consolidation." His experience of looking at the big picture benefitted him when it came to considering mergers in the lumber industry.[58]

William E. Boeing, then known more for his lumber activities than for his fledgling airplane company, proposed in 1928 the formation of what George Long described as "a large corporation with ample funds to get better control of the lumber business around Puget Sound and possibly Western Washington." To be included in the organization were the operations of Boeing, Reed, Polson, Merrill and Ring, and the Weyerhaeuser-affiliated Clemons Logging Company. The Butler and Bloedel interests to the north would also be brought in. Reed was particularly interested in the scheme because of the inclusion of Bloedel, although he did not agree with the Billingham lumberman's "methods of doing business at all." It was better, he said, "to tie him in than to have him bush-whacking on the outside." Discussions of the proposed merger were held throughout 1929.[59]

The attitude of Alex Polson proved decisive to the outcome of the negotiations. Polson, who had been one of the pioneer loggers in the region, was reluctant to surrender the independence of his company. "When it comes down to the final decision," Reed informed Long, "you will not find the Polson Logging Company inclined to join the group." Reed later noted that Polson's convictions were "firmly fixed in his mind" and "nothing could be said or done to change their conclusion." Long was in a difficult spot. He faced opposition to the merger idea from Minot Davis and other associates in the Weyerhaeuser operation. Long could not commit Clemons if its principal Grays Harbor competitor, Polson, refused to join. "Without Polson," Reed observed, "they could not hope to control the situation on Grays Harbor."[60]

Reed felt that Weyerhaeuser had never been "very keen" about the merger. But he believed that Long would have put Clemons in if Polson had agreed to join. With both Polson and Clemons out of the picture, Reed himself dropped the merger proposal. "We would not be interested," he told Long, unless "a strong controlling factor could be built up on Grays Harbor." By October 1929 the first serious effort to bring about a merger of major components of the industry had collapsed.[61]

The effort demonstrated once again the inability of the industry to act in unison for common benefit. The individual units had conflicting visions of their self-interest, making a reconciliation extremely difficult. Conditions in 1929 were not yet bad enough to force such a step. "The typical Northwest lumber manufacturer," commented the *West Coast Lumberman*, "has too independent a spirit to submerge himself in any one group whereby his identity or initiative may be lost." When the Great Depression engulfed the country, however, driving the lumber industry to new lows, mergers were more seriously considered.[62]

As the 1920s drew to a close Reed began to experience some health problems. He complained of "gastritis of the stomach" and sought remedies ranging from patent medicines to stays at a health resort in Oregon. He also began spending the winter months in the sunny climes of Arizona. Frustration over the economic problems facing the industry and the inability of lumbermen to confront them with effective action may well have contributed to Reed's stomach troubles. "The lumber business for the last year or two," he observed in late 1929, "has been going through what seems to me to be the most impossible situation that we have met in a great many years." The "mill end of the game" was in particular "just simply impossible." And while the rest of the nation enjoyed the last frenzied days of prosperity, unaware of the great economic catastrophe about to begin, Reed saw little hope for the immediate future. "It will take an extreme optimist to maintain a high-pressure courage under the existing conditions." Simpson and its affiliates were well run, efficient companies, able to cope with hard times better than most, but this was little cause for euphoria. "Let us hope," Reed commented, "that we will live long enough to see a stable lumber market at a fair margin of profit."[63]

In the first half of the 1920s Reed had sought to assert greater control over the market by erecting a mill at Shelton. But the efficient operation of one company was not enough, as the chaos of the closing years of the decade demonstrated. The industry itself needed to operate on a more efficient basis. Production had to be adjusted to demand and markets exploited on a large scale. The persistence of traditional methods, however, stood in the way. Most operators continued to work on the time-honored basis of short-term self-interest. The lumber industry could not solve its problems. Like other businessmen, many Northwest lumbermen turned to the government to do for them what they were unable to do for themselves.

CHAPTER 6

Reed, the Republicans,
and the Tariff

The tariff had been an important issue in American politics for over a century. Although the protective tariff concept was originally supported by some logic, politics soon became the predominant factor when it came to revision of duties. Republicans were generally thought to be protectionists and Democrats advocates of free trade, but what really mattered was where each individual congressman came from and what special interest group was able to gain his attention. Those industries able to exert enough pressure on Congress got what they wanted—usually rates freezing out foreign competitors—and those unable to do so did not. Whether or not a particular industry was actually in need of protection was of relatively minor importance. Following World War I many economists and businessmen favored a more rational approach to the setting of duties, one that would encourage foreign trade and strengthen the economic standing of the nation. The traditional approach to tariff-making, however, was not abandoned.

Three days after assuming the presidency in March 1929, Herbert Hoover called a special session of Congress to consider agricultural relief and "limited changes of the tariff." The assumption was that the changes recommended by Hoover would take little time to implement. But the special session provided an opportunity for industries desiring protection to lobby for beneficial duties. Mark Reed and other Northwest lumbermen, blaming much of their economic difficulty on competition from across the border in British Columbia, were among those lobbying for protection.[1]

The campaign to secure duties on imported forest products offers a good case study of Reed's preferred method of political operation. His involvement in the fight was all but unknown to the public. He was not on the scene in the nation's capital, but remained on the Pacific Coast throughout the long struggle and left direct lobbying to other representatives of the industry. But he was the man in charge during the entire affair, developing strategy and issuing instructions to lobbyists and members of Washington's congressional delegation. And he provided much of the financial support for the tariff campaign as well. Reed operated behind the scenes, attempting to control events while appearing to outsiders not to be involved at all.

1

The Fordney-McCumber Tariff of 1922 provided a rate of one dollar per thousand feet on logs, but placed lumber and shingles on the free list. The shingle industry was in particular need of assistance. The capacity of the two hundred Northwest shingle mills, eight billion shingles a year, approximated the rate of consumption. But three billion shingles a year were imported from British Columbia, an increase of 400 percent since 1913. The impact of imports on sawmills and loggers was less clear. British Columbia mills delivered Douglas fir to Atlantic Coast ports at a cost below that of their Washington and Oregon competitors, but lumber imports made up only 5 percent of U.S. consumption. Canadian logs sold for less than the price charged by Puget Sound operators. Imports were only partially responsible for the plight of the lumbermen, but import restriction was expected to provide some economic relief.[2]

With the congressional logrolling that would accompany a general revision of the tariff, lumbermen hoped to secure the desired assistance from the federal government. "We will never have a better opportunity to secure a tariff on lumber and its products," Reed contended, "then we will have at the coming special session." In order to organize a strong lobbying effort, however, the often conflicting interests within the industry had to be reconciled, a task that proved extremely difficult. Some operators, such as Bloedel-Donovan, owned large tracts of timber in British Columbia and did not wish to see retention of the tariff on logs. (American companies owned over a million acres of timber in the Canadian province.) Neither did those mills that had to purchase logs on the open market. "Log buying mills," the operator of one of these mills pointed out, "are frequently hard pressed to secure adequate quantities" of logs on Puget Sound and "as a result have to fall back on the only other available source of supply, namely, British Columbia." The shingle mills, while desiring a tariff on shingles, hoped to eliminate the prevailing duty on logs. Loggers, on the other hand, were primarily interested in keeping cheaper British Columbia logs off the market. The industry was thus divided. Lumbermen who opposed a tariff and those who fought for a tariff acted at cross-purposes.[3]

The differences within the industry rendered the usual avenues of publicity and political pressure useless. The National Lumber Manufacturers Association refused to take a stand on the tariff and only four of the nation's 107 lumber trade organizations took part in the fight. In the Northwest the West Coast Lumbermen's Association was similarly immobilized, as were the region's trade journals. The *Timberman* had previously stood for free trade, claiming that "it would be better for both Canada and the United States if all trade restrictions were removed. . . . Canada and the United States must be and are one economic unit and arbitrary trade restrictions are harmful to both countries." But now it avoided editorial comment, as did the *West Coast Lumberman*, and both gave the fight only limited coverage. None of these organizations could afford to alienate any of their supporters.[4]

Reed's friend and business associate Henry McCleary refused to take part in the tariff effort. "Northwest lumbermen in my opinion haven't a ghost of a show competing with other stronger political interests," he observed. Everett Griggs, of the St. Paul and Tacoma Lumber Company, one of the state's most important lumbermen and an officer of the national association, also opposed political action. "We are liable to get very little for our troubles," he argued. Owners of British Columbia timber would be opposed and so would American farmers and urban residents. The lumbermen, Griggs concluded, could "muster but few votes to meet the overwhelming arguments advanced by the middle west and the east." The loss of Grigg's support was a severe blow to the advocates of a tariff. "How any lumberman operating in the Northwest," Reed lamented, "can reach such a conclusion, especially such a clear thinker as Major Griggs is generally speaking, is something more than we can fathom." Deprived of the support of the trade organizations and of such leaders as Griggs, the lumbermen had to establish new institutional arrangements.[5]

A special lumber industry tariff committee was created to raise funds and provide for witnesses and lobbyists to be on hand in the nation's capital. The committee was chaired by Richard Condon of the Charles McCormick Lumber Company, Republican national committeeman for Washington. Reed was a member, as were Governor Roland Hartley, Joseph Irving, state chamber of commerce head Frank Lamb, and A. C. Edwards of the shingle industry. Although Condon was chairman, Reed was regarded as the real leader of the tariff fight. "You could not pick a better man to do it," one lumberman observed, pointing out Reed's political connections with the Hoover Administration.[6]

By late March, Condon had raised ten thousand dollars, and another six thousand dollars had been forwarded from Oregon by lumber broker C. E. Dant. Alex Polson raised five thousand dollars on Grays Harbor at Reed's request. Most of this money, and subsequent funds as well, came from a few large operators. "We would save time," Dant suggested, "by a few of us getting together and putting up $4000.00 or $5000.00 a piece." Money appeared to be no problem, although much of the eventual financial burden fell on Reed and George Long of Weyerhaeuser. Selection of the right person to send East, though was another matter.[7]

Several lumbermen urged Reed to make the trip and personally supervise developments. He declined, claiming that, the state legislature having just concluded its session, he needed to devote his attention to pressing business matters. Besides, he told William C. Butler, "I am not sure that I am as close personally with the administration as I was early in the Hoover pre-convention campaign." He had spoken out against methods "being pursued in antagonizing good Republicans who were not enthusiastically supporting Mr. Hoover" and as a result had lost favor with the president. "I have not heard from Mr. Hoover directly since his nomination." Reed suggested that Butler, an

influential Republican, go in his place. When reminded that
Butler had opposed Hoover's nomination, Reed conceded that
"some one else probably would be more effective in presenting
our case for a lumber tariff to the President."[8]

The committee chose Condon for the task, despite Reed's
misgivings, and he left for the East in early April. Condon was
"a tireless worker in local legislative affairs," Reed recognized,
and was considered to be "a man of good judgment and a
splendid mixer." His position as national committeeman made
him a logical choice. Unfortunately, he was not well acquainted
with the congressmen he would have to deal with. Condon
hired C. Bascom Slemp, a Washington lawyer-lobbyist who had
been secretary to President Coolidge, to assist him. "I am quite
pleased in getting the services of so prominent a man and so
able a man in this connection," Condon informed Reed. But
Reed also had misgivings over this move. "I am very fond of Mr.
Slemp personally and he is in a position to do good work," Reed
commented, but he doubted Slemp's ability to do such work.[9]

In his message opening the special session in mid-April,
President Hoover called for "limited changes" in agricultural
tariffs as part of his farm relief program. He also pointed out
that "there have been economic shifts necessitating a readjustment of some of the [other] tariff schedules." The test should be
"in the main whether there has been a substantial slackening of
activity in an industry during the past few years, and a conse-
quent decrease of employment due to insurmountable competition in the products of that industry." The lumber industry met
these criteria, at least as far as lumbermen were concerned.
Condon wrote that Hoover's message "appears to be more or
less satisfactory to our desires."[10]

An impressive series of witnesses appeared before the House
Ways and Means Committee. Representative Albert Johnson of
Washington told the committee that all the lumbermen wanted
was justice. "We are asking only the same measure of protection," he insisted, "that you have given and will continue to give
to hundreds of other industries." A. C. Edwards claimed that 50
percent of the shingle mills in Washington and Oregon had
failed and asked for a 25 percent ad valorem duty on imported
shingles. "This represents approximately the exact difference in

the cost of production in this country and our competing neighbor across the line." Frank Lamb conceded that the amount of lumber imported "in relation to the entire demand of this country, is . . . very negligible." But the "effect upon local parts of the country is more or less severe," as demonstrated by the fact that British Columbia was shipping to the Atlantic Coast "18 per cent as much lumber as we are shipping from the Pacific Coast."

The most important testimony against the tariff was presented by J. H. Bloedel, the Bellingham lumberman who owned extensive tracts of timber in British Columbia. "The Northwest does not need protection," he asserted. Canadian shingles were of higher quality and this fact, not price, made them "noncompetitive with American-made shingles." Congress, moreover, should remove the duty on logs. "It is a fallacy," Bloedel argued, to retain the duty "in the face of a receding supply. It influences only one section, Puget Sound, and serves to tighten the grip of the logger." Bloedel's testimony exasperated his fellow lumbermen, but was of little impact in the House.[11]

The lumbermen benefitted from some strategic advantages in that body. Willis Hawley of Oregon chaired the Ways and Means Committee and was wholeheartedly in favor of tariff protection for the industry. (The committee's fifteen Republican members wrote the tariff bill, imposing their will on the minority Democrats.) And Lin Hadley of Everett, Washington headed the three-man subcommittee charged with drafting the lumber section of the measure. "In times past," Reed noted, Hadley "has been somewhat criticized by the lumbermen in his district for not getting more effective results." Still, Reed believed that "he has done everything any mortal man can do" and was confident he would vindicate himself in this instance. As a result of Hawley's and Hadley's positions, the lumbermen expected satisfactory results from the committee.[12]

In his subcommittee Hadley secured retention of the log tariff and a duty on shingles and cedar lumber as well, but failed to gain a duty on softwood lumber. Moving to the full committee, Hadley and Hawley fought for the latter duty. "We could not swing that item into the program," Hadley noted, "largely I believe because of fear of the general political effect of doing so throughout the East as well as in the Middle West." His colleagues, Hadley continued, had told him that inclusion of the proposed duty would cause the defeat of the shingle, cedar, and log rates on the floor. Reed informed Hadley that some of the lumbermen were disappointed in his failure. "But those of us who have given more or less study to the situation," he wrote, "have felt that you would have difficulty in including this soft wood schedule, and that we should and would be satisfied" with what had been achieved.[13]

The House passed the tariff bill on 28 May by a vote of 264-147. "I feel that we have done exceedingly well," Reed noted, "in view of the pronounced and determined opposition from the Middle West and Eastern states to a tariff on lumber at all." It was unfortunate that a tariff on softwood lumber had not been achieved, another lumberman observed, but on "the positive side of that the tactical situation is that we have more friends for soft wood tariff in the House of Representatives then we had when we started." Such a duty might still emerge from the conference committee, of which Hawley would be a key member, and the House might then approve it. As for now, "the battle is only half won," commented Hadley.[14]

The lumbermen won in the House because of the strategic position occupied by members from lumber-producing states and because of that body's rules. Representative John Summers of Washington informed Reed that had the duties come up "on a separate vote, all indications are that the timber schedule would be wiped out by a very large majority." The impending fight in the Senate would be more difficult and the long-range outlook remained problematical. "Until the tariff bill has passed both houses and been signed by the president," commented the *Timberman*, "one man's guess is as good as another as to its final content."[15]

2

The contest in the Senate was expected to be strenuous. Reed believed that to fight for retention of the House duties and for a tariff on softwood lumber as well was essential. Only by fighting for the latter, he concluded, would it be possible to at least "retain what we now have in the Senate, and of course there is always a possibility that we may get what we are working for." The best that could be said, though, was that the lumbermen had a "good fighting chance" for success. The opponents of duties on forest products were ready to launch their main attack in the Senate.[16]

These opponents included Eastern lumber dealers, owners of Canadian timber, farmers, and urban consumers. The wholesale lumber trade associations on the Atlantic Coast had already gone on record against a tariff on lumber. It no doubt seemed "strange to you," one Eastern dealer wrote Reed's associate Chris Kreienbaum, "that we, who make our living out of American lumber, should oppose such a tariff, but we are trying to be honest in our opinion and try to look at it from an unselfish standpoint and for the general good of the entire community." The "general good," fortunately for the dealers, meant the continuation of cheap lumber imports from British Columbia.

Northwest lumbermen could expect little support from the East in the Senate. "I am fundamentally a protectionist," Senator Walter Edge of New Jersey noted. "Nevertheless, in these days I have been compelled . . . to ease off a good bit on the convictions in this regard I have held for many years." The lumbermen believed that the opposition resulted from propaganda spread by owners of Canadian timber. Representatives of these interests, according to one account, would attend meetings of trade associations, claim that a tariff would destroy trade with Canada "and so with a hurrah, without thought or study, over goes the resolution condemning the proposed tariff."[17]

Farmers, for whom the special session had ostensibly been called, also opposed the proposed schedules, particularly those on shingles. William Butler fumed that farm spokesmen like Senator Arthur Capper of Kansas evidently believed that "the purpose of this tariff bill is to have everybody contribute to the poor, down-trodden farmer, and that no other industries need consideration." Lumbermen felt that the opposition of farmers was unjustified, as only a small percentage of the region's shingle production was sold to farmers. Any increased cost for farmers resulting from a tariff, Reed asserted, would be "a negligible item of expense." The real source of the opposition, according to the lumbermen, came from the American owners of timber on the other side of the line. But that did not lessen the seriousness of the situation. "Unless one has been in the east and talked to dealers, farmers and lumber consumers," Frank Lamb reported to Reed, "he has no realization of the intense opposition there is to a tariff on lumber."[18]

The great problem was that the tariff was not a party or ideological matter. "There are comparatively few states especially interested in the tariff on shingles and lumber," Senator Wesley Jones of Washington observed. "The other states are consumers and it looks like we are going to be up against their unfriendly attitude." The economic problems of the lumbermen and the control of Congress by Republicans meant little in the face of this clash of competing interests. "As Hancock said years ago," Reed noted, referring to the 1880 comment by Democrat presidential candidate Winfield Scott Hancock, "the tariff issue is a local problem and it is pretty hard to satisfy all localities with any provisions that are written into a tariff bill." The truth of Hancock's observation soon became apparent to the tariff advocates.[19]

Reed and his friends were also concerned about the attitude of the president. Hoover's position would be crucial, Butler warned Reed, noting further that reports in the Eastern press suggested that Hoover opposed a tariff on forest products because the duties would increase the price of building materials. Reed informed Senator Jones that the rumors about Hoover's opposition represented the "most disturbing factor in this pending situation." He suggested that Jones, who was close to Hoover, determine the president's true intentions. Jones reported back that his discussion with the president had gone well and that Hoover "is all right." The president, observed Jones, "is unequivocally and earnestly for a tariff on shingles" and had remarked that he had "an open mind" as far as duties on logs and lumber were concerned. The lumbermen were relieved to hear this news, but many became embittered when Hoover, who was under intense pressure from opponents of the tariff, refused to do anything positive in their behalf.[20]

The lumbermen relied on Senator Jones for positive action.

First elected to the Senate in 1908, the austere Jones was chairman of the Commerce Committee. He was closely identified with the prohibition movement, promotion of the American merchant marine, and reclamation of the arid Columbia Basin. His seniority seemed to many to assure Senate passage of the tariff. But the Senator was a reluctant champion who shied away from aggressive tactics. "I cannot club a man to make him vote my way," he insisted. "Everything that is humanly possible for me to do to get this tariff. . . . I will do but when it comes right down to brass tacks I have just one vote."[21]

Jones had never been popular with lumbermen, many of whom regarded him as weak, indecisive and, despite his closeness to conservative G.O.P. senators, something of a progressive. Jones, wrote Butler, "has no idea of leadership, and his main trouble really is that at heart he is a La Folletteite." Butler contended that if Jones "would be as aggressive and militant in this important matter as he is in hunting anti-Volsteadites, there would be no question about securing a duty." Tariff advocates had to buck up the lethargic Jones if they wished to achieve success.[22]

"We must prod Senator Jones along," Reed informed George Long, and he meant to keep up the pressure. He told Jones that the lumbermen "are looking to you almost entirely to carry on this battle of success." Should Jones fail to secure a tariff, Reed continued in what amounted to a warning, "many who are not familiar with congressional procedure would place the blame for the defeat of this measure at your door. Nothing that any of your friends could do would convince them to the contrary." Writing to Butler, Reed noted that he had tried to phrase his letter to Jones "so that he could without much trouble read between the lines. He should understand that he is travelling on extremely shifty sands politically." Reed was only being fair in putting the Senator on notice that should he fail "he will have to stand the consequences." Butler supported this approach, observing that "it will be very embarrassing for him" if the industry did not receive protection.[23]

The Senator felt that more of the burden should be placed on his Democratic colleague from Washington, Clarence Dill of

Spokane. The latter had been elected to a second term in 1928, Jones reminded Reed, "largely because of the feeling on the part of the hundreds, and possibly thousands of our people, that he could render very efficient aid in this matter." Indeed, many staunch Republican lumbermen, including Mark Reed himself, had crossed party lines to provide support for Dill in 1928. And Dill had promised in return to support the demands for tariff protection. He assured Reed that he would secure "the support of at least fifteen Democrats" for the tariff.

But the tariff advocates did not trust Dill. Reed recalled that Dill had earlier promised twenty-five votes from the Democratic side of the aisle. While Dill vowed to fight for a tariff on shingles, moreover, he was not willing to do so for logs and lumber. Despite entreaties from Reed, Dill refused to exert any real effort on behalf of these items. "Senator Dill was very profuse in his promises during the campaign," Reed exclaimed, "but he lost little time in getting away from them." Dill's unreliability forced continued dependence on Jones, although the presence of Dill and his claims of Democratic support might at least stimulate Jones to a greater effort. Reed pointed out that if the tariff was saved "through Democratic support it is going to make it embarrassing politically in the state when Senator Jones comes up for re-election." The tariff advocates lacked effective leadership in the Senate. "If the opposition is not successful in eliminating the House provisions from the Senate bill," Reed wrote, "it will be their fault."[24]

The situation was exacerbated by the need for Jones, suffering from a kidney disorder, to undergo an operation, idling him during the crucial deliberations of the Finance Committee. Testimony before the committee mirrored that heard earlier in the House. A large contingent was on hand from the Northwest to call for protection. J. H. Bloedel again angered his Washington colleagues by testifying in opposition. "The problems of the business can not be settled by a tariff," he contended. The real problem, Bloedel observed, was "depletion of native timber. We are cuting it too fast now," he claimed. "We should permit the cutting of our neighbor's timber if they will let us." Still, the supporters of a tariff believed they had the best of the argument. Their witnesses, Condon reported to Reed, had made a "favorable impression on [the] committee." But impressions meant little in the face of political reality.[25]

The forest products schedules were considered by a five-man subcommittee chaired by the progressive Republican Senator James Couzens of Michigan. Couzens, Jones informed Reed, "is rather inclined against us." The Michigan Republican agreed that the shingle industry was in bad shape, but contended that this was not the fault of imports. The real problem was a shortage of raw material and therefore logs should be placed on the free list, a decision that would also eliminate any need for a shingle tariff. Happily, this diagnosis coincided with the best interests of Couzens' Midwest constituents. And it coincided as well with the desire of many senators to respond to complaints being voiced against the House duties by farmers and Canadian businessmen.[26]

The subcommittee recommended that the shingle and log duties be dropped from the bill. Reed was furious over this development. Couzens, he wrote, was "a 'lime-lighter' who made his money through a fortunate investment with the Ford Motor Company . . . and who since has conceived the idea that he is the Moses to lead the 'dear people' out of the wilderness." Rather than looking out for the interest of the nation as a whole, the Michigan senator was "more interested in keeping his political star to the fore-front locally." It was too bad, Reed concluded, that Couzens was not "inoculated somewhat with Senator Jones' idea of being a country-wide senator, and Jones had a little more of his spirit that he would look first after his own people." Reed's feelings were not aided by the knowledge that this defeat presaged difficulty in the full committee.[27]

The Finance Committee voted six to five to place logs and shingles on the free list. "The lumbermen of the Pacific Northwest, as you can well imagine," Reed wrote Jones, who was still recuperating from his operation, "were not only amazed but well nigh paralyzed" at this action. The amazement resulted in particular from the affirmative votes of Senators Reed Smoot of Utah, the committee chairman, and James Watson of Indiana, generally regarded as among the leading spokesmen for Republican protectionists. "It is incredible to me," Butler exclaimed, "that Senators Watson and Smoot will enlist under the banner of a renegade like Couzens and refuse to extend the fundamental basis of our party to the states of Washington and Oregon, which have supported the protective principle for two generations."[28]

Reed commented that the position of Smoot and Watson was "almost unbelievable." Smoot in particular was a hypocrite, as evidenced by his efforts to secure an increased tariff on sugar in order to protect the sugar beet interests of Utah. "An increased tariff on sugar," Reed pointed out, "will increase the cost of living for every consumer and the number to be benefited is almost infinitesimal." The votes of Smoot and Watson also threatened the unity of the party. "Why should these regular members of the finance committee," the Shelton lumbermen wondered, "line up with the so-called Republicans of the Couzens stripe to penalize a section of the country that has always been regular, for the evident purpose of currying favor with the renegades?"

Reed urged that Jones invite Smoot and Watson to his hospital room and insist that they reconsider. Because of Jones's seniority, Reed continued, "it is inconceivable that they can deny you this request." The merits of the lumbermen's case apparently were not sufficient and therefore the matter must "be handled from the inside, and to you only have we to look for leadership." Condon seconded this suggestion, telling Jones that Smoot and Watson must be made aware that their votes were a "severe blow . . . to your political prestige and party affiliation." But Jones declined to bring any pressure on his colleagues and the Finance Committee vote remained unchanged.[29]

Jones was to blame for this outcome, according to the tariff advocates. "We might just as well depend on a feather duster," Butler observed. The senator had done nothing on behalf of the lumbermen beyond writing a few "ladylike" letters. "So far as representing the State efficiently and effectively is concerned," Butler reiterated, "we might just as well have had a dummy or no Senator at all." Clarence Dill had also failed to do his part. "Rather than staying on the job and attempting to make good on his part promises," Reed noted, Dill had "hot-footed it for the more comfortable climatic conditions in the West and is repairing his political fences." The lumbermen had to rethink their strategy before the bill reached the floor.[30]

They looked to Senator Charles McNary of Oregon to assume leadership of the fight. McNary was popular with both conservatives and progressives and was one of the rising powers in the Senate. Condon visited McNary in Portland and told him that Jones would be unable, for reasons of health, to lead the tariff effort. The tariff advocates therefore counted on McNary to take over and the Oregon Republican agreed to do so. "I have a great deal of confidence in my friend McNary," Reed exulted. "He is not only a prince of good fellows but he is a 'fightin' fool.' He likes the game and knows how to ward off and take the blows that come with action." The low spirits of lumbermen revived somewhat with this change in leadership.[31]

Reed and George Long financed a trip to the nation's capital by Oregon lumbermen Russell Hawkins to aid McNary. Hawkins was close to McNary and had extensive political connections. Reed had more confidence in Hawkins than he had in Condon. "Most of our lumbermen had not given much attention to politics," he wrote Hawkins, "and do not understand political methods." It was "almost a super-human task to get over to them the necessity for certain activities." Reed felt that he and Long had to bear too much of the burden, but he intended to do everything possible to secure the desired tariff.[32]

That included maintaining the pressure on Jones, not as leader of the tariff fight but to back up the efforts of McNary. "I am keeping in close touch with Senator Jones," Reed noted, "and trying to stiffen him up from day to day. Jones wants to do the right thing but he is not much of a fighter." The senator, moreover, wrote that his doctors had told him to avoid strenuous labor. The real fighting would be left to McNary.[33]

The tariff advocates decided to organize a group of senators who would refuse to support any tariff bill that did not include the desired duties. Butler said that the pro-tariff group should "insurge until they force an acceptable compromise, and under no circumstances to respond to the party lash or be cajoled out of that position through vacant talk about loyalty to the party and administration." Reed observed that he had "always stood for organization and been what might be classed as a stand-patter in organization methods." Therefore, it felt "rather strange to be on the outside, insurging, but it does appear to be the only way that we can hope to bring about any recognition." Northwest senators, with the notable exception of William E. Borah of Idaho, held a series of meetings to concert tactics. Jones was attending these meetings, Reed noted in amazement, "and seems to be participating in the deliberations of the 'insurgents.'"34

Unfortunately, other senators were equally determined to prevent a tariff on forest products. A coalition of progressive Republicans, led by Senator Borah, and Democrats dominated the scene as the bill reached the floor. They hoped to limit tariff revision to farm products. "The Republican party is not in control," Reed observed, "and the policies that it advocates can at any time be turned down by coalition of the Democrats and mongrel so-called Republicans." The lumber senators could not easily oppose this effort, as they represented states in which the importance of agriculture matched that of the lumber industry.35

The lumbermen were especially outraged at the position of Borah, leader of the effort to limit revision to farm products and the only legislator from the Northwest to oppose the wood duties. "I had rather hoped that Senator Borah would be with you," Reed wrote Jones. Officials of the Weyerhaeuser Timber Company tried but failed to persuade the senator to drop his opposition. Borah "suffers so from megalomania," said Butler, "that he is practically impossible." Jones agreed with this assessment of his colleague, noting that Borah was able but "very peculiar."36

Reed and his friends recognized that they would have to expand their forces if they were to preserve the duties won in the House. A number of companies operating in the Northwest, such as Long-Bell, also had holdings in the South and some influence with Southern Democrats. And Dill, whom Reed was now referring to in his personal correspondence as "Pickles," also endeavored to line up Southern support in order to meet his promises.37

Tariff advocates hoped to attract the support of conservative senators by focusing attention on lumber imports from the Soviet Union. Russian lumber undersold American by two to three dollars per thousand feet in New York but, as imports were small, the real competitive danger was potential. The Soviets planned to expend over three million dollars on construction of sawmills in their Five Year Plan and, Reed noted, "our greatest menace for the future is the Russian competition." The Seattle *Business Chronicle* pointed out that "students of the lumber future see in Russia a competitor of menacing potentiality and one of the best reasons for a lumber tariff." This argument seemed to present some prospect for success. Emphasis on the "Russian menace," an industry lobbyist wired, "is going to enhance chances for securing votes [of] southern Senators."[38]

In the final analysis, however, hope for success rested on the positions held in the Republican leadership by Jones and McNary and on Dill's influence with the Democrats. Referring to the two Washington senators, the *Seattle Times* observed that "the time has come when the people who keep them in the Senate are more interested in what they do than in what they intend to do." In late October the elevation of Jones to the Senate leadership (James Watson being forced to step aside because of ill health) and the selection of McNary as assistant leader boosted the chances for a tariff. Little action was expected of Jones, so the real importance of the move was the enhanced status of McNary.[39]

The Senate made slow progress with the bill, preoccupied by the Democratic-progressive efforts to restrict it to agriculture. The coalition failed by a narrow margin to limit revision but did succeed in attaching an amendment providing bounties for agricultural exports, the so-called export debenture plan. President Hoover opposed the plan, as well as failure of the Senate to provide a flexible clause allowing him to raise or lower rates acording to advice from the Tariff Commission. Discussion of the actual schedules did not begin until late October. "We are going very slowly," Jones reported and many observers began to despair over the whole process. "Everything here is submerged in the miserable tariff bill," Hiram Johnson of

California grumbled. Senator Bronson Cutting of New Mexico noted that "every day it seems more impossible to pass a tariff bill in the special session."[40]

The lumber industry "insurgents" could not achieve their aim in the Senate. The opposition was too strong and the group could not hold out against a bill that contained benefits for farmers. Tariff advocates had previously agreed on action to be taken should Senate approval of the desired rates be deemed impossible. The "wisest course," Jones had written Reed, was to make an argument for the duties, but to avoid a record vote. Jones was confident that House members of the conference committee "will stand strongly for the House provision and I believe that if our conferees are not bound by a record vote, that we stand a much better chance" of securing the duties in the conference report. "Individual senators," Reed, a shrewd observer of legislative behavior, argued, "would consider themselves bound by the original vote, if a record vote had been taken, to a greater extent than they would if the senate in passing on the question did not make the record." By avoiding outright defeat in the Senate, the duties might be obtained in the final bill.[41]

This approach meant abandonment of the desired tariff on softwood lumber, as neither the House nor the Senate bill would contain such a provision and it could not be considered in conference. But the rates in the House bill would be saved, particularly the crucial shingle and cedar duties. Reed commented that the "shingle problem is the most serious problem that we have in the lumber industry." Cedar made up as much as 50 percent of the production in some logging operations, making it absolutely necessary to preserve a healthy shingle industry. At the moment the shingle mills in British Columbia "can knock our business in the head any time they want to and still make a profit." Unfortunately, the shingle rate was the most difficult to put over, as 90 percent of the nation's shingles were produced in Washington and Oregon and the other forty-six states had only a consumer's interest. The precarious position of shingles made it necessary to adopt the no-record-vote course, abandoning softwoods in hopes of preserving the shingle tariff. "Shingles and cedar lumber," Reed informed Jones, "should not be sacrificed if it is impossible to secure all asked for."[42]

Debate on the wood schedules began in the second week of November. Jones led off with a speech he was unable to complete because of his frail condition. "Protection is a principle or policy," he argued, "that should be applied wherever needed." Dill spoke particularly to the fears of conservationists. "The greatest need to-day in order to conserve the timber of that great region," he spoke of the Northwest, "is a protective tariff high enough to make it worth while to reforest those lands which will produce new timber more rapidly than any other part of the civilized world."[43]

Dill, however, insisted on a roll call vote on his amendment providing a 10 percent ad valorem duty on shingles. He was encouraged in this step by Condon and shingle lobbyist Edwards, both of whom admired Dill and felt that the amendment would be approved. In addition, Condon and Edwards represented log-buying mills whose owners desired free logs. A record vote on shingles might force a similar vote on logs and elimination of the duty on the latter item from the final bill. (This was a good example of the conflicting interests within the industry.) Dill would not listen to the arguments of McNary or of Reed. "I have done everything I could to make him see the proposition in the right light," Reed noted, "but I frankly admit my influence with the gentleman is not pronounced to say the most."[44]

Dill's amendment was defeated 49-29, making eventual retention of the House shingle tariff all the more difficult. "This vain display," Hawkins reported to Reed, "has convinced Dill he only had a few votes on his side." The Senator's only justification was that he had promised to fight for the shingle tariff. Dill, "Slippery Dick [Condon] and Edwards . . . are much chagrined," concluded Hawkins. Dill attempted to put the best light on his defeat by informing Reed that it had produced an "excellent" impression and convinced many senators "that we have a just cause."[45]

Reed observed that he was "not surprised" at Dill's action. "It is selfish and he has more thought of his own political future than he has of the success of the program." Writing to George

Long, Reed contended that all Dill "was working for was 'lime light' and words for the CONGRESSIONAL RECORD, so that he could say to his constituents that he made a valiant fight." His effort resulted in a serious setback, as the Senate went on to vote against a tariff on logs as well. Tariff advocates would have to dispense with reliance on Dill and his promises of Democratic assistance. And, as far as Reed was concerned, they would also have to dispense with the services of Condon as chief lobbyist. "I do not believe that value has been returned on that investment," he stated.[46]

Two weeks after this debacle another organizational change took place in the Senate. Senator Jones, after a month as majority leader, surrendered that post to become chairman of the Appropriations Committee and McNary assumed the leadership. "It would certainly look as if we were getting all the breaks," Butler observed. "No regular, Democrat or Progressive would care to antagonize the chairman of the Senate Committee on Appropriations." All that was needed was to prod Jones into taking advantage of his new position. We have "all the necessary cards to win the game," Butler explained, "if we play them and play them right." Reed noted that Butler was "of the old school and seems to think that about all there is to it is for our representatives to assert their demands and the issue is won." Still, Reed was encouraged over the organizational change. As a result of McNary's new influence, "some of those hard-boiled Yankees will realize shortly that the West has a vitality and ability."[47]

The Senate failed to pass the tariff bill before the end of the special session, two weeks before the regular session of the Seventy-first Congress was due to convene. This failure gave the tariff advocates time to regroup and plan new approaches to the Senate. The "delay in consideration," noted one lobbyist, "is greatly enhancing our prospects for success as many potent influences not enjoyed before are now being exerted and all new developments seem to strengthen our case and give wider support." Another lumberman contended that "there is coming to be a general appreciation of the fact that the lumber industry is in a very bad way."[48]

If the lumbermen were to benefit from that "appreciation,"

however, they would have to revamp their lobbying effort. Condon and Hawkins had not gotten along well hampering the tariff campaign. As far as Reed was concerned, this was not Hawkins' fault. "I am quite familiar with Mr. Condon's temperament," Reed wrote. "Generally speaking, he is not inclined for 'team work.'" Reed had learned that Condon, in the time he was supposed to be handling matters on the scene, had failed to contact any senators from outside the Northwest. These factors as well as Condon's role in the shingle affair prompted Reed to drop him.[49]

Since Reed and Long were financing the efforts of Hawkins and recently of Condon as well, they felt entitled to make the move on their own. Henceforth, Hawkins would head the lobbying effort. The change was made despite a warning that congressional opponents of the tariff contemplated an investigation of lobbying focusing on the activities of Hawkins. "He had better be advised," wrote lumberman John W. Blodgett, "that there had been a little gossip, and that our opponents might take action to discredit the lumber tariff through him."[50]

Reed and his friends enjoyed little satisfaction over their efforts of the past year. They had succeeded in getting much of what they wanted in the House, although this was due to the makeup of that body rather than the merits of their case. The same advantages had not prevailed in the upper chamber and the political weakness of Northwest lumbermen had been amply demonstrated. The damage done fostered further disasters in the months ahead.

3

Mark Reed exercised less direct supervision over the final tariff deliberations. William Butler urged that the Shelton lumberman go East, "as you were the personal and political friend of the president and could no doubt, if there, through daily and hourly application, stimulate Jones to use the power of his new chairmanship to win this fight." But Reed departed instead for Arizona in mid-January, to spend six weeks resting in the sun. He had been, he informed a Weyerhaeuser official, "directed by one of these czar-ist doctors to do so." There was nothing seriously wrong, but he had been told that "the grind is too steady and the nervous condition is something that only sunshine and rest can best do away with."⁵¹

Since it was no longer necessary to sacrifice softwood lumber in order to preserve the duty on shingles, attention focused on lumber in the regular session. Reed believed that there was "a reasonable fighting chance" of securing a duty of two dollars per thousand feet on lumber. If achieved, all the desired duties would be considered by the conference committee, "and in my judgment an agreement will be reached by the majority of the conference to give some relief on all these products, possibly compromise rates." The stock market crash in the fall of 1929 increased the likelihood of this outcome. Condon noted that the industry representatives on the scene were stressing in their contacts with senators "the question of unemployment and loss to the working man—or voter, as you might put it—by this continued reduction in employment. This seems to affect them a great deal more than the fact neither you nor anyone else is making any money."⁵²

His health restored, and worried about his chances for re-election in 1932, Senator Jones stirred himself into action. "I have done everything I can possibly do to bring about a favorable result," he informed Reed, noting that he had exerted pressure on a number of his colleagues. "I will say to you frankly, but confidentially, that I have done what I do not believe in generally." It had taken "some maneuvering," Reed noted, "to get Senator Jones into a trading attitude," but he was at last being an effective spokesman for the industry. The resurgence of Jones was especially important, as McNary failed to live up to expectations. The Oregon Republican was preoccupied with his duties as Senate leader and, reported one observer, "is not prepared and does not want to take the burden of the fight on the floor." The tariff advocates were back where they had started in the summer, depending on Wesley Jones.⁵³

On 20 March, 1930 Jones argued for his amendment providing a duty of $1.50 per thousand feet on lumber. "The situation with reference to the lumber industry in my State is a very bad one," he contended. Jones continued that in admitting duty-free lumber from British Columbia "we are admitting

Chinese or oriental labor free. The labor that we say can not come into this country at all we are allowing to come in indirectly by having their products brought in." The Senate narrowly approved Jones's amendment, 39–38, with all members from lumber states voting in the affirmative except Borah.[54]

Four days later the Senate passed the tariff bill, relieving the pressure that had built up over the preceding months. "Those senators who have really conscientiously tried to do their work," observed Hiram Johnson, "are in a very wretched state." The Senate had denied the protection for wood approved in the House. Although disappointed over this development, the lumbermen consoled themselves with their success in securing a lumber duty. They also consoled themselves with the knowledge that all the duties would be before the conference committee.[55]

Unfortunately, disaster again interposed. In the House, progressive and urban Republicans joined with the Democrats to force a separate vote on forest products before consideration of the conference report. "I have never heard of an attitude like this before," Jones exclaimed, "where one House puts an item in the bill and then, when it has been disagreed to by the other House, that House insisting upon its having a vote on the item before any agreement is reached." Lumbermen recalled with dismay that the duties had originally been approved only because they had not been brought up on a separate vote. Now that vote was being held after all. "Some of the Eastern States have 45 or 46 members on their delegations," Jones pointed out, "when we have only 5, so you can appreciate the situation the boys are up against there."[56]

The tariff advocates detected the hand of J. H. Bloedel behind the House decision. The Bellingham lumberman had organized a group of Puget Sound log-buying mills to petition the House for deletion of the duty on logs. He claimed that 75 percent of the mills in Washington had to purchase logs on the open market and that the duty was "a tax on a raw material much needed by one of the largest American industries." In a brief circulated to all members he maintained that log prices had increased 10 to 25 percent since 1928; thus, there was no need to protect the loggers. Supporters of the tariff were outraged by this claim, which they contended went against all the facts. Reed pointed out that logs were selling for "less than any period since early nineteen fourteen."[57]

The House voted in early May to delete the log and shingle items from its bill, preventing their consideration in conference. "We have lost the fight," Reed laments, "but at least we know who our friends are." And at least the Senate's lumber duty was included in the conference report, although reduced to one dollar. Reed contended that the lumber duty was "of little value" but that it should be fought for, especially as rumors had progressives and Democrats demanding its deletion in return for their support of the bill. At Reed's urging the G.O.P. state convention, meeting in Bellingham in mid-May, resolved that the Washington delegation "actively oppose the passage of the tariff bill unless lumber products were included." The state's congressmen adopted this stance, and apparently so did Senator Dill. Jones, however, refused to go along, noting that if the final bill did not include lumber to vote against it "will not put any tariff on lumber."[58]

Lumber remained in the final bill, which passed the Senate 44-42 on 13 June, and the House the following day by a vote of 222-153. All senators from the Western lumber states voted for the tariff, with the exception of Borah and Dill. The latter had promised that he would vote for the bill if it was necessary to secure passage and the lumber duty. Nineteen of the twenty congressmen from those states also voted in the affirmative, providing the most significant support outside the industrial Northeast. Jones had been pressed to vote against the bill by shinglemen and lumbermen who felt the duty was worthless. "The dollar a thousand is not all we should have," he conceded, "nor does it cover all the lumber it should cover but it surely will be a benefit as far as it goes." Under the flexible provision it could be raised to $1.50. Most of the lumbermen agreed with this analysis and accepted the outcome as better than nothing.[59]

President Hoover signed the tariff, although the measure went well beyond his original call for "limited" revision and despite the contrary advice of many of the nation's leading economists and bankers. (The bill raised the average ad valorem rates from 33 to 40 percent, the highest in U.S. history.) "No tariff bill has ever been enacted or ever will be enacted under the present system," he noted, "that will be perfect." The Smoot-Hawley Tariff provided the desired protection for agriculture, Hoover contended, and the flexible provision allowed for correction of any inequities.[60]

Tariff advocates had little to say about the results of their lengthy fight. "While the immediate benefits from the small pittance that we got may not be noticed," George Long remarked, "yet it certainly is worth all it cost probably to win out against the unfair fight that was put up against the tariff asked for." Reed observed that "I do not feel that our efforts were all lost but of course we cannot be entirely satisfied with the result." Facing the political consequences of his failure to achieve the lumbermen's desires, Jones suggested that "when one has done the best he can, there is that satisfaction anyhow."[61]

The best, though, had not been sufficient to secure victory over the combined forces opposing the duties on forest products. The whole affair demonstrated that economic hardship alone was not sufficient to obtain protection. Nor was fidelity to the organization that professed to be the party of protection. "I hope this will be the last time of dealing with the tariff in this way," Jones wrote with some distaste. "We should adopt some other way and none that we adopt can be worse than the method we follow now." Tariff advocates could also blame themselves for their failure. Operating under a handicap, they worked at cross purposes with each other and were unable to find a leader in the nation's capital to provide vigorous direction of their efforts.[62]

The efforts of over a year had produced nothing but the small duty on lumber. These efforts again demonstrated the lack of unity in the industry. The tariff fight failed in part because the different sections of the industry had different and often conflicting interests, preventing the kind of cooperation necessary for effective action. The fight also had important political repercussions, as the era of one-party domination of Washington politics was coming to an end. The Great Depression was primarily responsible for the Democratic resurgence, but the Republican failure to benefit the region's principal industry lessened the party's ability to withstand the challenge. The Republican party seemed to many lumbermen to be a poor investment. Above all, their failure to secure a tariff indicated to lumbermen that the government would not be able to help them in their plight. They would have to save themselves by themselves, if they could.

CHAPTER 7

The Collapse of the Old Order

Arnold George, a twenty-nine-year-old ex-marine from Texas, had nursed a grievance in the Shelton hospital for nearly two years since an accident at one of the Simpson logging camps had cost him one leg and a severe fracture of the other. Driven insane by his ordeal, he had determined that the Reed family was somehow responsible for his suffering. On an evening late in June 1930, George observed Sol Reed, Mark Reed's eldest son, chatting with his brother Frank in front of the latter's home opposite the hospital. George wheeled himself across the street, calling to Sol as Frank entered the house. The crippled logger pulled out a pistol, purchased through the mail, and shot Sol four times before turning the gun on himself. Young Reed died shortly after being carried to the hospital, while George remained alive for half an hour.

Mark Reed was crushed by the murder. Sol's death, Reed wrote, was "a most terrible blow to me." He "was shattered," his youngest son recalls. "My father never fully recovered his drive." Sol was in the process of taking over much of the responsibility for management of Simpson, in accordance with his father's wishes. The shooting, Reed grieved, "has for all time annulled an ambition I have cherished for many years, feeling as I did that the young man would be able to successfully handle our business affairs after the time arrived for me to retire."[1]

The death of his son forced Reed to make a number of changes in his plans. George Drake, a promising Forest Service worker, was hired to replace Sol as logging superintendent. Frank Reed assumed the role of future successor to his father as president. But Frank had health problems and was not very interested in the business, so Reed placed his reliance on his youngest son, William G. Reed. Will, who had just finished a year of study at the Harvard Business School in preparation for his anticipated career in banking, was put through a crash course at the University of Washington forestry school, then became his father's principal assistant. The two had never been close, but their relationship changed considerably as Will gained the confidence of the elder Reed. "One time just made me thunderstruck," he recalls. "We were driving . . . somewhere and he offered me a cigarette and up until that time I'd been told that if he ever caught me smoking I'd have my head chopped off." Will, however, lacked Sol's experience, which meant that Mark had to take a more active role in the business than he had planned.[2]

Sol's murder was one example of the latent violence of the logging industry. On the day of Sol's death, William Renfroe, a hooktender at one of the camps, suffered a fractured skull in a fall. Eleven months later he shot and killed the camp foreman, twenty-four year old Joseph Grisdale, a cousin of the Reeds and a close friend of Will. Renfroe then returned to his home and shot his wife and two daughters before killing himself. Ironically, Renfroe had been charged with murder in Grays Harbor County in 1929 and had won acquittal with the aid of Sol Reed and the father of Joseph Grisdale. "This young man who brought all this sorrow and grief to those who are left behind," Mark Reed wrote, "has had nothing but the most helpful acts extended to him, not only by the company but its officers personally." Anguish over these senseless murders led Reed to abandon Shelton in 1932, moving his home to Seattle. "We've had enough," he told Will. "It is just too awful to contemplate."[3]

1

On Thursday, 24 October 1929 the New York Stock Exchange, scene of so much exhilaration and profitmaking over the previous decade, was the scene of panic and despair. The following Tuesday over sixteen million shares were traded and the *New York Times* industrial averages dropped a staggering forty-three points. By mid-November the value of stocks listed on the New York Exchange had fallen by 40 percent, and the nation was entering the greatest economic crisis in its history.

Reed had long been concerned by the wild stock-market speculation. The principal cause of the crash, he believed, was the draining off into stock speculation of funds usually invested in construction and business expansion. "We were running hog-wild," Reed later recalled, "expecting a large margin of profit to continue forever, and did not stop to realize that all things equalize." "Funds that should be invested in business, should be used to promote industry," he had pointed out in early 1929, "are being used for speculation; and as this situation is prolonged there can be no other result, . . . but a slowing down of business activity." During this speculative period, he noted following the crash, construction had fallen off, "and it will take some time to change the operating plans of the investor as well as to change the psychology of the investor's mind."[4]

Still, businessmen had no cause to panic. "There is no occasion for the business interests of this country to feel alarmed at the general situation," Reed contended a few weeks after the crash. The crash was merely one of "those periods of natural and necessary re-adjustment" in the nation's economy, a period that had been "brought upon us through the outgrowth of a wonderful period of development." The United States possessed "incalculable" resources and as a creditor nation occupied the strongest position in the world economy. And there was nothing fundamentally wrong with the New York Stock Exchange. "New York is the financial hub of the world and by constructive management it will so remain for all time," Reed wrote. "There may be some weak spots which should be corrected in our financial organization but they are not outstanding."[5]

In viewing the economy as basically sound and discounting the possibility of a serious depression, Reed voiced the opinion held by most businessmen and by President Herbert Hoover. Like the president, he believed that all that was necessary was to maintain confidence in the economy. "Faith," he observed, "that's the big thing we need these days." Reed was prepared to act on this belief. "Now is a splendid time to show our confidence in our industrial development by investing in stocks and bonds," he argued, as he purchased several thousand shares of blue chip stocks. His refusal to panic was no doubt the result of his experience coping with economic difficulties in the lumber industry.[6]

The national collapse compounded the problems facing the industry, ending any hopes for recovery. Demand and prices had been falling for several years and the downward pressure was likely to continue. "Just how lumbermen can expect to make a profit in 1930" one operator pondered, "is beyond my ability to figure out." The answer was that they could not, although Reed remained confident that the industry would rebound as the national economy shook off the impact of the crash. For the time being, however, the lumbermen would have to watch their situation closely. "All of us who expect to stay in the game," Reed pointed out, "must watch our operating costs and build up our efficiency to the highest degree possible."[7]

Fortunately, Reed's careful management of Simpson had put the company in a strong position to withstand the Depression. In fact, argues William G. Reed, the company's "position was . . . strengthened by it [the Depression] because Mark Reed had followed a very conservative policy of operating without debt and with the surplus amount of cash and most of the other companies were relatively short of cash, if not actually in debt and most of them had higher cost operations." Still, Reed was faced with severe problems. By early May 1930 he had reduced log prices, and his actions were followed immediately by requests for further reductions. "There just does not seem to be any bottom to the market," he noted.[8]

Lumbermen again turned to curtailment as the most promising solution. "A limited cut with prices predicated upon making a profit at the lessened volume," contended the *Timberman*, "is the essential remedy." In early June 1930 lumbermen representing 80 percent of Washington's production met in Tacoma to work out a voluntary program. Under the scheme, two-shift mills, including such large operators as Weyerhaeuser and Long-Bell, would go to one shift, while one-shift mills would run only five days a week. This would cut production by one fouth, a rate Reed feared would not be sufficient because "the market is absorbing somewhere from 40 to 50%." Loggers should, he calculated, cut their output by half.[9]

Curtailment, combined with maintenance of that elusive

commodity, confidence, would, most lumbermen hoped, restore the health of the industry. "All we have to do," Reed wrote, "is to keep a stiff upper lip . . . and keep the wheels turning, if we can." The *Timberman* urged a similar course. "Public lamentation by lumber manufacturers and Monday morning newspaper economists will not improve the situation," the Portland trade journal pointed out. "Such statements cause the public, business men in other lines and bankers to regard the industry unfavorably. Public utterances by lumber manufacturers decrying their own industry have recently had an unfavorable effect in financial circles." It was, however, difficult to avoid facing the economic facts.[10]

By the end of 1930 the lumber industry had been curtailed to a point where it was running at less than half of normal capacity. But even this was insufficient to meet the crisis as demand was falling even faster. "There is an immense stock of lumber on hand at the mills," Reed informed a friend, "with a constantly depreciating value due to the fact that prices fall so that in many instances the actual lumber inventory in a mill, if converted, will not pay the cost of producing the log, to say nothing of sawing and handling the lumber." In his thirty-five years in the industry, he continued, "it is the only time I ever knew of lumber being offered that could not be sold at any price. It isn't a question of price—it is just not being consumed."[11]

Curtailment was no real solution to the long-standing problems of the industry. What was needed, Reed believed, was a fundamental reorganization of the industry, allowing more efficient control of prices and production. "We are attempting to arrive at a cure of our ills by homeopathic remedies," he observed. These were "easier to take but . . . the time for cure will be extended for a much longer period." Perhaps, Reed and other lumbermen hoped, the exigencies of the moment would lead to recognition of this point. The industry, Minot Davis of Weyerhaeuser pointed out, would "have plenty of leisure time" in which to consider such a course.[12]

Reed had lost his illusions about the state of the economy and the prospects of the industry. "These are most trying times," he observed, "and are wearing on the patience of us all." Everything possible had to be done to cut costs, including the inevitable reduction of wages. Nationally, the refusal of labor organizations, backed by the Hoover administration, to accept wage reductions, Reed contended, was "one of the fundamental reasons for the lack of proper co-ordination in bringing us out of the industrial depression." Real wages, he noted, had increased as a result of declining prices. Those in positions of authority "should show some backbone" and support the public interest "rather than an organized minority."

At the end of 1930 Reed began to institute a series of wage reductions that left the minimum daily wage in Simpson camps at $2.75. (Company officials also took salary cuts.) This scale was more in line with prevailing prices, but was still higher than wages paid by most companies. Reed regretted having to make the reductions: "It does seem impossible for a man with a family at least to live on any such wage." But wage cuts were preferable to shutting down operations, which would leave the employees with no income at all.[13]

Simpson's long-time policy of encouraging development of a stable work force with roots in the community had succeeded, as most of its employees lived in Shelton with their families and worked year after year in the camps and mills. While such economic masterminds as Secretary of Treasury Andrew Mellon advised the "liquidation" of labor in order to combat the Depression, Reed determined to keep his most important workers on the job. "They helped us lay by a reserve for just such an emergency," he pointed out, "and why shouldn't they be in on it when the time comes for us to use it? They are entitled to this consideration and if we can carry on and maintain the proper thoughts in the minds of these workman [sic] we will have done something worth while." Chris Kreienbaum recalled Reed telling him that "we can come through this mighty bent, but if we play our cards right, we should make it and nobody will starve."[14]

These efforts, while socially responsible, also reflected sound business sense. By providing work during hard times, Reed retained his skilled labor in anticipation of returning prosperity and discouraged the development of radical political ideas. "When a man is out of work and his family is getting hungry," he observed, "you cannot blame him for getting some pretty radical ideas." Even if the mill was shut down, moreover, financial loss could not be avoided. "We are losing money every day and plenty of it," Reed informed a friend, "but that isn't so serious if you stop to think that even if we close our operation tight we would be losing to the extent of about $35,000 per month, including taxes and overhead."[15]

In late 1931 Chris Kreienbaum told Reed that costs could not be cut further and that the mill would have to be closed. "Chris, you'd better think about this," Reed responded. The two men discussed the number of people who had come to Shelton along with their families to work in the mill. Reed pointed out that these people had "bought or built homes, and they mortgaged them. The banks hold the mortgages. The merchants are carrying these people on their current purchases; and the banks are carrying the merchants. A lot of these people have growing families; they have hospital and doctor bills and they are behind in their payments. The hospital is beginning to suffer. And remember, without payrolls we have no taxes to support the town or county. So . . . why don't you go home and think about that for a few days; then come back and talk to me again." More was at stake then the balance sheet of the sawmill; the life of the community was involved. Kreienbaum agreed that shutting down the mill would damage Shelton, so he resolved to find some way to continue operating.[16]

By the middle of 1932, however, it was no longer possible to cut lumber because there was no place left to store it. Reed had to order Kreienbaum to shut down. "But," he decided, "let's notify the employees that anyone who wants to continue trading with the Lumberman's Mercantile Company can do so. We'll extend credit to these families, and we'll give it in proportion to the size of each family." Will Reed and George Drake were put in charge of supervising the credit operation. "I used to get the grocery bills and go over them," Drake recalled. "If I found that John Smith was buying too much yeast to make beer or buying too many cigarettes, I told him that wasn't in the picture, that we were giving him this credit, but we expected that they were going to pay for it and the less they borrowed, the less they'd have to pay back." Efforts were made to see that men who had car payments to make to the State Bank of Shelton did not lose their autos.[17]

When the mill was started up again to cut chips for the Rainier pulp mill, Reed had his employees sign notes for the money owed. "He put those notes away," Kreienbaum remembered, "and told the men that their credit rating would revert to what it had been before the shutdown. They could go on buying from the Lumberman's Mercantile Company and begin payment on the notes as they could afford it." As time passed most of the notes were paid off, but some workers with large families had considerable difficulty making payments. Kreienbaum called this to Reed's attention and the two of them went over the accounts. "Let's wipe these off the books and forget about them," Reed concluded, "and tell the people to go ahead and get back on their feet again." The whole episode again demonstrated Reed's concern for his employees and for the community of Shelton.[18]

Meanwhile, the industry's economic standing had continued to decline. "There is no denying the fact," Reed wrote in mid-1931, "that economically the lumber industry is going from bad to worse." National lumber production for the year was expected to exceed fifteen billion feet and some twelve billion feet remained unsold from 1930. But demand was predicted to be only seventeen billion feet, leaving a huge surplus to drag down the market. "The weak point now," wholesaler C. E. Dant stated in a rather severe understatement, "is a lack of business." Only 12 percent of the lumber workers on the Pacific Coast were employed full time. Hemlock prices had declined 30 percent since 1929, and Douglas fir prices 40 percent. "If any one had said to me two years ago that we would be selling our commodity for the prices we are," Reed noted, "I would have thought him a fit personality for the insane asylum."[19]

Curtailment could not stem the tide. Washington and Oregon mills cut half the lumber in 1931 that they had turned out in 1929, but this drastic reduction was far from sufficient. Reed determined to make a severe cut in the price of Simpson logs, a step he had long resisted. "The log inventory . . . was entirely out of balance with the cutting activity of the mills," he observed, "with the result that distress logs were being offered to the mills continually." As a result, the market could not be stabilized. By reducing his price two dollars a thousand feet, Reed hoped to force his weaker competitors to close down, reducing log supply and possibly leading to improved prices for lumber. The new prices meant that "we are sacrificing our stumpage," but over the long haul this could produce good results. "If we can keep the surplus of log supply within reasonable bounds in all the competitive markets," Reed concluded, "we may be in a position to start on the upward grade with our prices for lumber."[20]

Conditions continued to worsen in 1932, however. "There is no visible sign of business improvement in this section," Reed informed an Eastern correspondent. West Coast lumber production slumped to a third of what it had been in 1929. Shipments from Washington mills were reduced by eight hundred million feet from 1931. Prices of both logs and lumber were half of what they had been a decade earlier. "I just do not see how lumber can be sold for any less than it is now," Reed observed. There seemed to be little hope for the immediate future. Even with a slight upswing in demand, Chris Kreienbaum noted, "price would respond but production would immediately knock it down."[21]

The situation was equally bleak on the logging front. Reed's customers pressed him to reduce his prices to meet the cheaper logs available from the north and to the south in the Columbia River district. Reed took his men and equipment out of the woods in an effort to avoid adding to the surplus, but refused for the time being to drop his prices below the reductions made in the previous year. "Mark said," Tiff Jerome of the Merrill and Ring Lumber Company reported to that organization's president, "if logs were reduced lumber would be reduced accordingly, so there is nothing to be gained by reducing prices and it makes it just that much harder to get a fair price later on."[22]

Finally, though, Reed agreed to reduce his prices to seven, ten, and fourteen dollars for fir. This reduction was necessary to prevent his customers from acquiring logs elsewhere. "It is our intention," Reed informed R. D. Merrill, "to feed out these logs slowly so as not to break the market any more than is now being done." The new prices were below the "irreducible minimum" and would be maintained, Reed warned, only until he had disposed of most of his surplus. When he started his camps up again in the fall of 1932 prices would revert to their previous levels.[23]

By the end of 1932, three years after the stock market crash, the fortunes of the lumber industry reached bottom. "These are desperate times," Reed pointed out, "and frankly there is not very much that can be called tangible which is in the offing that promises for a prompt improvement." The only hope for the future that Reed could divine was the fact that the Depression was driving much of the industry into bankruptcy, reducing the number of competing units. "We doubt very much whether anything can be accomplished that isn't brought about under the law of economics," he noted. "It is unfortunate for some but things seem to be drifting that way."[24]

The industry, pressed by the vicissitudes of the economic collapse, had achieved a relatively successful degree of curtailment. But curtailment had not been sufficient to counteract the downward pressure of the economy. In these circumstances many operators were now willing to give serious consideration to plans to revamp the industry. "It is a helpful sign," observed Reed, "to see those who have been on the outside all these years, drifting along without any co-operation in association work of any nature, ready to come in and sit down around the table."[25]

2

In the lumber industry, Minot Davis noted large operating units were going to be inevitable, "because if properly organized and managed, they will permit us to improve the product and the service which we can give our customers, and they will afford better protection to employees and to stockholders." While perhaps inevitable, however, this development had not been possible during good times, or even during the period prior to the collapse of the national economy. "It is quite evident," Davis had written Reed, "that a mill merger cannot be formed successfully until such time as mill owners are right up against a necessity for doing something." Valuable information had been gained in the abortive 1929 negotiations. And now that the industry was really up against the wall a large scale merger was a distinct possibility.[26]

J. D. Tennant of Long-Bell took the lead in 1930 in urging the merger of properties on a large scale as the best solution to the industry's problems. Tennant's scheme would bring together a number of Northwest sawmills, forming a new company with an annual capacity of five billion feet of lumber. The company would enter into a twenty-year contract with the independent loggers as a means of assuring a stable supply of logs. It would be financed by an issuance of fifty million dollars in bonds. Although his Shelton operation was an integral part of Tennant's plan, Reed was not very enthusiastic. His friends among the loggers informed him of their distrust of the plan, as did operators of log-buying mills. Chris Kreienbaum, Reed's principal adviser in such matters, argued that the new company could not succeed because of the presence on the outside of such competitors as Weyerhaeuser, Bloedel-Donovan, and the British Columbia mills. Moreover, the financing was unsound, as it would be extremely difficult to meet the annual payments on the bond issue. "With no weak spots," Kreienbaum observed, the merger "would be a wonderful line-up." But the Tennant plan was, in the final analysis, too weak.[27]

Reed informed Tennant that, despite his concern with the problems the Longview lumberman was attempting to alleviate, he could not accept the proposal. "I do not believe our people would be interested in even encouraging you with the thought that we might give favorable consideration later," he wrote. Because of the economic crisis, Reed did not feel that the bonds could be sold. Besides, "we would not consider the merger of our hemlock mill with any other mills and thereby become a minority factor in the control of the property." His mill was too important to the Simpson logging operation to allow others to have a voice in its management. Finally, the plan required that the Simpson Logging Company negotiate an exclusive contract with the new mill organization. This would terminate its connections with long time customers remaining on the outside:

"Certainly we do not feel that we should kick them out the back door and say to them that we have made other arrangements." In order to succeed, a merger would have to be on a much larger scale.[28]

Reed did, however, involve himself in efforts at industry cooperation. Early in 1931, for example, he took the Reed Mill Company into a reorganized Douglas Fir Exploitation and Export Company. "This," reported the *Mason County Journal*, "is the result of efforts which have been under way for months to get the largest mill concerns together and selling through one sales agency, and end the demoralization which has ruled the lumber business for a year or more." Reed served on the governing body of the DFE and E, although continuing to have misgivings about its policies. Still, he believed that if the Shelton mill and other operations had not strengthened the company, "the market of the product throughout the competitive points of the Northwest would have been at a much lower price level than even we have realized during this recent period of deflation." The strengthening of the industry was the important question. "While we have not always agreed as to policies," Reed noted, "we have not 'sulked in our tent' but rather have tried to help carry on successfully for the general benefit of the industry."[29]

Reed also helped establish the Puget Sound Associated Mills, a group of mill organizations trading with the Atlantic Coast. With Chris Kreienbaum as its president and experienced lumber broker Robert Seeley as manager, the association was meant to bring some rationality to the Atlantic Coast market, pooling shipments and handling sales direct without the requirement of middlemen. "We hope [it] will become a very efficient agency," Reed observed, "and will be the forerunner towards the organization of similar agencies at other competitive points, with the end in view that the heads of these agencies can sit down around the table and reach a better understanding than can be done through so many individual operations." These efforts focused on the distribution end of the industry, but Reed was also giving attention to a new, more ambitious merger scheme.[30]

This effort began to take shape at a meeting of the state's

leading lumbermen in Tacoma in February 1931. On the Olympic Peninsula, the merger would include the Bloedel and the Merrill and Ring operations in the north and Polson, Simpson, and the Weyerhaeuser-affiliated Clemons Logging Company in the south. "These operations brought under one controlling unit would dominate effectively for all time probably the Olympic Peninsula situation," Reed noted. To the east of Puget Sound the merger would take in the Bloedel-Donovan mills at Bellingham, the various interests of William Butler, and, probably, the St. Paul and Tacoma Lumber Company. Also included as the most significant aspect of the plan would be the Weyerhaeuser mills at Everett and that company's logging operation at Vale.

The merger would leave western Washington with two major companies, Weyerhaeuser and the new giant firm, which would be known as the Washington Timber Company. "The purpose," William G. Reed, who represented his father in the negotiations, later recalled, "was to reduce competition, control production, and try to get prices at a liveable level." The first series of meetings was concerned with gathering information about the values of the respective companies, preparatory to serious discussions. Those participating agreed on the hiring of Carl Stevens, the experienced Portland forestry consultant, to supervise the entire process. "He is very keen," Weyerhaeuser's Minot Davis informed Reed, "and will, I think, develop the information just the way we want it."[31]

Reed was enthusiastic over the scope and object of the plan, but less so over its prospects. Many lumbermen who should have been devoting their energies to the working out of such constructive schemes were failing to do so. "Life is too short," Reed observed to William Butler, "to engage in an undertaking where those that should help and are just as largely interested, or more so, than those who are willing to help, stand on the outside and say 'let George do it.'" Once again a number of lumbermen were refusing to act responsibly. "I am very much disgusted," Reed said, "with the attitude of some of those who should know that it is a crime to allow this industry to proceed in the throes of despair as it is at the present time."[32]

The Shelton lumberman also feared that the proposed combination might violate the antitrust laws. There was no such law in Washington. Although the state constitution prohibited combinations in restraint of trade, the legislature had never provided a means of enforcing this provision. The national laws, however, were a more serious matter. Many of the potential participants in "the getting-together program," observed Reed, feared that "they might be assuming liability under the anti-trust laws." This was especially important because of the planned participation of Weyerhaeuser, a tempting target for antimonopolists. "We are not at all anxious to become law breakers," Reed insisted.[33]

The merger, moreover, could not succeed unless a similar competition-reducing development was worked out in Oregon. The potential timber production of that state, which would soon supplant Washington at the forefront of the industry, was too great. "If Oregon cannot be welded into a concrete arrangement," Reed cautioned, "then we are just throwing ourselves wide open for a cut throat operation that will wreck our plans." Although discussions among Oregon operators were underway in Portland, they appeared unlikely to lead to a consolidation. Oregon lumbermen, John W. Blodgett informed Reed, had been concentrating on the minute details of their own individual operations for so long "that they have lost all sense of perspective. . . . This is not because they lack ability but because they have looked down at one spot for so many years without raising their heads and taking a broad view, that it has grown to be a habit." Reed contended that the situation in Oregon had to be "buttoned up tight before constructive action could actually be undertaken in Washington."[34]

But the most serious obstacle proved to be the attitude of Weyerhaeuser, which was reluctant to disrupt its own organization. The success of the merger, Reed believed, required that the company contribute its Everett mills and logging operations. "With such an interest on their part," Chris Kreienbaum pointed out, "it would be necessary that they give serious consideration to the welfare of a much larger part of the industry than they seem to have done recently." Weyerhaeuser was the most important organization in the region, Reed maintained, "and if those of us who put in our properties (the result of a lifetime of work) cannot feel that they are personally interested in the success and upbuilding of the new organization, there is no reason for us to make the change." This was precisely the sticking point in the negotiations.[35]

"Nothing effective can be accomplished," Reed argued to Weyerhaeuser officials, unless they took an "active and concrete part in the organization of such a consolidated unit." The company, however, failed to agree with this assessment. Weyerhaeuser had been expending considerable energy in maximizing the efficiency of its operation, Frederick Weyerhaeuser informed Reed, "and naturally, any change in this set up might seriously disrupt the organization we have been creating over the years." Carl Stevens, negotiating with the company's executive committee in St. Paul, reported that "they all immediately think and talk about 'dismemberment' of the Weyerhaeuser Timber Company in tones of shock and consternation." The committee members, though, agreed to visit the Northwest and take part in serious discussions of the proposal.[36]

This willingness indicated to Reed that Weyerhaeuser might be ready to go into the merger. The company's new attitude was the result, he observed, of "a state of affairs which they have not heretofore realized in their operations; that is, one of actually losing money." After their visit, however, the executive committee members informed Reed that they would not contribute the Everett mills or the Vale timber to the merger. They did agree to put in Clemons and other timber operations on Grays Harbor, and would consider adding their recently organized operation on Willapa Bay. Reed told Butler that the committee was adamant in refusing to "entertain anything that would tend to be destructive of their present operating set-up." Although this decision was disappointing to the merger advocates, they continued to negotiate on the basis of the Weyerhaeuser offer.[37]

Discussions continued throughout 1932. Laird Bell, Chicago attorney and son of Weyerhaeuser president F. S. Bell, journeyed to the coast on at least three occasions to handle negotiations for the company, particularly on the vital effort to organize the Oregon industry. That task remained a rather difficult undertaking. "The Columbia River situation is rather like a kalaidoscope [sic]," Reed noted, "one day they seem to be working on a constructive policy and the next you hear is that they are at loggerheads." Efforts were also underway to promote a merger in British Columbia, not an easy task in itself. These preconditions remained essential for the working out of the Washington plan. "It would be rather hopeless and probably hazardous," Reed cautioned, "to attempt to put through our organization in Washington and leave us open on both flanks."[38]

Closer to home, the merger plans hit a snag when the Polson Logging Company repeated its 1929 refusal to join. Robert Polson, who had taken over management of the Hoquiam company from his ailing brother, listed a number of technical objections. But the real reason, Reed informed Bell, was "that he [Polson] had put in his whole life in buiding up the organization which he now has, . . . and that he just did not feel he should join a larger organization and possibly lose their identity and discard the plans they had been working on and building on for the future." Polson's withdrawal meant that its competitor, Bloedel-Donovan, was not likely to put in its Olympic Peninsula properties, destroying what Reed described as "an airtight arrangement" in that region. "The Peninsula is still intensely competitive territory."[39]

Reed was determined to continue negotiations however, although the chaotic conditions in Oregon and British Columbia prevented fruition of the merger plan. His interest, along with that of other Washington lumbermen, indicated how deeply the Depression had effected the traditional means of operation in the industry. Their efforts also demonstrated the severe obstacles that those traditional means and the often conflicting interests within the industry placed in the way of rationalizing the industry's structure. Reed continued to contemplate the prospects for a merger. In the meantime, however, his attention was diverted by a return to politics.

3

Mark Reed had spent some time in Olympia in early 1931 lobbying on behalf of tax and forestry matters before the legislature. Except for that instance, however, he had devoted little time to state politics since his retirement as Mason County's representative. Many of his friends and business associates now urged him to run for governor in 1932. "To my notion," wrote J. H. Bloedel, Reed's one-time opponent in the tariff fight, "there never was a better opportunity than now." Mark Reed "is and will always be a power in the politics of this state," the Seattle *Argus* observed. "If nominated he could be elected, even at a time when there is much dissatisfaction with conditions in the country, and the unthinking are laying that trouble to the Republican administration." Others were urging him to run for the Senate. "You are the logical candidate for the toga now worn by Senator Jones," a Seattle businessman argued.[40]

Reed refused to become a candidate for either office, stressing that his business affairs would not permit him to do so. Privately, he informed a friend on a "very confidential" basis that at sixty-five, "I do not feel that my health would stand up under the strenuous campaign that would be necessary, and the subsequent developments if I should be elected." Reed's announcement that he would not be a candidate, the *Argus* commented, "came as a painful shock to many of his friends all over the state who honestly had cherished the idea he would be the next governor of the commonwealth." It did not, however, mean that he would refuse to become involved in politics during 1932.[41]

The position of Republican national committeeman traditionally went to a man of wealth, who could afford to spend a great deal of time traveling on party business. Thus, it was not unusual that many Republicans desired Reed to assume the post in 1932. One friend with political connections warned him not to accept: "It is quite probable that the men who have been meeting with indifferent success in financing the party will pass the whole load to you." Reed did not take this advice, though, and was elected to the position at the state convention in May. "Were a vote to be taken today to find the most influential man in the Republican party in this state," the editor of the *Argus* observed, "Mark Reed would, I believe, win by a handsome majority."[42]

Reed's main responsibility as national committeeman was to manage the reelection campaign of President Hoover in the state, a somewhat sobering task in the midst of the greatest depression in the nation's history. The two had held a lengthy meeting at the White House in late 1931, discussing the economic and political situation. "His problems have been even greater than I had thought," Reed informed William Butler. "He is trying to lead the country into a favorable reconstruction period and will be satisfied if he can do that, without regard to his political future." Hoover had "some really constructive ideas," Reed continued, "but unfortunately, as I see it, he is not a leader of men and has very few followers who are disposed to carry out his program." As for the political situation, Reed concluded after this trip east that "the Republicans do not have a Chinaman's chance."[43]

The odds did not lessen Reed's determination to do everything possible for the president. In March 1932 he received a letter from Chicago attorney and former Progressive Harold Ickes asking for assistance in an effort to dump Hoover. "I see no reason why the Republican Party should deliberately run into a smashing defeat merely to satisfy one man's ambitions," Ickes wrote. Rather, the party should nominate Ickes's one-time Progressive party colleague, Governor Gifford Pinchot of Pennsylvania. "I would not support Mr. Pinchot on a bet," Reed responded. "I do not have any sympathy with those who are sailing under our flag of Republicanism and attempting to tear down the party from within." Hoover, moreover, should be supported, not rebuked, by members of his party. "History," Reed asserted, "does not record any administration during times of depression when more constructive leadership came from the administration in power than has originated during President Hoover's term."[44]

Hoover's reelection would not be easy. "Our most serious problem is unemployment," Reed pointed out. Sixty thousand people were on relief in Seattle alone, and banker W. H. Parsons reported that the city was "more or less a hot bed for the Communists, Socialists and other foreign 'isms' that are sure to make trouble unless something can be done to find employment for these people." This was unfortunate, Reed noted, but "people under those conditions just do not think normally" and such confusion would be a decisive factor on election day. The best that Republicans could hope for would be that the people would in the end "take note of the problem which has confronted him [Hoover] and finally . . . believe that he has done a remarkable job in keeping his feet on the deck and steering the ship as well as he has."[45]

The proper conservative policies, Reed believed, would bring the Depression to an end. The federal budget must be balanced "before business will take heart and go ahead." This required that the cost of government be pared to the bone. "We must do in government what we do in private business," Reed argued. "We are getting down to fundamentals in private life and we must do so in government." But new taxes were also required to balance the budget. These levies could not be raised from the personal or corporate income tax, "no matter how high the rates are made, as the earnings are not there to tax." On the contrary, these "confiscatory taxes" had to be reduced in order to encourage new investment. "Business is now carrying about all the load it can in the way of taxation," Reed insisted. The only solution to the revenue problem, the only means of balancing the budget, he concluded, was establishment of a national sales tax.[46]

Reed also supported Hoover's action in approving creation of the Reconstruction Finance Corporation to provide financial assistance to the nation's banks and railroads. Some had criticized the R.F.C for not aiding the poor, Reed noted, "but what is being done when the railroads and banks are saved, except helping the people?" In the final analysis, however, the nation must depend on individual initiative for recovery. "The more you depend on government for the support of the individual," he pointed out, "the more you are breeding trouble. There are times when government must step in and help but it is not the function of government to provide the means of life." These policies, though, would take some time to be effective and could have no impact on the fortunes of Republicans in 1932.[47]

In late July, Reed moved to Seattle, ostensibly to devote full attention to the campaign. Actually, the move resulted from his continuing anguish over the violent events that had taken place in his hometown. The *Mason County Journal* said that Reed would not return to Shelton after the election.[48]

Reed's first effort in the campaign was to call a meeting of the state's elected Republican officials, at which he stressed the need for harmony if the party was to avoid defeat in November. Governor Roland H. Hartley, Land Commissioner Clark Savidge, and Secretary of State J. Grant Hinkle agreed to terminate their long feud in the face of a severe threat to their mutual political survival. "Mark said that the meeting was entirely harmonious," political commentator J. H. Brown reported, and "that he believes the officials recognized how necessary to party success it was that they present a united front in the campaign." Unfortunately, the agreement encompassed only those officials previously involved in the party dispute and Hartley soon began attacking his principal opponent for renomination, Lieutenant Governor John Gellatly, with his accustomed vigor and venom. The impending Democratic challenge could not paper over the divisions within the party.[49]

Nationally, Reed was encouraged by the selection of Governor Franklin D. Roosevelt of New York as the Democratic candidate. Along with many other observers, he contended that Roosevelt was the weakest possible choice of the opposition. "If Roosevelt is nominated," he had written prior to the Democratic convention, "in my judgment Hoover will be re-elected without question." But his perception that the public desired a change soon convinced Reed that F.D.R., despite his weakness, would be difficult to defeat. "These times do not bring about peace of mind in the citizenship of the country," he noted, "and there is too much of a disposition to want to change, which naturally increases liberalism as against conservatism." Even the *Seattle Times* had come out for Roosevelt, giving him a monopoly of support in the Seattle daily press. Reed, noting that William Randolph Hearst was backing the Democratic ticket, pressed *Times* publisher C. B. Blethen to reconsider. "I do not know of a time since 1896," he argued, "when the fundamentals of our government were so seriously involved in a questionable program as is the case at the present time. Suffice it to say if Roosevelt and [John Nance] Garner should be elected it means Hearst domination in the White House."[50]

As the general election campaign got underway, Reed held another meeting of Republican candidates for statewide office. The most notable feature of this meeting was the absence of Governor Hartley, who had been soundly defeated in the G.O.P. primary by Gellatly. The chances of the party's ticket were threatened by the refusal of the governor to endorse the ticket. Hartley was a poor sport, one Republican complained. "He ought to tell his friends to line up. He asked this for himself eight and four years ago, and, generally, got this support." With any chance of achieving party unity ended, Reed devoted most of his energy to the Hoover campaign, exerting himself to prevent the defeat of the safe and sane Republican administration.[51]

Reed traveled the state in the closing days of the campaign, speaking out for the "retention of the principles in government that we believe in." Returning to Shelton, he reminded his former neighbors that "no statesman, no leader in the history of our country, has been more maligned, more misrepresented, and has shown greater fortitude, greater patience and greater feeling for his people than our great leader," Herbert Hoover. The voter, he insisted, should "think it over again carefully, and unless you can see some reasonable assurance of bettering the conditions in any wild theories that are contrary to the principles and policies that have made this country great," your vote should go to Hoover. Things might be bad, in other words, but they could be infinitely worse under a Democratic administration.[52]

Reed professed to see some hope as the campaign neared its end. When he assumed control of the Hoover effort, he wrote his old friend Henry Suzzallo, "it looked as if this state was hopelessly Roosevelt" by a margin of at least 150,000 votes. But "it has gotten down to a point now where the gamblers are offering wagers on the board this morning ten to seven that Roosevelt carries the State." After a trip east of the mountains, Reed informed an associate that "we are making headway and if the situation keeps on improving as it has for the last two weeks, we will carry the state beyond any doubt." There is, another Republican observed, "an unmistakable drift back to Hoover."[53]

The results of what Reed called "the most strenuous campaign" in Washington's history, however, brought a Democratic sweep. Franklin Roosevelt, winning nationally, carried every county in the state. Democrat Clarence Martin matched F.D.R.'s 57 percent of the vote to win the governorship, carrying all but two counties. Homer Bone, Reed's one-time opponent in the public power fight, defeated Senator Wesley Jones in the latter's bid for a fifth term with 60 percent of the vote. Democratic candidates swept Republican congressmen from office, won all but one statewide race and secured control of the state legislature. The election results, observed Reed, came as "a wild tornado." An era in state politics had come to an end.[54]

Reed accepted the outcome as foreordained. "It was just out of the question," he pointed out, "to overthrow the tremendous sentiment existing in the minds of the people against the depression and its results." Putting the best light on the situation, he noted that "we have gotten rid of the renegades who have used the Republican party only as a means for furthering their ends. . . . If the Democratic party which has taken over the radical element in our party will only keep it, they will have performed a wonderful service to the Republican party and the country." Moreover, the Democrats would now have the responsibility for ending the Depression, and their inevitable failure in this task would lead to a Republican comeback. "There will be plenty of trouble ahead for the next two years, at least," Reed contended, "and before the 1934 election rolls around, the Democratic leadership will be thoroughly discredited in the minds of the people."[55]

Following the death of Senator Jones a few days after the election, Reed was widely mentioned as a successor to serve out the remaining months of Jones's term. The Shelton lumberman had "long cherished" a desire to serve in the Senate, claimed the *Argus*. But Governor Hartley passed over Reed to appoint another lumberman, E. S. Grammer of Seattle. The governor apparently believed that Reed had undermined his efforts for a third term by informing Republican county chairmen before the primary that renomination of Hartley would lessen Hoover's chances in the state. Had it not been for this belief, for which no supporting evidence can be found, Reed might well have been named to the Senate, concluding his political career with brief service in that august body.[56]

As it was, Reed had finished his political career by presiding over the most massive Republican defeat in the state's history. It was a defeat, though, that he was not responsible for, as the Depression had upset all traditional modes of political behavior. It was a defeat that ended the period of one-party rule in the state, the period in which Mark Reed had come to power in the Republican party and in the state it dominated.

4

Change was in the air as the nation entered the fourth year of the Depression. Herbert Hoover served out his last dispirited months in the White House, as Franklin Roosevelt prepared to launch the New Deal. In Washington state the Democrats assumed control in Olympia. New expectations were the order of the day, with most Americans expecting significant developments, some for the worst but most for the better. No noticeable signs of improvement were apparent to Northwest lumbermen, but many of those not totally driven to despair by the Depression expected better times. "We feel . . . a sense of relief that the past three years are behind us," Reed wrote, "and it does seem as if we are over the worst of our difficulties. We hope so at any rate."[57]

Reed's expectations received a partial blow when the merger negotiations collapsed early in 1933. They had been going along during the months devoted to the political campaign, concentrating on the situation in Oregon. At the beginning of January, however, the Weyerhaeuser-affiliated Clemons Logging Company instituted a drastic reduction in the price of its Grays Harbor logs. Minot Davis, who was responsible for management of Clemons, asserted that this lower price was necessary because mills in the Grays Harbor region were at a competitive disadvantage with those on Puget Sound. It was essential, he informed Reed, that Clemons sell logs at prices that would allow its customers to compete. The action did not, he indicated, mean that Weyerhaeuser no longer believed in cooperation within the industry.[58]

That was not the attitude perceived by Reed. The lumber industry, he informed Laird Bell, "is in a deplorable situation which can be helped to some extent by a spirit of co-operation in trying to stabilize prices at some low level." Prevailing prices were too low as it was "and it does not help any to appear wobbly' in our attitude as to prices." The situation provoked by the Clemons reduction, Reed told Bell, "only serves to prove that there should be better control; and as I see it, this control will have to be invoked by the Weyerhaeuser Timber Company, otherwise chaos will prevail." William Butler observed to Reed that there was little use "trying to cooperate when the major activity permits destructive sniping in almost every branch of the industry which they should dominate and control."[59]

The Grays Harbor affair convinced Reed that Weyerhaeuser was not seriously interested in cooperation and that there was thus no point in continuing the merger negotiations. "Frankly," he observed, "I am so thoroughly disgusted with the whole situation that I am just about in the frame of mind that it is useless for me to waste time and effort in an attempt to help stabilize the industry." Referring to Weyerhaeuser, he criticized the "last of a disposition to co-ordinate among those whom we should look up to for leadership." Reed concluded that he would no longer waste his time on "useless and fruitless activities. I think we shall devote more of our time to our own affairs and try to pull ourselves through this depression period with our losses minimized as much as possible." Again, the conflicting interests within the industry had prevented the working out of schemes to rationalize its operation in the interest of maximum efficiency and market control.[60]

The hopes for a better year collapsed along with the negotiations. The Northwest lumber industry operated at about 18 percent of normal capacity during January, and there seemed to be little prospect of improvement in the coming months. "Certainly," Reed wrote to an associate, "general business conditions do not indicate that we are to have very much improvement for the ensuing year." But by June the situation had improved significantly as confidence in the future of the economy, buoyed up by the heady feelings of Roosevelt's first months in office, returned. Northwest lumber shipments were up for the first six months of the year, and one operator reported that "lumber prices are gradually strengthening in all markets." Confidence was "being restored," Reed noted, "rehabilitation of buildings is going on, and a generally better feeling is prevalent all around."[61]

Although the volume of orders for the spring months was the greatest since 1928, Reed feared that the apparent recovery was not genuine. "A considerable proportion of these new orders," he pointed out in late June, "are being placed from a speculative standpoint in that the yards are stocking up before there has been a material increase in price." Already, Chris Kreienbaum had reported a downturn in demand. Therefore, Reed hesitated to increase the price of logs, a step that he had been looking forward to for a considerable period of time. "It would be a mistake to advance the price of logs at this time," he observed, "until we have a better understanding of the reasons behind the recent demand for lumber." At this point of uncertainty a new force entered the picture, offering at last a mechanism by which the lumbermen could bring their industry under control: the federal government in the form of Roosevelt's National Recovery Administration.[62]

Reed had regarded the early months of the New Deal with considerable distaste. The government was interfering directly in the operations of the nation's industry and agriculture, its banks and stock exchanges—all anathema to Reed's conservative temperament. He confessed that he could not predict how things would turn out, but the "present trend in Washington seems to be one of tearing down all the principles of government which have made this country great." Still, there was a good chance that this dangerous trend could be sidetracked. He retained his faith, Reed concluded, that "the majority of the people . . . are fundamentally sound in their thinking and that we will not go so far in the changes of fundamentals in this 'new deal' that we cannot still feel that our form of government is to survive."[63]

This attitude caused Reed to regard the establishment of the

N.R.A. with some misgivings. The National Industrial Recovery Act authorized individual industries to establish under government guidance codes regulating production, prices, hours of labor and wages. Thus, each industry would be brought, ideally speaking, under a system of rational control that would allow recovery. "There have been sporadic attempts on the part of certain industries to adjust production to the approximate demand," noted the *Timberman*, "but the results have often been nullified through the lack of authority to compel adherence to any prescribed formula. This is the crux of this far-reaching departure from the hitherto accepted principle of free competition." But the federal government would also be involved in industry matters through the N.R.A., a point that troubled Reed, as did the problems involved in working out a code that would protect the interests of all the component units of the lumber industry.[64]

"We are moving out into uncharted waters in the new industrial program which is proposed under the government regulatory act," Reed observed, "and just what the outcome will be nobody seems to know." Nevertheless, he concluded, "there doesn't seem to be anything to do but to go along, and in any event it cannot be much worse than it has been for the past three years." Although he was still recovering from injuries suffered in a fall taken while horseback riding, Reed was determined to participate in the development of the lumber code. This would take palce in a Chicago meeting called by the National Lumber Manufacturers Association. (That organization would administer the code on the national level, with the West Coast Lumbermen's Association deputized to handle it on the Pacific Coast.) "I would feel it my obligation to serve," Reed told Kreienbaum.[65]

Reed served on the committee that worked out the lumber code in Chicago and then traveled to Washington, D.C. to participate in the negotiations with the government for acceptance of the code. The minutes of these meetings indicate that Reed was not one of the more active members of the committee, but he did attempt to make the code more effective and more acceptable to General Hugh Johnson, head of the N.R.A. He was successful, for example, in winning deletion from the proposed

code of a section providing for "a fair profit" in the detremina-
tion of prices. "Mr. Reed stated his belief," according to the
minutes, "that the Administration would look with great alarm
on a code provision for the first natural resource industry based
on the principle of guaranteeing the profit." He failed, however,
in an effort to prevent removal of a provision establishing code
control over the installation of new capacity in existing mills.
Above all, he insisted, the code must be quickly devised and put
into effect in order to prevent the further growth of labor
discontent in the Northwest industry. A strike currently underway on Grays Harbor, he claimed, was the result of labor
uncertainty over the code.[66]

The principal problems in the working out of the code
involved establishment of wage and hour scales that would not
"disturb the long standing relationship between the South and
the West" and would be acceptable to the Roosevelt administration. In a meeting with the lumbermen, General Johnson,
according to an account of the discussion, "pointed out that the
Recovery Act was primarily a measure for industry self-
government; that temporarily and only because of the emergency, wages and hours had assumed an immediate importance
and were being stressed." As finally determined, the code
established machinery empowered to set production quotas and
minimum prices for each division of the industry. It guaranteed
the right of workers to join unions of their choice and set the
maximum hours of labor per week on the West Coast at forty
and the minimum wage at sixteen dollars per week in the mills
and twenty dollars in the logging camps. And it committed the
lumber industry to the practice of conservation.[67]

Although most lumbermen expected some uncertainty in the
early months of the code's operation and believed that it would
result in a good deal of hardship for marginal producers, its
signing by President Roosevelt on 19 August received wide-
spread approval in the Northwest. "The theory of the lumber
code is to reduce production to a point where the demand will
naturally force prices upward to a point equal to the increased
cost of production," the *Timberman* pointed out. "We must exercise patience and let these new economic theories sought to be
tested out under the lumber code, have a fair trial." The area's

lumbermen, commented the *West Coast Lumberman*, "are convinced the new lumber code will be of positive benefit to the entire lumber industry." Reed never had a chance to comment in the aftermath of the code's approval. His attitude no doubt was rather lukewarm, as he recognized the practical difficulties facing efforts to administer the code. "Any code that is now agreed upon," he had earlier noted, "can be looked upon as tentative and probably will have to be changed later to meet operating conditions as they develop."[68]

Reed returned to Seattle from the nation's capital in early August in a state of complete physical exhaustion and soon entered the city's Providence Hospital. Along with several other lumbermen, it turned out, he had contracted amoebic dysentery while staying at the Congress Hotel in Chicago. But doctors of the day had little understanding of this debilitating disease and, as Reed failed to recover, they apparently determined that he had cancer. In late August they operated, discovering no cancer but furthering his weakened condition. On the morning of 5 September after nearly a month in the hospital, Reed died. Funeral services were held the next day at the First Presbyterian Church of Seattle, with the Reverend Mark Matthews presiding, and Reed was buried in the family's vault in Tacoma.[69]

Tribute to Reed poured in from throughout the Northwest. Governor Clarence Martin said that he had been "loved by his followers and respected by his competitors and opponents." The *Seattle Times* mourned the loss of "the first citizen of his state." Reed's old friend Alex Polson observed that "his leadership in politics and the lumber industry and his sacrifices for his own men and the laboring men everywhere can hardly be fully appreciated," while the Seattle *Town Crier* commented that "there could be no greater monument to Mr. Reed than the fact that no one ever begrudged him his millions."

Reed's death, noted the *West Coast Lumberman*, "brought to an untimely end the career of the Northwest's most outstanding lumberman." He "could have been governor of Washington, or United States Senator," the editor of the *Argus* pointed out. "Not one word to his detriment has ever been printed, or, so far as I know, uttered." The Portland *Oregonian* claimed that "as a timberman he did not conform to type, nor as a politician. . . .

The reason underlying this difference appears to be in the possession of uncommon vision." "Men may grow and men may go," reflected the *Mason County Journal*, "but there rarely comes into being a man who can measure up to the many calls of diversified activities, and yet find time out of a busy life to be neighborly, friendly, sociable and considerate of the little affairs of others."[70]

The last three years of Reed's life had witnessed the overturning of most of the fundamental institutions of importance to him. The murder of his son was a shattering personal blow and destroyed his plans for the future of his business affairs. Politically, the 1932 election brought to an end the long period of Republican domination of state politics. The coming of the New Deal meant a significant departure from the traditional role of the federal government. The impact of the Depression, moreover, exposed the weaknesses of the Northwest lumber industry, demonstrating that it could no longer be operated as it had been since its founding in the nineteenth century. The old order had come to an end by the time Reed died.

Mark Reed had clearly been one of the major figures in the history of the state and the forest industry. His stewardship of the Simpson Logging Company marked the beginning of its transformation from a supplier of logs to an integrated forest products enterprise and set the stage for its expansion in the years after World War II. In his effort to organize the company's operations on an efficient basis, he represented a major development in modern American business enterprise. In striving to improve working conditions, he showed that a businessman could also be a reformer and that reform, contrary to conventional wisdom, could well be a benefit to business. And in the fusion of his roles as businessman and politician, he demonstrated the ways in which political activity could be utilized to further business goals and, moreover, that it was possible to serve the public interest as well as the private.

Notes

Notes to Introduction

1. George Drake oral history interview with Elwood R. Maunder, 22-23 February 1967, Forest History Society, p. 145; *Seattle Times*, 12 September 1926. There is no mention of Reed in the most commonly used text on Northwest history: Dorothy O. Johansen and Charles M. Gates, *Empire on the Columbia*. For an introduction to Reed's career, see Robert E. Ficken, "Mark E. Reed," *Journal of Forest History* 20 (January 1976):4-19. Also see Norman H. Clark, *Washington, A Bicentennial History*, pp. 126-34, 139, 141-44.

2. See Joseph F. Tripp, "Progressive Labor Laws in Washington State (1900-1925)," (Ph.D. dissertation), pp. 302, 304.

3. Shelton *Mason County Journal*, 22 March 1928.

Notes to Chapter 1

1. Olympia *Pacific Tribune*, 29 December 1866.

2. Reed Family Information Book, Simpson Reed & Co., pp. 1-4; Hubert Howe Bancroft, *History of Washington, Idaho, and Montana, 1845-1889*, p. 312; Julian Hawthorne, ed., *History of Washington, the Evergreen State*, 1:694-95; Mrs. George E. Blankenship, *Early History of Thurston County, Washington*, pp. 78-79, 306-9; Clarence B. Bagley, *History of Seattle, from the Earliest Settlement to the Present Time*, 2:829-34; Olympia *Tribune*, Souvenir Edition, May 1891; Thomas M. Reed, *Pioneer Masonry: A History of the Early Days of Freemasonry on the Pacific Coast*.

3. *West Shore* 2(January 1877):108, 3(December 1877):64.

4. Reed Family Information Book, pp. 3-4; Blankenship, *Early History of Thurston County*, pp. 308-9.

5. Olympia *Tribune*, Souvenir Edition, May 1891; Gordon R. Newell, *So Fair a Dwelling Place*, p. 39; *R. L. Polk & Co.'s Olympia City and Thurston County Directory, 1902-03*, pp. 31, 152.

6. Mark E. Reed to James H. Davis, 18 April 1922, Simpson Logging Co. Papers, Simpson Timber Co.; *Pacific Mason* 3(June 1897):184; Edwin P. Conklin, "Logging on Puget Sound, As Illustrated in the Lives of Sol Simpson and Mark E. Reed," *Americana Illustrated* 29(April 1935):271; Stewart H. Holbrook, *Green Commonwealth*, p. 55; Harry W. Deegan, *History of Mason County*, p. 89.

7. *Pacific Mason* 3(June 1897):184; James L. Fitts, "The Washington Constitutional Convention of 1889," (master's thesis), pp. 59, 100, 128,

177; Hawthorne, ed., *History of Washington*, 1:695; Bagley, *History of Seattle*, 2:832; Lloyd Spencer and Lancaster Pollard, *A History of the State of Washington*, 1:414, 416.

8. Newspaper clipping, Mark E. Reed folder, Washington State Biography File, Northwest Collection, University of Washington Library; Holbrook, *Green Commonwealth*, p. 55.

9. Conklin, "Logging on Puget Sound," p. 271; *Pacific Mason* 3(June 1897):184; Olympia *Tribune*, Souvenir Edition, May 1891; Blankenship, *Early History of Thurston County*, pp. 367-68. Mark also had a half-brother, Avery, who later worked for many years as a clerk in Shelton area businesses, and a half-sister who married a prominent Olympia physician.

10. Newell, *So Fair a Dwelling Place*, pp. 29-31; Olympia *Tribune*, Souvenir Edition, May 1891; Roger Sale, *Seattle, Past to Present*, p. 51.

11. Spencer and Pollard, *History of the State of Washington*, 2:23; Deegan, *History of Mason County*, pp. 5-11, 19-27; Holbrook, *Green Commonwealth*, 23-29; Grant C. Angle and William D. Walsh, *A Brief Historical Sketch of Shelton Washington*, pp. 7-8, 10-11; Dave James, *Big Skookum*, n.p.; James W. Phillips, *Washington State Place Names*, pp. 87, 98, 129; Washington State, *An Official Report of the Resources of the State*, 1894, p. 43.

12. Holbrook, *Green Commonwealth*, pp. 55-56; Deegan, *History of Mason County*, p. 89; Conklin, "Logging on Puget Sound," p. 272.

13. Washington State, *Biennial Report of the Board of State Land Commissioners, 1896*, pp. 3, 11; *Pacific Mason* 3(June 1897):184; Conklin, "Logging on Puget Sound," pp. 271-72; Holbrook, *Green Commonwealth*, p. 56.

14. Shelton *Mason County Journal*, 28 February 1919; Reed to W. T. Andrews, 10 July 1922, Simpson Logging Co. Papers; Reed to Stephen B. L. Penrose, 23 January 1928, Mark E. Reed Papers, Manuscripts Collection, University of Washington Library.

15. Conklin, "Logging on Puget Sound," p. 272; Holbrook, *Green Commonwealth*, p. 56.

16. Grant C. Angle, "Sol Simpson, Pioneer Logger," *Simpson Lookout* 5(May 1951):2, 10; Conklin, "Logging on Puget Sound," pp. 262-64; Shelton *Mason County Journal*, 11 May 1906; William G. Reed Draft Memoirs, n.p., copy in author's possession; Holbrook, *Green Commonwealth*, pp. 30-31.

17. Thomas R. Cox, *Mills and Markets*, pp. 61-63, 101-26, 208-9, 211-12; Edmond S. Meany, Jr., "The History of the Lumber Industry in the Pacific Northwest to 1917," (Ph.D. dissertation), pp. 84-124; Richard C. Berner, "The Port Blakely Mill Company, 1876-89," *Pacific Northwest Quarterly* 57(October 1966):158-71; Olympia *Washington Standard*, 18 October 1901. For a useful glossary of logging terms, see Dubuar Scrapbook, no. 27, pp. 10-11, 13-14, 16-18, Northwest Collection, University of Washington Library.

18. U.S. Bureau of Corporations, *The Lumber Industry*, Pt. 1, *Standing Timber*, 1913, p. 156; Meany, "History of the Lumber Industry in the Pacific Northwest," pp. 1-46; Adele M. Fielde, "Lumbering in the State

of Washington," *Independent* 63(7 November 1907):1108; Julian Ralph, "Washington—The Evergreen State," *Harper's New Monthly Magazine*, 85(September 1892):595; F. I. Vassault, "Lumbering in Washington," *Overland Monthly* 20(July 1892):24; W. D. Lyman, "The State of Washington," *Atlantic Monthly* 87(April 1901):508.

19. James N. Tattersall, "The Economic Development of the Pacific Northwest to 1920," (Ph.D. dissertation), pp. 179, 183, 186; Meany, "History of the Lumber Industry in the Pacific Northwest," pp. 134-42; *West Shore* 6(August 1888):415-16; Charles M. Gates, "A Historical Sketch of the Economic Development of Washington since Statehood," *Pacific Northwest Quarterly* 39(July 1948):216-17; Victor H. Beckman, "Lumber Resources of Washington," *Pacific Monthly* 19(April 1908):385; Washington State, *Agricultural, Manufacturing and Commercial Resources and Capabilities of Washington, 1901*, p. 110; Olympia *Washington Standard*, 18 October 1901.

20. F. W. Clayton to Port Blakely Mill Co., 13 May 1886; Sol Simpson to Port Blakely Mill Co., 5 May 1888, Port Blakely Mill Co. Papers, Manuscripts Collection, University of Washington Library; Berner, "Port Blakely Mill Company," pp. 163-64, 171; Cox, *Mills and Markets*, p. 208-9; Ralph W. Andrews, *Heroes of the Western Woods*, pp. 102-6; W Reed Draft Memoirs.

21. Holbrook, *Green Commonwealth*, pp. 31-36; James, *Big Skookum*, n.p.; H. Tilly Browne to Port Blakely Mill Co., 2 May 1886, Port Blakely Mill Co. Papers.

22. Simpson to William Renton, 13 January and 23 March 1888, Port Blakely Mill Co. Papers; Holbrook, *Green Commonwealth*, pp. 52, 57; Olympia *Washington Standard*, 15 September 1893.

23. Holbrook, *Green Commonwealth*, pp. 36, 52, 57; Reed to Agnes H. Anderson and Mary M. Simpson, 20 June 1925, Simpson Logging Co. Papers; W. Reed Draft Memoirs.

24. Simpson to John A. Campbell and James Campbell, 14 June 1902; Simpson Logging Co. to Port Blakely Mill Co., 16 September 1899; Arthur B. Govey to Port Blakely Mill Co., 29 April 1901; Simpson to Port Blakely Mill Co., 28 April 1902, Port Blakely Mill Co. Papers; Shelton *Mason County Journal*, 21 and 28 October 1898; 24 March 1899; 11 May 1906; Andrews, *Heroes of the Western Woods*, p. 107.

25. Conklin, "Logging on Puget Sound," p. 273; Holbrook, *Green Commonwealth*, p. 56; Reed Family Information Book; Shelton *Mason County Journal*, 7 December 1923.

26. Olympia *Washington Standard*, 14 October 1898; Shelton *Mason County Journal*, 3 March 1899; August 1905 special edition.

27. Washington State, *A Review of the Rosources and Industries of Washington, 1909*, p. 94; Shelton *Mason County Journal*, 27 January and 2 June 1899.

28. Holbrook, *Green Commonwealth*, pp. 60, 62; Andrews, *Heroes of the Western Woods*, p. 107.

29. Govey to Port Blakely Mill Co., 17 May 1898; 20 September

1899; 29 April 1901, Port Blakely Mill Co. Papers; Reed to Edwin G. Ames, 17 January 1913, Edwin G. Ames Papers, Manuscripts Collection, University of Washington Library; Holbrook, *Green Commonwealth*, p. 57.

30. Sol Simpson also owned a controlling interest in the State Bank of Shelton and was an important stockholder in the Seattle National Bank. Shelton *Mason County Journal*, 16 February, 2 March and 24 Augus 1900; Conklin, "Logging on Puget Sound," pp. 273-74.

31. Thomas M. Reed, Jr., to Reed, 5 September 1900, Simpson Timber Co. Papers, Simpson Reed & Co.; Holbrook, *Green Commonwealth*, pp. 62-63; Andrews, *Heroes of the Western Woods*, p. 107.

32. Olympia *Washington Standard*, 12 April 1901; Andrews, *Heroes of the Western Woods*, p. 104; W. Reed Draft Memoirs.

33. Simpson to Reed, 2 September 1901, Simpson Timber Co. Papers; W. Reed Draft Memoirs; Shelton *Mason County Journal*, 17 June 1904. For more information on Sol Simpson's various business activities, see Robert C. Nesbit, *"He Built Seattle,"* pp. 238-39; Alan Hynding, *The Public Life of Eugene Semple*, p. 167.

34. Shelton *Mason County Journal*, 12 February 1904, 17 February 1905, August 1905 special edition.

35. Ibid., 26 January and 11 May 1906; *Timberman* 7(May 1906):37.

36. W. Reed Draft Memoirs; William G. Reed, ed., "The Katheryn Wilson Memoirs," Simpson Reed & Co., p. 33; Seattle *Argus*, 25 February 1972; Shelton *Mason County Journal*, 4 March 1907.

37. Shelton *Mason County Journal*, 4 March 1907; Lyman, "State of Washington," pp. 513-14; Lawrence Rakestraw, "A History of Forest Conservation in the Pacific Northwest, 1891-1913," (Ph.D. dissertation), pp. 301-2; Harold K. Steen, "Forestry in Washington to 1925," (Ph.D. dissertation), pp. 169-70; Gordon Newell, *Rogues, Buffoons & Statesmen*, pp. 212-13.

38. Tattersall, "Economic Development of the Pacific Northwest," pp. 183, 207-8; Meany, "History of the Lumber Industry in the Pacific Northwest," p. 147; Edwin T. Coman, Jr. and Helen M. Gibbs, *Time, Tide and Timber*, pp. 220-26; Steen, "Forestry in Washington," pp. 132-34, 200-1; *Timberman* 9(January 1908):19.

39. Shelton *Mason County Journal*, August 1905 special edition; Olympia *Washington Standard*, 9 May 1902; W. Reed Draft Memoirs.

40 *Review of the Resources and Industries of Washington, 1909*, p. 71; Shelton *Mason County Journal*, 9 July 1915; Deegan, *History of Mason County*, p. 50; Holbrook, *Green Commonwealth*, p. 130.

41. Deegan, *History of Mason County*, p. 35.

42. C. H. Kreienbaum and Elwood R. Maunder, *The Development of a Sustained-Yield Industry*, pp. 21, 100; George Drake oral history interview with Elwood R. Maunder, 19 January 1968, Forest History Society, pp. 15-16; *Timberman* 7(December 1950):20, 16(November 1914):48E; Edmond S. Meany, "Western Spruce and the War," *Washington Historical Quarterly* 9(October 1918):257.

43. Shelton *Mason County Journal*, 24 April 1914, 9 July 1920.

44. Kreienbaum and Maunder, *Development of a Sustained-Yield Industry*, p. 30; Reed to J. W. Pace, 25 June 1923, Reed Papers; Shelton *Mason County Journal*, 1 June 1923.

45. Shelton *Mason County Journal*, 7 August 1914.

46. Ibid., 1 June 1923.

47. Ibid., 16 January 1914.

48. Ibid., 7 August 1914, 8 January 1915, 7 February 1919; Reed to Ames, 10 January 1913, Ames Papers; Reed to Calvin S. Hall, 20 January 1920, Reed Papers; *Timberman* 14(May 1913):35, 16(April 1915): 36-37; *West Coast Lumberman* 25(15 March 1914):19; P. C. Leonard to Ernest Lister, 6 October 1913, Ernest Lister Papers, Washington State Archives.

49. Shelton *Mason County Journal*, 21 August, 9 and 16 October and 13 November 1914. In the early 1920s Reed helped Kingery obtain a position as manager of a demonstration farm in the Soviet Union. Shelton *Mason County Journal*, 7 December 1923. Reed was opposed by a Farmer-Labor candidate in 1920.

50. Reed to Louis F. Hart, 28 December 1920, Louis F. Hart Papers, Washington State Archives; Alfred T. Renfro, *The Fourteenth Session*, n.p.; *West Coast Lumberman* 27(15 November 1914):22; Washington State, *House Journal*, 1915, pp. 24-27; C. H. Kreienbaum and Elwood R. Maunder, "Forest Management and Community Stability," *Forest History* 12(July 1968):9-10.

51. Shelton *Mason County Journal*, 22 and 29 January, 12 and 26 February and 5 and 12 March 1915; *House Journal*, 1915, pp. 74, 160.

52. Shelton *Mason County Journal*, 12 February, 12 March and 22 September 1915.

53. *Seattle Post-Intelligencer*, 9 January 1923; *Seattle Times*, 20 January 1927; Shelton *Mason County Journal*, 28 March 1929.

54. Reed to Russell Hawkins, 7 October 1929, Simpson Logging Co. Papers; Herman W. Ross and Richard Seelye Jones, *The Fifteenth Session*, n.p.

55. Shelton *Mason County Journal*, 29 January, 12 and 19 March, and 16 April 1915.

56. Washington State, *House Journal*, 1917, pp. 101-2, 239-40; Joseph F. Tripp, "Progressive Labor Laws in Washington State (1900-25)," (Ph.D. dissertation), pp. 31-51, 139, 141-43; Robert D. Saltvig, "The Progressive Movement in Washington," (Ph.D. dissertation), pp. 431-32; *Timberman* 18(December 1916):48; (February 1917):73; *West Coast Lumberman* 31(1 March 1917):26; (15 March 1917):33; Reed to J. F. McGoldrick, 3 April 1922, Simpson Logging Co. Papers.

57. Shelton *Mason County Journal*, 2 February and 16 March 1917; Ames to Reed, 9 March 1917, Ames Papers; *House Journal*, 1917, p. 239. At the end of the session house members presented Reed with the poem "I'm Just a Plain Logger," written by the daughter of Representative Ina Williams of Yakima. The first lines went:

There are men with ambition a-pushing them on;
There are men with a great work to do;
They are good, they are bad,—and perhaps they are right,
I have some respect for them, too;
Their wagons are hitched to the stars up above,
But no such connections are mine—
I'm just a plain logger,—a friend of mankind;
The rest is outside of my line.

Shelton *Mason County Journal*, 23 March 1917.
58. Shelton *Mason County Journal*, 16 February and 9 March 1917.
59. Ibid., 13 April, 8 and 15 June, and 3 August 1917; Reed to Ames, 14 June 1917, Ames Papers.
60. Ames to Alfred Rose, 21 December 1914; Ames to Howard C. Littlefield, 14 March 1914; Ames to William Walker, 28 March 1914, Ames Papers; *Timberman* 15(October 1914):61; 16(April 1915):36; Shelton *Mason County Journal*, 18 December 1914, 15 October 1915.
61. Shelton *Mason County Journal*, 26 November 1915, 25 February 1916; Reed to Ames, 27 December 1915; Ames to Reed, 29 December 1915, Ames Papers; *West Coast Lumberman* 32(1 May 1917):19.
62. Meany, "Western Spruce and the War," pp. 255-58.
63. Olympia *Washington Standard*, 18 October 1901; Alvin Hovey-King, "The Lumber Industry of the Pacific Coast," *American Monthly Review of Reviews* 27(March 1903):322-23; Stewart H. Holbrook, "The Logging Camp Loses Its Soul," *Sunset* 56(June 1926):19. For a view of a Mason County logging camp which, although not identified, appears to have been a Simpson camp, see S. Allis, "As Seen in a Logging-Camp," *Overland Monthly* 36(September 1900):195-208.
64. Robert L. Tyler, *Rebels of the Woods*, p. 90; Ralph Philip Boas, "The Loyal Legion of Loggers and Lumbermen," *Atlantic Monthly* 127(February 1921):221-26; George L. Drake and Elwood R. Maunder, *A Forester's Log*, p. 16; Meany, "History of the Lumber Industry in the Pacific Northwest," pp. 332-33.
65. Tyler, *Rebels of the Woods*, pp. 85-91 (quote on p. 86); George Drake oral history interview with Elwood R. Maunder, 10 November 1958, Forest History Society, pp. 14-18.
66. Conklin, "Logging on Puget Sound," p. 272; Holbrook, *Green Commonwealth*, pp. 56-57; Shelton *Mason County Journal*, 15 February 1918; Drake and Maunder, *Forester's Log*, p. 14.
67. *Timberman* 18(December 1916):51.
68. Tyler, *Rebels of the Woods*, pp. 91-94; Vernon H. Jensen, *Lumber and Labor*, pp. 124-27; Shelton *Mason County Journal*, 27 July 1917.
69. Reed to Wesley L. Jones, 11 May 1918, Reed Papers; Shelton *Mason County Journal*, 27 July 1917.
70. *West Coast Lumberman* 33(15 October 1917):19; *Timberman* 19(23 August 1918):28; Shelton *Mason County Journal*, 22 June 1917; *American*

Lumberman quoted in Ralph W. Hidy, Frank Ernest Hill, and Allan Nevins, *Timber and Men*, p. 341.

71. Reed to T. P. Fisk, 25 March 1922, Simpson Logging Co. Papers.

72. Shelton *Mason County Journal*, 13 July and 10 and 24 August 1917; Reed to Fisk, 25 March 1922, Simpson Logging Co. Papers; Harold M. Hyman, *Soldiers and Spruce*, pp. 64-104; Tyler, *Rebels of the Woods*, pp. 94-100; Jensen, *Lumber and Labor*, pp. 125-26.

73. Seattle *Argus*, 15 September 1917; Shelton *Mason County Journal*, 21 September 1917.

74. Tyler, *Rebels of the Woods*, pp. 97-98; Jensen, *Lumber and Labor*, pp. 127-29; Bulletin no. 3 of men who "strike on the job," 26 January 1918, Reed Papers.

75. Hyman, *Soldiers and Spruce*, pp. 40-63, 112-30.

76. Long and Polson quoted in ibid., pp. 123, 159.

77. Ibid., pp. 123-25, 159, 278-79; Shelton *Mason County Journal*, 22 February, 19 April and 23 August 1918. Harold Hyman recognizes Reed's important role, but offers no details of his wartime activities.

78. Reed to Fisk, 25 March 1922, Simpson Logging Co. Papers; Howard W. Allen, "Miles Poindexter," (Ph.D. dissertation), p. 449.

79. Reed to Henry Suzzallo, 14 and 28 December 1917, Henry Suzzallo Papers, Manuscripts Collection, University of Washington Library.

80. Seattle *Argus*, 15 December 1917; Shelton *Mason County Journal*, 25 January and 1 February 1918; *West Coast Lumberman* 33(1 February 1918):19; Hyman, *Soldiers and Spruce*, pp. 204-22.

81. Shelton *Mason County Journal*, 15 February 1918; Hyman, *Soldiers and Spruce*, p. 217.

82. Hyman, *Soldiers and Spruce*, pp. 222-24; Tyler, *Rebels of the Woods*, pp. 105-7; Jensen, *Lumber and Labor*, pp. 131-32; Shelton *Mason County Journal*, 1 March 1918; *West Coast Lumberman* 33(1 March 1918):19; Reed to Fisk, 25 March 1922, Simpson Logging Co. Papers; Robert W. Vinnedge, *The Pacific Northwest Lumber Industry and Its Development*, p. 18; George S. Long to Frederick E. Weyerhaeuser, 8 March 1918, quoted in Hidy et al., *Timber and Men*, p. 345.

83. Hyman, *Soldiers and Spruce*, p. 334; Tyler, *Rebels of the Woods*, pp. 107-9, 115; J. W. Grisdale to Reed, 22 April 1918, Reed Papers.

84. Reed to Jones, 11 May 1918; Reed to Miles Poindexter, 11 May 1918, Reed Papers; Hyman, *Soldiers and Spruce*, pp. 253-322; Tyler, *Rebels of the Woods*, pp. 109-10; William S. Forth, "Wesley L. Jones," (Ph.D. dissertation), pp. 393-96.

85. Tripp, "Progressive Labor Laws in Washington State," pp. 144-62. Reed maintained friendly relations with Short during the following years. Reed to W. W. Short, 1 July 1925, Washington State Federation of Labor Papers, Manuscripts Collection, University of Washington Library; J. H. Godfrey to Reed, 10 December 1928, Reed Papers.

86. Tripp, "Progressive Labor Laws in Washington State," p. 144.

Notes to Chapter 2

1. Grant C. Angle and William D. Welsh, *A Brief Historical Sketch of Shelton Washington*, p. 12.

2. William G. Reed Draft Memoirs, n.p., copy in author's possession.

3. Edwin G. Ames to W. C. Furber, 10 May 1920, Edwin G. Ames Papers, Manuscripts Collection, University of Washington Library; U.S. Bureau of the Census, *Historical Statistics of the United States, Colonial Times to 1957*, pp. 313, 317. Washington's lumber payroll fell from $114 million in 1920 to $58 million in 1921. Shelton *Mason County Journal*, 19 October 1923.

4. Shelton *Mason County Journal*, 16 January 1920, 21 January 1921.

5. W. Reed Draft Memoirs.

6. *Historical Statistics*, p. 313; Shelton *Mason County Journal*, 19 October 1923; Mark E. Reed to W. Yale Henry, 19 April 1922; Erik Back to Reed, 4 September 1922, Simpson Logging Co. Papers, Simpson Timber Co.; *Four L Bulletin* 4(June 1922):12.

7. E. B. Benn to Reed, 26 September 1922; Reed to C. H. Springer, 9 November 1922; J. J. Donovan to Reed, 2 August 1922; Reed to foremen, 19 October 1922, Simpson Logging Co. Papers.

8. Benn to Reed, 13 April 1923; Reed to Benn, 14 April 1923; Reed to Agnes H. Anderson, 27 April 1923, Simpson Logging Co. Papers; Shelton *Mason County Journal*, 27 April 1923; Robert L. Tyler, *Rebels of the Woods*, pp. 201-6; Vernon H. Jensen, *Lumber and Labor*, p. 145; *Four L Bulletin* 5(April 1923):44.

9. Justice Department Bureau of Investigation Confidential Reports, 29 April and 2 June 1923, Simpson Logging Co. Papers.

10. Donovan to Reed, 2 August 1922, Simpson Logging Co. Papers. A number of Wobblies, of course, received severe prison sentences for their part in the "massacre," and one was lynched by a mob.

11. Mark A. Matthews to Reed, 29 September and 16 November 1922; Reed to Matthews, 18 November 1922, Simpson Logging Co. Papers.

12. John Anderson to Reed, 31 December 1921; 18 February 1922; 28 November and 17 December 1924; 7 December 1925; 5 January 1929; Anderson to Simpson Logging Co., 13 August 1923; 27 March 1924; Anderson circular, n.d.; Reed to Anderson, 18 December 1924; 16 May and 10 December 1925; 7 January 1929, Simpson Logging Co. Papers; *Camp and Mill News* 6(November 1923):13.

13. Reed to George V. Bonat, 25 May 1923, Simpson Logging Co. Papers; Shelton *Mason County Journal*, 16 January 1920.

14. *Four L Bulletin* 1(January 1919):17; 2(April 1920):14; (May 1920):7; 3(August 1921):27.

15. W. Reed Draft Memoirs; C. H. Kreienbaum and Elwood R. Maunder, "Forest Management and Community Stability," *Forest History* 12(July 1968):10; George L. Drake and Elwood R. Maunder, *A Forester's Log*, p. 130.

16. *Four L Bulletin* 2(October 1920):31; 3(June 1921):17; *Camp and Mill News* 5(November 1922):15; 6(August 1923):16; (September 1923):16; 9(February 1926):9; Drake and Maunder, *Forester's Log*, p. 14; Stewart H. Holbrook, *Green Commonwealth*, pp. 134-35.

17. *Camp and Mill News* 7(January 1924):17-18; *Four L Bulletin* 2(January 1920):10; 3(January 1921):7; Shelton *Mason County Journal*, 8 September 1920; 29 December 1922; Reed to Ed Davis, 5 April 1929, Mark E. Reed Papers, Manuscripts Collection, University of Washington Library.

18. Drake and Maunder, *Forester's Log*, pp. 130-31; Dave James, *Big Skookum*, n.p.; W. Reed Draft Memoirs.

19. Reed to T. P. Fisk, 25 March 1922; Alex Polson to Reed, 28 May 1924, Simpson Logging Co. Papers; Polson to Reed, 28 August 1923, Reed Papers; *Four L Bulletin* 2(November 1920):11, 3(November 1921):13.

20. Reed to Arthur B. Govey, 7 March 1922; Reed to Bonat, 25 May 1923; Walter W. Whitbeck to Reed, 24 January 1924, Simpson Logging Co. Papers. Reed had supported state regulation of employment agencies in the previous decade. Govey to Ernest Lister, 18 December 1916, Ernest Lister Papers, Washington State Archives.

21. *Four L Bulletin* 1(June 1919):13; Reed to Fisk, 25 March 1922, Simpson Logging Co. Papers; Polson to Reed, 28 August 1923, Reed Papers.

22. Reed to Polson, 22 August 1923, Reed Papers; Reed to Benn, 14 April 1923, Simpson Logging Co. Papers.

23. Irving Bernstein, *The Lean Years*, p. 142; Bonat to Reed, n.d., but ca. January-February 1923, Simpson Logging Co. Papers.

24. Reed to J. J. Hewitt, 1 September 1927, Reed Papers; Federated Industries Weekly Business Letter, 7 January 1924; Reed to Eastern Railway & Lumber Co., 28 July 1922; Reed to E. C. Kaune, 26 August 1922, Simpson Logging Co. Papers; Shelton *Mason County Journal*, 19 October 1923; *Four L Bulletin* 4(June 1922):12.

25. Kaune to E. P. Blake, 30 January 1922; Reed to John Snyder, 20 September 1922; Reed to J. C. Buchanan, 23 November 1922, Simpson Logging Co. Papers; *Four L Bulletin* 1(September 1919):17.

26. Reed to Kaune, 3 and 19 August, and 15 December 1922; Kaune to Reed, 23 August 1922; Reed to Henry, 13 May 1922; Reed to Herbert J. Clough, 23 November 1922, Simpson Logging Co. Papers. Reed's political foe, Roland H. Hartley, was an important figure in the operation of Clark-Nickerson.

27. Reed to Clough, 2 May 1924; Reed to P. L. Reese, 7 October 1926; Reed to Anacortes Box and Lumber Co., 5 June 1924; Ralph Shaffer to Reed, 3 July 1924, Simpson Logging Co. Papers.

28. Reed to C. J. Lord, 20 February 1922; Lord to Reed, 21 February 1922; Reed to L. L. Knapp, 15 February 1926, Simpson Logging Co. Papers; Reed to Lord, 18 January 1930, Reed Papers.

29. Reed to Kaune, 20 and 26 December 1922; 25 June and 23

October 1924; Kaune to Blake, 30 January 1922; Kaune to Reed, 21 October 1924; 31 January and 18 April 1925, Simpson Logging Co. Papers.

30. Kaune to Reed, 13 and 16 December 1922; 31 May and 15 June 1923, Simpson Logging Co. Papers.

31. Reed to W. A. Whitman, 14 May 1925, Simpson Logging Co. Papers. "The logger is in somewhat of a different position from the mill when it comes to assuming a loss," Reed explained on another occasion, noting that the mill could run as long as it could obtain logs. But if the logger "continues to cut the timber and cannot operate at a profit he will probably end up with the timber supply exhausted and no profit from his activities. It would seem to be the part of good judgment and common sense for the logger if he cannot maintain a price for his product that would meet the cost of stumpage and operation, to rest up a bit until he can at least get his money back from his investment and the results of his activities." Reed to Kaune, 14 February 1925, Simpson Logging Co. Papers.

32. Kaune to Reed, 28 September 1922; Reed to Kaune, 29 September 1922; Clough to Reed, 9 November 1925; Frost Snyder to Reed, 26 October 1926, Simpson Logging Co. Papers.

33. Reed to Kaune, 29 August 1922, 22 September 1923; Kaune to Reed, 30 August 1922; Reed to Harry Ramwell, 29 August 1922; Reed to Buchanan Lumber Co., 10 April 1922, Simpson Logging Co. Papers.

34. Reed to R. C. Force, 1 November 1922; Reed to W. H. Abel, 31 July 1922; Joseph W. Fordney to Reed, 14 June 1922; Reed to A. Anderson, 17 April 1922; Reed to R. M. Calkins, 24 April 1922, Simpson Logging Co. Papers.

35. Polson to Reed, 24 June 1929; Reed to American Lumberman, 15 May 1922; Reed to George Drake, 17 December 1932, Simpson Logging Co. Papers; Kramer A. Adams, Logging Railroads of the West, p. 54.

36. Camp and Mill News 5(February 1922):24; U.S. Bureau of Labor Statistics, Monthly Labor Review 28(April 1929):97; Polson to John McIntosh, 19 September 1923, Reed Papers; H. L. Hughes to Reed, 14 February 1923, Simpson Logging Co. Papers. Forester George Drake recalled that safety measures were "good business, let alone the human phase of it. . . . It is just bad business to have an accident. You can't have a fatal accident without it upsetting production for that day. People naturally are upset. So it's just good business." George Drake oral history interview with Elwood R. Maunder, 10 November 1958, Forest History Society, p. 20.

37. Historical Statistics, p. 318; Harold K. Steen, "Forestry in Washington to 1925," (Ph.D. dissertation), pp. 85-89, 168-69; Lawrence Rakestraw, "A History of Forest Conservation in the Pacific Northwest, 1891-1913," (Ph.D. dissertation), pp. 280-83, 285-86; Stewart H. Holbrook, Burning an Empire, pp. 196-97; Howard M. Brier, Sawdust Empire, pp. 42-43.

38. Reed to William Corkery, 9 August 1924; Corkery to Reed, 8 August 1924; George C. Joy to Reed, 28 July 1924; Reed to Conovan-Corkery Logging Co., 29 August 1925, Simpson Logging Co. Papers.

39. Kaune to Reed, 4 March 1924; Reed to Snyder, 5 March 1924; Reed to Kaune, 7 May 1924; Reed to Shaffer, 19 and 28 June 1924, Simpson Logging Co. Papers.

40. Reed to Snyder, 5 March 1925; Reed to Timberman, 10 March and 8 July 1924, Simpson Logging Co. Papers.

41. A. A. Scott to Reed, 27 September 1924, Simpson Logging Co. Papers.

42. Kaune to Reed, 5 March 1925; Thomas Bordeaux to Reed, 10 June 1925; Polson to Reed, 26 January 1925; Reed to Timberman, 16 May 925; Reed to Clough, 13 November 1925, Simpson Logging Co. Papers.

43. Charles M. Gates, "A Historical Sketch of the Economic Development of Washington since Statehood," *Pacific Northwest Quarterly* 39(July 1948):228.

44. C. H. Kreienbaum and Elwood R. Maunder, *The Development of a Sustained-Yield Industry*, pp. 46-47; W. A. Tenney, "Evolution of the Northwest," *Overland Monthly* 35(April 1900):330; Olympia *Washington Standard*, 16 September 1892. A more perceptive observer commented that "it is not the wood that is used, but the wood that is wasted that gives the observer cause for much thought." Adele M. Fielde, "Lumbering in the State of Washington," *Independent* 63(7 November 1907):1111.

45. Gifford Pinchot to Thomas Burke, 30 December 1897, Thomas Burke Papers, Manuscripts Collection, University of Washington Library.

46. George S. Long to Ames, 11 January 1921, Ames Papers; *Nation* 88(28 January 1909):80; Shelton *Mason County Journal*, 8 December 1922, 1 October 1926, 5 December 1927.

47. David T. Mason to Reed, 7 October 1922; Carl M. Stevens to Reed, 6 December 1922; Reed to A. E. McIntosh, 7 October 1926; Reed to Mason County Logging Co., 15 March 1924, Simpson Logging Co. Papers; David T. Mason and Elwood R. Maunder, "Memoirs of a Forester," *Journal of Forest History* 13(April-July 1969):28-39.

48. *Literary Digest* 81(28 June 1924):16; Douglas R. Pullen, "The Administration of Washington State Governor Louis F. Hart, 1919-1925," (Ph.D. dissertation), pp. 80, 128; Ralph W. Hidy, Frank Ernest Hill and Allen Nevins, *Timber and Men*, pp. 383-84; Senate Committee on Reforestation, *Hearings*, 67:4, p. 850; Shelton *Mason County Journal*, 26 May 1922; Reed to Grant Angle, 29 March 1932, Mark E. Reed Personal Papers, Simpson Reed & Co.; *West Coast Lumberman* 60(January 1933):5.

49. Long quoted in Hidy et al., *Timber and Men*, p. 383; *Sunset* 36(April 1916):35; Reed to Mason, 16 October 1922, Simpson Logging Co. Papers; Reed to J. T. Gear, 15 December 1928; Reed to Hewitt, 1 September 1927; E. L. Farnsworth to Reed, 20 June 1928; Stevens to

Reed, 29 September 1923, Reed Papers; Steen, "Forestry in Washington," pp. 242-43, 266-68. Cf. Carl M. Stevens, "The Taxation of Forest Property in the State of Washington," *Journal of Forestry* 22(May 1924): 464-72.

50. Reed to Mason, 18 April 1927, Simpson Logging Co. Papers; W. Reed Draft Memoirs.

51. Clark M. Savidge to Reed, 30 June 1922, Simpson Logging Co. Papers; Steen, "Forestry in Washington," pp. 217-19, 221, 263-65; Shelton *Mason County Journal*, 15 July 1921; 29 October 1926; I. M. Howell to Reed, 24 October 1918, Reed Papers; Bill G. Reid, "Franklin K. Lane's Idea for Veteran's Colonization, 1918-1921," *Pacific Historical Review* 33(November 1964):447-61.

52. Shelton *Mason County Journal*, 9 January 1920; Reed to George M. Brinton, 3 January 1922; Reed to T. B. Bowmar, 27 March 1922; Reed to Ben Banner, 28 August 1922; Long to Reed, 22 May 1925, Simpson Logging Co. Papers; *Four L Bulletin* 5(February 1923):36.

53. George Drake oral history interview with Elwood R. Maunder, 22-23 February 1967, Forest History Society, p. 141; Seattle *Argus*, 11 December 1964; Reed to J. J. Anderson 30 April 1923, Simpson Logging Co. Papers; Senate Committee on Reforestation, *Hearings*, 67:4, p. 850; Reed to Gear, 5 December 1928, Reed Papers; *Simpson Diamond* 3(October-November 1963):4; Hidy et al., *Timber and Men*, p. 383; Holbrook, *Green Commonwealth*, pp. 144-45, 155-63.

54. Shelton *Mason County Journal*, 5 December 1924; C. A. Lyford, "Standing Timber Yield Tax Plan Proposal for State of Washington," *West Coast Lumberman* 60(January 1933):18-19. The county assessor, writes one historian, was "the weakest link in the administration" of the state's tax system. Pullen, "Administration of Washington State Governor Louis F. Hart," p. 129.

55. *Timberman* 31(April 1930):23; W. Reed Draft Memoirs; Reed to J. B. Shelton, 28 July and 20 September 1922; W. B. Nettleton to Reed, 8 August 1922; Reed to Nettleton, 9 August 1922; James G. Eddy to Reed, 13 May 1932; Reed to Eddy, 16 May 1932, Simpson Logging Co. Papers; Reed to Ed Sims, 26 March 1928, Reed Papers.

56. Reed to Polson, 17 August 1922; Reed to Frank Lonsberry, 11 September 1922; Reed to Donovan, 17 August 1928; Reed to J. Anderson, 30 April 1923; Abel to Simpson Logging Co., 10 April 1922, Simpson Logging Co. Papers; Shelton *Mason County Journal*, 26 November 1915, 26 May 1922.

57. Abel to Reed, 29 August 1922; Reed to Abel, 2 and 6 September 1922; R. A. Lathrop to Reed, 28 August 1922; Reed to Lathrop, 29 August 1922; Reed to Lonsberry, 11 September 1922; J. E. Calder to Reed, 8 August 1924, Simpson Logging Co. Papers. Also see *Timberman* 15(September 1914):97, and 17(July 1916):74.

58. Kreienbaum and Maunder, *Development of a Sustained-Yield Industry*, pp. 20, 38-42; F. I. Vassault, "Lumbering in Washington," *Overland Monthly* 20(July 1892):27; Edmond S. Meany, "Western Spruce and the

War," *Washington Historical Quarterly* 9(October 1918):255; Reed to Herbert Hoover, 26 November 1926, Simpson Logging Co. Papers.

59. Reed to Hoover, 26 November 1926; Reed to E. B. Wight, 2 May 1924; Reed to Polson, 28 April 1924, Simpson Logging Co. Papers; Reed to C. C. Crow, 30 October 1925, Reed Mill Co. Papers, Simpson Timber Co.; *Timberman* 27(December 1925):46. Polson noted that "we couldn't operate at all if we didn't own a mill today." Polson to Reed, 29 April 1924, Simpson Logging Co. Papers.

60. Minutes of Trustees Meeting, 25 July 1918, Douglas Fir Export Co. Papers, Oregon Historical Society; Reed to Force, 16 February 1922, Simpson Logging Co. Papers; Everett Griggs to Reed 22 September 1927, St. Paul & Tacoma Lumber Co. Papers, Manuscripts Collection, University of Washington Library.

61. Shelton *Mason County Journal*, 4 February 1921; 8 December 1922; 10 September 1926.

62. Newspaper clipping, Mark E. Reed folder, Washington State Biography file, Northwest Collection, University of Washington Library; Drake and Maunder, *Forester's Log*, p. 130; Holbrook, *Green Commonwealth*, pp. 142-43.

63. W. Reed Draft Memoirs; Shelton *Mason County Journal*, 26 January 1923, 7 March 1924. Reed always took a detailed interest in the operation of local schools. Reed to Edmond S. Meany, 1 May 1923, Edmond S. Meany Papers, University of Washington Archives.

64. Henry Suzzallo to Reed, 28 July 1923; Reed to F. R. Clarke, 24 November 1928; Reed to Eddy, 17 September 1929, Reed Papers.

65. Reed to Davis, 5 April 1929; Savidge to Reed, 27 August 1923, Reed Papers; Reed to George T. Kennedy, 5 June 1926, Simpson Logging Co. Papers; Shelton *Mason County Journal*, 26 January 1923; Harry W. Deegan, *History of Mason County*, p. 90. "It seems to me," suggested tugboatman Henry Foss, "that they ought to call it 'Reedsville', or 'Reedview.'" Henry Foss to Govey, 26 April 1924, Simpson Logging Co. Papers.

66. W. Reed Draft Memoirs.

67. Shelton *Mason County Journal*, 25 April, 18 July and 22 August 1924; Reed to District Forester, 19 November 1926, Simpson Logging Co. Papers; Kreienbaum and Maunder, "Forest Management and Community Stability," p. 9.

68. Reed to Katheryn Wilson, 14 March 1928, Reed Papers.

69. Shelton *Mason County Journal*, 31 March 1922; 13 June 1924; 13 November 1925; Reed to Calkins, 3 April 1922, Simpson Logging Co. Papers; Kreienbaum and Maunder, *Development of a Sustained-Yield Industry*, pp. 25-27.

70. *Pacific Pulp and Paper Industry* 1(June 1927):26; Reed to Calkins, 25 November 1929, Reed Papers; Reed to R. D. Merrill, 11 April 1929, Merrill & Ring Lumber Co. Papers, Manuscripts Collection, University of Washington Library; Reed to Henry McCleary, 23 May 1925, Simpson Logging Co. Papers.

71. Shelton *Mason County Journal*, 22 January 1926; Reed to McCleary, 9 October 1925; Reed to Clough, 18 March 1926, Simpson Logging Co. Papers; *Camp and Mill News* 9(May 1926):21.

72. Shelton *Mason County Journal*, 21 May 1926; E. M. Mills to Reed, 16 October 1926, Simpson Logging Co. Papers; *Pacific Pulp and Paper Industry* 1(June 1927):12-15.

73. Reed to Mills, 9 December 1926; Reed to District Forester, 19 November 1926, Simpson Logging Co. Papers; Kreienbaum and Maunder, *Development of a Sustained-Yield Industry*, p. 26; Shelton *Mason County Journal*, 4 June 1926.

74. Reed to Wilson, 10 December 1925, Reed Mill Co. Papers; Reed to Calkins, 25 November 1929, Reed Papers; Allen H. Hodgson, "Going After that Forty Per Cent," *Pacific Pulp and Paper Industry* 1(July 1927): 11-13, 48.

75. Newspaper clipping, Reed folder, Washington State Biography File; J. Orin Oliphant, "Legislative Reapportionment in Washington," *Washington Historical Quarterly* 22(January 1931):6-7.

76. William Howard Taft to S. A. Perkins, 19 September 1925, S. A. Perkins Papers, Washington State Historical Society.

Notes to Chapter 3

1. Shelton *Mason County Journal*, 12 March 1915.

2. One other complaint, according to this view, "grows out of the booze and poker parties, which continue to be quite the customary weapons of many lobbyists. . . . This is the one place and time where any legislator so inclined, may indulge himself." Seattle *Argus*, 24 October 1925.

3. Douglas R. Pullen, "The Administration of Washington State Governor Louis F. Hart, 1919-1925," (Ph.D. dissertation), pp. 1-79, 339, 372-73; F. A. Bird to Mark E. Reed, 4 April 1922, Simpson Logging Co. Papers, Simpson Timber Co.

4. William G. Reed Draft Memoirs, n.p., copy in author's possession; C. H. Kreienbaum and Elwood R. Maunder, *The Development of a Sustained-Yield Industry*, p. 49.

5. W. Reed Draft Memoirs; Norman H. Clark, *The Dry Years*, pp. 149-78; Reed to J. H. Easterday, 28 May 1930; J. E. Knapp to Reed, 7 December 1923, Mark E. Reed Papers, Manuscripts Collection, University of Washington Library; Reed to D. A. Doyle, 13 April 1932, Mark E. Reed Personal Papers, Simpson Reed & Co.; Reed to Bernard H. Hicks, 16 November 1926, Simpson Logging Co. Papers.

6. Seattle *Argus*, 12 March 1921, 31 October 1925; Maude Sweetman, *What Price Politics*, p. 76; Reed to Wesley L. Jones, 11 March 1930, Simpson Logging Co. Papers.

7. Pullen, "Administration of Washington State Governor Louis F. Hart," pp. 128, 137; *Seattle Times*, 6 January 1921.

8. Reed to J. H. Bloedel, 30 June 1923, Simpson Logging Co. Papers; Alex Polson to Louis F. Hart, 30 December 1921, Louis F. Hart Papers, Washington State Archives. "The legislature," Reed contended on another occasion, "will not cease making appropriations for new activities until the people cease making demands upon them for these additional funds to meet the proposed new activities." Reed to Thorpe Babcock, 13 June 1922, Simpson Logging Co. Papers.

9. Reed to E. P. Blake, 28 August 1922, Simpson Logging Co. Papers.

10. Hart to Albert C. Ritchie, 23 August 1921, Hart Papers; *Seattle Post-Intelligencer*, 16 January 1921; Pullen, "Administration of Washington State Governor Louis F. Hart," pp. 81, 89-94.

11. *Seattle Post-Intelligencer*, 19 and 20 January 1921; *Seattle Times*, 19 January 1921; Reed to E. B. Chinn, 3 April, 1922, Simpson Logging Co. Papers; Pullen, "Administration of Washington State Governor Louis F. Hart," pp. 95-101, 107-15.

12. William c. Butler to Edwin G. Ames, 29 January and 3 February 1914; Ames to Butler, 2 February 1914, Edwin G. Ames Papers, Manuscripts Collection, University of Washington Library.

13. Reed to Chinn, 3 April 1922; J. J. Donovan to Reed, 4 April 1922; Donovan to Bird, 4 April 1922, Simpson Logging Co. Papers; *Seattle Times*, 16 February 1921.

14. Joseph F. Tripp, "Progressive Labor Laws in Washington State (1900-1925)," (Ph.D. dissertation), pp. 241-46; J. C. H. Reynolds to Reed, 6 April 1922, Hart Papers; Manager, Timber Products Manufacturers, to unnamed person, 13 April 1922; Reed to Chinn, 13 April 1922, Simpson Logging Co. Papers.

15. Reed to Polson, 7 November 1921, quoted in Pullen, "Administration of Washington State Governor Louis F. Hart," p. 153; Hart to John Carmode, 15 March 1921, Hart Papers.

16. Hart to Carmode, 15 March 1921; Frank W. Hull to Hart, 19 March 1921, Hart Papers; Shelton *Mason County Journal*, 9 June 1922; Pullen, "Administration of Washington State Governor Louis F. Hart," pp. 146-56. One correspondent informed the governor that if the poll tax was instituted, "there will not be enough republicans in the next legislature to make up a whist game." H. Blair to Hart, 2 March 1921, Hart Papers.

17. Pullen, "Administration of Washington State Governor Louis F. Hart," pp. 225-43, 253; J. Vincent Roberts to Hart, 15 February 1923, Hart Papers; S. Frank Miyamoto, "The Japanese Minority in the Pacific Northwest," *Pacific Northwest Quarterly* 54(October 1963):145-46.

18. *Seattle Post-Intelligencer*, 24 February 1921; Shelton *Mason County Journal*, 2 July 1926; Pullen, "Administration of Washington State Governor Louis F. Hart," pp. 239-41. Some historians have incorrectly stated that Reed supported the alien land bill. Pullen, "Administration of Washington State Governor Louis F. Hart," pp. 244-45; Norman H. Clark, *Washington, A Bicentennial History*, p. 133.

19. Seattle *Argus*, 5 March 1921; *Seattle Post-Intelligencer*, 26 February 1921; Pullen, "Administration of Washington State Governor Louis F. Hart," p. 243-47.

20. Shelton *Mason County Journal*, 17 November and 1 December 1922.

21. *Seattle Post-Intelligencer*, 8 and 9 January 1923; *Seattle Times*, 8 and 9 January 1923; Hamilton Cravens, "A History of the Washington Farmer-Labor Party, 1918-1924," (master's thesis), p. 187.

22. Shelton *Mason County Journal*, 1 and 22 December 1922; *Seattle Times*, 8 and 9 January 1923. One legislator urged Reed to make his committee assignments "for the best interests of the state, the Republican party and all concerned." Victor J. Capron to Reed, 14 December 1922, Reed Papers.

23. R. W. Vinnedge to Reed, 19 July 1922, Simpson Logging Co. Papers; Shelton *Mason County Journal*, 1 and 29 December 1922; Pullen, "Administration of Washington State Governor Louis F. Hart," pp. 162-64.

24. Shelton *Mason County Journal*, 1 and 8 December 1922; Pullen, "Administration of Washington State Governor Louis F. Hart," p. 163.

25. Pullen, "Administration of Washington State Governor Louis F. Hart," pp. 162-64; Reed to W. H. Latimer, 9 March 1923, Simpson Logging Co. Papers.

26. W. Reed Draft Memoirs.

27. Donovan to Reed, 4 April 1922, Simpson Logging Co. Papers; *Seattle Times*, 8 and 9 February 1923.

28. *Seattle Post-Intelligencer*, 29 January 1923; Tripp, "Progressive Labor Laws in Washington State," pp. 251-54; Reed to R. E. Anderson & Co., 6 January 1927; Reed to George Cornwall, 7 January 1927, Simpson Logging Co. Papers.

29. *Seattle Post-Intelligencer*, 2 March 1923; *Seattle Times*, 18 February 1923; Tripp, "Progressive Labor Laws in Washington State," pp. 254-55; Cravens, "History of the Washington Farmer-Labor Party," pp. 192-93.

30. William O. Sparks, "J. D. Ross and Seattle City Light, 1917-1932," (master's thesis), pp. 80-83.

31. Shelton *Mason County Journal*, 2 February 1923; *Seattle Post-Intelligencer*, 11 January 1923; Pullen, "Administration of Washington State Governor Louis F. Hart," p. 311; Cravens, "History of the Washington Farmer-Labor Party," p. 189.

32. *Seattle Post-Intelligencer*, 19 January and 2 February 1923; *Seattle Union Record* quoted in Pullen, "Administration of Washington State Governor Louis F. Hart," p. 312; *Seattle Times*, 25 February 1923.

33. Shelton *Mason County Journal*, 1 and 13 October 1922.

34. *Seattle Post-Intelligencer*, 3, 6, 15, 26, and 17 February 1923; Pullen, "Administration of Washington State Governor Louis F. Hart," p. 316; Cravens, "History of the Washington Farmer-Labor Party," p. 192.

35. *Seattle Post-Intelligencer*, 1, 9 and 10 1923; Pullen, "Administration of Washington State Governor Louis F. Hart," pp. 316-17.

36. I. M. Kurtz to Jones, 22 March 1926, quoted in Sparks, "Ross and Seattle City Light," p. 86; Cravens, "History of the Washington Farmer-Labor Party," p. 190; *Seattle Post-Intelligencer*, 19 February 1923.

37. E. Mills to Reed, 16 September 1926; Reed to Mills, 20 September 1926; Reed to W. H. Abel, 14 February 1925; Reed to Homer T. Bone, 7 December 1931, Simpson Logging Co. Papers; Reed to John A. Rea, 25 June 1923, Reed Papers. William O. Sparks illustrates the typical confusion. The Reed bill, he says, "was unfavorable to the interests of the public ownership group." A page later, however, we find that the bill "achieved a minor victory, for the measure still allowed the sale of municipal power outside the city limits." Sparks then concludes that Reed was interested only in killing off the expansion of public power. Sparks, "Ross and Seattle City Light," pp. 84-86.

38. *Seattle Times*, 11 March 1923; Shelton *Mason County Journal*, 16 March 1923; Reed to Latimer, 9 March 1923, Simpson Logging Co. Papers; Seattle *Argus*, 10 March 1923.

39. *Seattle Times*, 9 and 11 March 1923; *Seattle Post-Intelligencer*, 10 and 11 March 1923; Stephen B. L. Penrose to Reed, 31 May 1923, Reed Papers; Shelton *Mason County Journal*, 16 March and 6 April 1923.

40. Reed to Penrose, 5 June 1923, Reed Papers.

41. Pullen, "Administration of Washington State Governor Louis F. Hart," pp. 355-56.

42. *Seattle Post-Intelligencer*, 20 November 1923; *Seattle Times*, 20 November 1923; *Tacoma News Tribune*, 19 November 1923; Charles B. Welch to Reed, 19 November 1923, Reed Papers.

43. Polson to Reed, 20 November 1923, Reed Papers; *Seattle Union Record*, 20 November 1923.

44. *Seattle Star*, 20 November 1923; Spokane *Spokesman-Review*, 20 November 1923.

45. *Seattle Post-Intelligencer*, 23 November 1923; Spokane *Spokesman-Review*, 20 November 1923. Alex Polson told Reed that Hartley "should be for you if he hasn't lost all his political sense." Another correspondent asked by a friend how Reed compared to Hartley, said: "I asked him how Christ compared with a Chinaman and told him there was that much difference." Polson to Reed, 20 November 1923; J. H. Sexsmith to Reed, 27 November 1923, Reed Papers.

46. Shelton *Mason County Journal*, 23 November 1923; *Seattle Post-Intelligencer*, 20 November and 2 December 1923; Spokane *Spokesman-Review*, 20 November 1923; Reed to Rufus Woods, 21 November 1923, Reed Papers.

47. *Seattle Times*, 2 December 1923; *Seattle Post-Intelligencer*, 2 December 1923; Reed to Woods, 21 November 1923; undated statement on the governorship, Reed Papers; Pullen, "Administration of Washington State Governor Louis F. Hart," p. 357.

48. Reed to Thomas M. Reed, Jr., 1 December 1923, Reed Papers.
49. Ralph Shaffer to Reed, 3 December 1923, Simpson Logging Co. Papers; *Tacoma News Tribune*, 3 December 1923; Shelton *Mason County Journal*, 7 December 1923.
50. Reed to Belle Reeves, 16 November 1923, Reed Papers.
51. Shelton *Mason County Journal*, 25 June 1920; 6 July 1923; Reed to Elmer Dover, 20 January 1922, Simpson Logging Co. Papers; Reed to T. Reed, Jr., 2 August 1923, Reed Papers. On Harding's fateful visit to the region, see Robert E. Ficken, "President Harding Visits Seattle," *Pacific Northwest Quarterly* 66 (July 1975):105-14.
52. Reed to Polson, 3 March 1924, Simpson Logging Co. Papers; Shelton *Mason County Journal*, 4 and 11 January 1924; C. C. Koehler to Reed, 27 June 1923, Reed Papers.
53. Seattle *Argus*, 5 January 1924; William S. Forth, "Wesley L. Jones," (Ph.D. dissertation), pp. 623-24.
54. Reed to W. Lon Johnson, 12 July 1924; Johnson to Reed, 11 November 1924, Lon Johnson Papers, Manuscripts Division, Washington State University Library; J. McIntosh to Reed, 23 September 1924, Simpson Logging Co. Papers; Shelton *Mason County Journal*, 1 August 1924. The race was much closer than nationally, where Coolidge had nearly a two-to-one margin over Davis and La Follette finished third with 17 percent of the vote. La Follette received 36 percent of the vote in Washington, including 40 percent in Reed's own Mason County.
55. Reed to George T. Reid, 23 June 1923, Simpson Logging Co. Papers; Shelton *Mason County Journal*, 1 June and 19 October 1923.
56. Shelton *Mason County Journal*, 31 October and 14 November 1924; Polson to Reed, 11 July 1924, Simpson Logging Co. Papers; *Seattle Post-Intelligencer*, 30 December 1925; Pullen, "Administration of Washington State Governor Louis F. Hart," pp. 319-29; Sparks, "Ross and Seattle City Light," pp. 88-93; Wesley A. Dick, "Visions of Abundance," (Ph.D. dissertation), pp. 252-53.
57. Pullen, "Administration of Washington State Governor Louis F. Hart," pp. 361-68.

Notes to Chapter 4

1. Roland H. Hartley to Austin Mires, 25 September 1924, Austin Mires Papers, Manuscripts Division, Washington State University Library; Albert F. Gunns, "Roland Hill Hartley and the Politics of Washington State," (master's thesis), pp. 1-72; Norman H. Clark, *Mill Town*, pp. 60ff.
2. Hartley to New York Graphic, 8 April 1925, Roland H. Hartley Papers, Washington State Archives.
3. Hartley to Mires, 25 April 1927; 21 November 1928, Mires Papers; Maude Sweetman, *What Price Politics*, p. 82; J. Grant Hinkle to Knute Hill, 16 October 1930, Knute Hill Papers, Manuscripts Division,

Washington State University Library. "The cocky little lumberman," writes his biographer, "thirsted for public office and enjoyed nothing so much as a good political battle." Gunns, "Hartley and the Politics of Washington State," p. 38.

4. *Seattle Times*, 21 and 22 January 1925.

5. Ibid., 23 January and 3 February 1925; Gunns, "Hartley and the Politics of Washington State," p. 84.

6. *Seattle Times*, 23 January and 10 February 1925; Gunns, "Hartley and the Politics of Washington State," pp. 84-86.

7. *Seattle Times*, 15 February 1925.

8. Gunns, "Hartley and the Politics of Washington State," pp. 86-95; Seattle *Argus*, 17 October 1925.

9. Hartley to Members of the Legislature, 1 October 1925, Hartley Papers; Mark E. Reed to W. Lon Johnson, 12 October 1925, Lon Johnson Papers, Manuscripts Division, Washington State University Library.

10. *Seattle Times*, 10 November 1925; Gunns, "Hartley and the Politics of Washington State," pp. 97-103.

11. *Seattle Post-Intelligencer*, 11 and 18 November 1925; Seattle *Argus*, 28 November 1925.

12. Olympia *Morning Olympian*, 18 November 1925; *Seattle Times*, 10 and 15 November 1925; Shelton *Mason County Journal*, 20 November 1925.

13. *Seattle Times*, 10 November 1925; Reed to Herbert J. Clough, 12 November 1925, Simpson Logging Co. Papers, Simpson Timber Co.

14. Shelton *Mason County Journal*, 21 February 1919; *Washington Alumnus* 17(February 1926):3-7. Although defending the University of Washington and its controversial president, Henry Suzzallo, Reed did have some doubts about the course of higher education in the state. The university did not, he believed, encourage academic excellence in its students. "If I had it to do over again," Reed stated a few years later, "I would send my boys to a smaller institution and situated in a smaller town than is the case with our University." Reed to Stephen B. L. Penrose, 23 January 1928, Mark E. Reed Papers, Manuscripts Collection, University of Washington Library.

15. *Seattle Times*, 20 November 1925.

16. Ibid.; Gunns, "Hartley and the Politics of Washington State," p. 107.

17. *Tacoma News Tribune*, 20 November 1925; Spokane *Spokesman-Review*, 24 November 1925. In a rare instance, the *Mason County Journal* did not agree with Reed's position: the Banker bill "does not square with Governor Hartley's expressed desire to encourage more economy in state affairs, and if the state is to go slow to avoid greater financial ills reclamation is a good place to begin." Shelton *Mason County Journal*, 4 December 1925.

18. *Seattle Post-Intelligencer*, 2 December 1925; W. B. Price to Mires, 6 December 1925, Mires Papers.

19. Ed Sims to Reed, 3 October 1928; 14 April and 4 May 1930; Sims to E. B. Deming, 4 May 1930, Reed Papers; Sweetman, *What Price Politics*, pp. 76-80; Seattle *Argus*, 2 January 1926; Olympia *Morning Olympian*, 22 January 1926. Gordon Newell contends that Sims "operated the most successful crimping operation in the Pacific Northwest" at Port Townsend. Gordon Newell, *Rogues, Buffoons & Statesmen*, pp. 257-58.

20. *Seattle Times*, 6 December 1925; *Seattle Post-Intelligencer*, 3, 4, and 5 December 1925.

21. *Seattle Post-Intelligencer*, 5 December 1925; Charles W. Hall to Hill, 16 October 1930, Hill Papers.

22. Price to Mires, 6 December 1925, Mires Papers; *Seattle Times*, 11 December 1925; *Seattle Post-Intelligencer*, 8 December 1925; Gunns, "Hartley and the Politics of Washington State,", p. 112.

23. Gunns, "Hartley and the Politics of Washington State," pp. 112-15.

24. Shelton *Mason County Journal*, 18 December 1925; *Seattle Times*, 8 December 1925; *Seattle Post-Intelligencer*, 11 December 1925; Clark Savidge to Johnson, 11 November 1928, Johnson Papers; Gunns, "Hartley and the Politics of Washington State," pp. 115-18.

25. *Seattle Post-Intelligencer*, 3 January 1926.

26. Shelton *Mason County Journal*, 18 December 1925, 7 May 1926.

27. Olympia *Morning Olympian*, 20 January 1926; Seattle *Argus*, 9 January 1926; Arthur G. Cohen, "Resume of Legislative Action on Appropriations for Higher Educational Institutions," n.p., Northwest Collection, University of Washington Library.

28. *Seattle Union Record*, 5 January 1926.

29. Reed to W. H. Abel, 13 April 1929, Simpson Logging Co. Papers; Seattle *Argus*, 22 May 1926; Shelton *Mason County Journal*, 28 January 1927; Elmo R. Richardson, "Olympic National Park," *Forest History* 12(April 1968):7.

30. *Seattle Times*, 22 and 30 December 1925; *Seattle Post-Intelligencer*, 22, 23 and 30 December 1925; Seattle *Argus*, 26 December 1925; Gunns, "Hartley and the Politics of Washington State," pp. 121-25.

31. *Seattle Times*, 4 January 1926; Gunns, "Hartley and the Politics of Washington State," pp. 125-28; Shelton *Mason County Journal*, 20 November 1925. Hartley, the *Argus* commented, had blown "up like a toy balloon touched with a hot cigar." Seattle *Argus*, 9 January 1926.

32. *Seattle Times*, 4 January 1926; *Seattle Post-Intelligencer*, 5 January 1926; *Seattle Star*, 4 January 1926.

33. *Seattle Times*, 5 and 6 January 1926; *Seattle Post-Intelligencer*, 5 and 6 January 1926; *Seattle Star*, 5 January 1926; Gunns, "Hartley and the Politics of Washington State," pp. 128-30. One legislator said that he had "known Mark Reed for 40 years and if any man would tell me that there is any chicanery, trickery or double-crossing in his life I would say he is a liar." Spokane *Spokesman-Review*, 5 January 1926.

34. *Tacoma News Tribune,* 5 January 1926; Shelton *Mason County Journal,* 8 January 1926; *Seattle Times,* 7 January 1926.

35. Olympia *Morning Olympian,* 17 January 1926; Spokane *Spokesman-Review,* 6 and 7 January 1926.

36. *Seattle Times,* 7 and 10 January 1926; *Seattle Star,* 5 and 9 January 1926.

37. Seattle *Argus,* 9 January 1926.

38. Mark E. Reed et al., "A Statement by the 'Majority,'" Northwest Collection, University of Washington Library.

39. Shelton *Mason County Journal,* 29 January 1926.

40. *Seattle Star,* 8 January 1926; Cohen, "Resume of Legislative Action;" William M. Landeen, *E. O. Holland and the State College of Washington, 1916-1944,* pp. 306-8.

41. Olympia *Morning Olympian,* 10 February 1926; *Seattle Times,* 22 March 1926; Spokane *Spokesman-Review,* 7 January 1926.

42. *Seattle Times,* 22, 23, and 24 March 1926.

43. Shelton *Mason County Journal,* 7 May 1926; Seattle *Argus,* 3 April 1926; Gunns, "Hartley and the Politics of Washington State," p. 166.

44. *Seattle Times,* 21 May 1926; *Seattle Post-Intelligencer,* 21 May 1926.

45. Shelton *Mason County Journal,* 20 August 1926.

46. Ibid., 27 August and 17 September 1926; Gunns, "Hartley and the Politics of Washington State," pp. 173-77.

47. Gunns, "Hartley and the Politics of Washington State," pp. 138-39, 142-43; Sweetman, *What Price Politics,* p. 131; Landeen, *Holland the the State College,* pp. 241-47.

48. Gunns, "Hartley and the Politics of Washington State," pp. 143-62; Henry Suzzallo to Johnson, 5 November 1926, Johnson Papers.

49. Shelton *Mason County Journal,* 8 and 22 October 1926; *Literary Digest* 91(30 October 1926):11-12; Suzzallo to Johnson, 5 November 1926, Johnson Papers.

50. Gunns, "Hartley and the Politics of Washington State," pp. 177-83 (Flood quoted on p. 183n); Shelton *Mason County Journal,* 19 November 1926.

51. Johnson to W. W. Robertson, 4 December 1926, Johnson Papers.

52. *Seattle Times,* 29 and 31 January and 1 February 1927; *Seattle Post-Intelligencer,* 1 February 1927.

53. Reed to Miles Poindexter, 19 March 1923, Reed Papers; Sweetman, *What Price Politics,* pp. 78-79. Gordon Newell, relying on Sweetman's account, contends that Reed was "moody" and motivated by "reasons apparently known only to himself." Newell, *Rogues, Buffoons & Statesmen,* p. 324.

54. Frank C. Jackson to Hill, 28 March 1927, Hill Papers.

55. *Seattle Times,* 3 February 1927; *Seattle Post-Intelligencer,* 4 February 1927; Reed to Harry Ramwell, 4 August 1928, Simpson Logging Co. Papers; Ralph W. Hidy, Frank Ernest Hill, and Allan Nevins, *Timber and Men,* p. 385.

56. *Seattle Times*, 23 and 24 February 1927; *Seattle Post-Intelligencer*, 20 February 1927.

57. *Seattle Post-Intelligencer*, 6 March 1927.

58. Shelton *Mason County Journal*, 22 July 1927. The ambiguous nature of the Reed-Hartley relationship, however, continued. When Reed applied for a quarter-section of state capitol timber he claimed that the cruise was too high. Hartley told the other committee members to accept Reed's estimate of the timber: "Mr. Reed would not misrepresent anything." Shelton *Mason County Journal*, 7 May 1928.

59. Reed to Johnson, 23 July 1927, Johnson Papers; Reed to D. F. Trunkey, 5 March 1928, Reed Papers.

60. Robertson to Johnson, 6 June 1927; Reed to Johnson, 3 June 1927; Johnson to N. C. Richards, 28 April 1927; Johnson to C. W. Ryan, 28 August 1928, Johnson Papers.

61. Johnson to Reed, 6 June 1927; Reed to Johnson, 3 and 10 June 1927; Sims to Johnson, 25 March 1927, Johnson Papers.

62. Reed to Johnson, 23 July 1927, Johnson Papers.

63. Alex Polson to Reed, 14 January 1928, Simpson Logging Co. Papers; J. J. Donovan to Polson, 20 March 1928; John A. Gellatly to Reed, 28 March 1928, Reed Papers.

64. Donovan to Reed, 20 March 1928, Reed Papers; Shelton *Mason County Journal*, 7 October 1927. French did lead Hartley in Mason County. Shelton *Mason County Journal*, 13 September 1928.

65. Shelton *Mason County Journal*, 12 August 1927; 21 June and 12 July 1928; Sims to Reed, 5 September 1928, Reed Papers.

66. George S. Long to Reed, 26 July, 13 August and 22 October 1928; Reed to Long, 12 October 1928; Reed to E. M. Mills, 4 August 1928; Reed to C. S. Chapman, 12 November 1927; Reed to Ramwell, 4 August 1928, Simpson Logging Co. Papers; Reed to R. D. Merrill, 18 April 1929, Merrill & Ring Lumber Co. Papers, Manuscripts Collection, University of Washington Library.

67. Seattle *Argus*, 8 September and 13 October 1928; Shelton *Mason County Journal*, 13 September 1928.

68. Robert L. Cole, "The Democratic Party in Washington State, 1919-1933," (Ph.D. dissertation), pp. 181-216; Shelton *Mason County Journal*, 29 October and 18 November 1928; Scott Bullitt to Reed, 3 December 1928, Reed Papers.

69. Reed to Trunkey, 5 March 1928, Reed Papers; Shelton *Mason County Journal*, 10 December 1928; Reed to Charles A. Murray, 12 November 1928, Simpson Logging Co. Papers; Reed to Merrill, 8 April 1929, Merrill & Ring Lumber Co. Papers.

70. Shelton *Mason County Journal*, 10 and 13 December 1928; Reed to Donovan, 26 March 1928, Reed Papers.

71. *Seattle Times*, 16 January and 19, 20, and 28 February 1929; *Seattle Post-Intelligencer*, 17 March 1929; Shelton *Mason County Journal*, 24 January and 28 February 1929. J. H. Brown speculated that Reed and Hartley

had reached agreement to divide the Olympic Peninsula timber between themselves. Seattle *Argus*, 13 April 1929.

72. William C. Butler to Reed, 9 and 22 July 1930; Reed to Savidge, 10 July 1930, Simpson Logging Co. Papers. On Butler, see Clark, *Mill Town*, pp. 158-67.

73. Shelton *Mason County Journal*, 4 and 28 March 1929; Reed to Ed Davis, 5 April 1929; Samuel R. Buck to Reed, 12 March 1930; Sims to Reed, 14 April 1930, Reed Papers.

Notes to Chapter 5

1. Mark E. Reed to District Forester, 19 November 1926; Reed to Arthur Govey, 12 February 1928, Simpson Logging Co. Papers, Simpson Timber Co.; Shelton *Mason County Journal*, 21 May 1926; 10 May 1927; Reed to Katheryn Wilson, 25 July 1928; 16 June 1930, Mark E. Reed Papers, Manuscripts Collection, University of Washington Library; *Pacific Pulp and Paper Industry* 1(May 1927):14.

2. Thomas R. Cox, *Mills and Markets*, pp. 71-100, 138-60; Charles M. Gates, "A Historical Sketch of the Economic Development of Washington since Statehood," *Pacific Northwest Quarterly* 39(July 1948):216-17; Minutes of Trustees Meetings, 25 July 1918; 7 September 1921, Douglas Fir Export Co. Papers, Oregon Historical Society; Victor H. Beckman, "Lumber Resources of Washington," *Pacific Monthly* 19(April 1908):385-89; Robert W. Vinnedge, *Pacific Northwest Lumber Industry and Its Development*, pp. 13-15; Harold K. Steen, "Forestry in Washington to 1925," (Ph.D. dissertation), pp. 132-34, 200-1.

3. Reed to George Cornwall, 18 May 1926, Simpson Logging Co. Papers; Minutes of Executive Committee Meeting, 13 July 1925, Douglas Fir Export Co. Papers; Shelton *Mason County Journal*, 21 August 1925; 14 May 1926; U.S. Bureau of the Census, *Historical Statistics of the United States, Colonial Times to 1957*, p. 313.

4. Minutes of Trustees Meeting, 31 August 1925, Douglas Fir Export Co. Papers; Shelton *Mason County Journal*, 5 February 1926; R. S. Fox to S. E. Ganges, 2 April 1925; Alex Polson to Reed, 15 November 1926, Simpson Logging Co. Papers.

5. Fox to Ganges, 2 April 1925; Fox to Feed, 14 May and 2 June 1925, Simpson Logging Co. Papers; Fox to Reed Mill Co., 11 October 1925, Reed Mill Co. Papers, Simpson Timber Co.

6. Minutes of Trustees Meeting, 29 April 1925, Douglas Fir Export Co. Papers; Reed to Douglas Fir Exploitation & Export Co., 25 April 1925, Simpson Logging Co. Papers; C. H. Kreienbaum to Reed, 3 march 1926; Polson to Reed, 5 March 1926; Reed to Polson, 8 March 1926, Reed Mill Co. Papers; Vinnedge, *Pacific Northwest Lumber Industry and Its Development*, pp. 17-18.

7. Reed to Eureka Lumber Co., 31 January 1925, Simpson Logging Co. Papers.

8. Shelton *Mason County Journal*, 9 July 1925; 5 February and 8 October 1926; *Camp and Mill News* 9(September 1926):23.

9. Reed to Cornwall, 18 May 1926, Simpson Logging Co. Papers; Reed to F. Nakagawa, 24 May 1929, Reed Mill Co. Papers; Shelton *Mason County Journal*, 12 March, 14 May and 4 June 1926. The Reeds also visited China. According to the *Mason County Journal*, Reed told his friends that "the natives seemed to be without initiative, except in a few cases, and civilization might be said to be going backwards, . . . Ignorance is apparent on every side, sanitation is practically unknown, and begging a recognized profession, parents even being known to have maimed their children so that they might be more proficient in this line." Shelton *Mason County Journal*, 2 July 1926.

10. *Timberman* 28 (February 1927):198; Fox to Kreienbaum, 16 November 1926; Fox to Reed and Kreienbaum, 25 December 1926; Reed to Fox, 16 December 1926, Reed Mill Co. Papers.

11. Minutes of Executive Committee Meeting, 15 October 1926, Douglas Fir Export Co. Papers; Kreienbaum to Fox, 11 November 1926; Fox to Kreienbaum, 16 November 1926; Reed to Fox, 2 March and 7 and 16 December 1926; Fox to Reed Mill Co., 17 December 1925, Reed Mill Co. Papers.

12. Kreienbaum to Reed, 9 December 1925; Reed to Kreienbaum, 10 December 1925, Reed Mill Co. Papers; Kreienbaum to Reed, 5 August 1927, Simpson Logging Co. Papers.

13. *Timberman* 31(February 1930):118; Kreienbaum to D. E. Hillier, 25 July 1929; Kreienbaum to Reed, 13 September 1929, Simpson Logging Co. Papers; Reed to C. E. Dant, 13 May 1929, Reed Mill Co. Papers; Minutes of Trustees Meeting, 27 June 1929, Douglas Fir Export Co. Papers; Reed to E. G. Griggs, 26 September 1927, St. Paul & Tacoma Lumber Co. Papers, Manuscripts Collection, University of Washington Library. Some observers felt that such actions as passage of Washington's alien land law caused the Japanese government to retaliate on the tariff front. "In plain English," the *Mason County Journal* commented, "we desire their trade and money but don't fancy their people. . . . it is remarkable that the Japanese have any trade or business relations with the United States." Shelton *Mason County Journal*, 13 November 1930.

14. Polson to Reed, 26 October 1928, Simpson Logging Co. Papers.

15. *Lumberman's and Logger's Guide, 1919*, p. 122; Edwin G. Ames to William Walker, 23 and 28 March 1914, Edwin G. Ames Papers, Manuscripts Collection, University of Washington Library.

16. William G. Reed Draft Memoirs, n.p., copy in author's possession.

17. Ibid.; Reed to Frank Reed, 14 January 1928, Reed Papers; *Four L Bulletin* 6(August 1924):43.

18. C. H. Kreienbaum and Elwood R. Maunder, "Forest Management and Community Stability," *Forest History* 12(July 1968):9-10;

George L. Drake and Elwood R. Maunder, *A Forester's Log*, p. 137; W. Reed Draft Memoirs.

19. Reed to Wilson, 24 October 1928, Reed Papers; Kreienbaum to Fox, 17 November 1925, Reed Mill Co. Papers; Cornwall to Reed, 17 May 1926, Simpson Logging Co. Papers.

20. C. H. Springer to Reed, 12 October 1926; Kreienbaum to Reed, 19 April, 1927, Simpson Logging Co. Papers.

21. C. H. Kreienbaum and Elwood R. Maunder, *The Development of a Sustained-Yield Industry*, pp. 38-42; Kreienbaum to Reed, 22 December 1927; Henry Schott to Reed, 27 May 1926, Simpson Logging Co. Papers; Shelton *Mason County Journal*, 22 December 1927.

22. *Timberman* 28 (February 1927):198; Kreienbaum to Reed, 20 January and 22 December 1927, Simpson Logging Co. Papers.

23. Reed to Kreienbaum, 2 February 1926, Reed Mill Co. Papers; C. H. Kreienbaum, "Price Warfare in Waterborne Markets," *Timberman* 32(April 1931):109.

24. Kreienbaum to Reed, 6 and 31 August 1927, Simpson Logging Co. Papers; Kreienbaum to Reed, 27 January 1926, Reed Mill Co. Papers; Shelton *Mason County Journal*, 20 December 1928.

25. *Timberman* 31(February 1930):118; Reed to F. R. Clarke, 24 March 1928, Reed Papers; Shelton *Mason County Journal*, 8 March 1928; Kreienbaum to Hillier, 25 July 1929; Kreienbaum to Reed, 13 September 1929, Simpson Logging Co. Papers.

26. E. J. Van den Ven to Simpson Logging Co., 13 November 1926; Reed to Van den Ven, 20 October, 1926; T. E. Ripley to Reed, 19 October 1926, Simpson Logging Co. Papers; *Timberman* 30(May 1929):202; Shelton *Mason County Journal*, 22 November and 13 December 1928.

27. Reed to R. D. Merrill, 11 April 1929, Merrill & Ring Lumber Co. Papers, Manuscripts Collection, University of Washington Library; Shelton *Mason County Journal*, 4 October and 27 December 1928, 30 September 1929.

28. Reed to E. M. Mills, 8, 13, 24 and 29 October 1928; Mills to Reed, 15 October 1928, Simpson Logging Co. Papers; Shelton *Mason County Journal*, 20 December 1928.

29. Harry W. Deegan, *History of Mason County*, pp. 18-19; Shelton *Mason County Journal*, 21 January 1927. The *Journal* quoted with approval an article from the Port Angeles *News* claiming no damage from that city's Washington Pulp Mill. "Dump your liquor waste in our bay," the *News* invited, "and the cleansing tides will purify it. Clams, oysters, crabs and devil fish may have been frightened for a time, but they are back on the reservation and fattern' ever." Shelton *Mason County Journal*, 23 July 1928.

30. Shelton *Mason County Journal*, 5 July 1928; 29 August and 7 and 10 October 1929; Reed to Martha Deer, 5 August and 14 October 1929, Reed Papers.

31. Shelton *Mason County Journal*, 26 May and 18 December 1930; Mills to Reed, 5 December 1930, Simpson Logging Co. Papers. Reed seems to have been grasping at straws when he claimed that "the oyster growers have had a very satisfactory year. . . . I feel that the situation as to the law suits has become considerably improved by this bettered propagation condition." Reed to Mills, 3 December 1930, Simpson Logging Co. Papers.

32. Mills to Reed, 17 December 1930; Reed to Mills, 26 December 1930, Simpson Logging Co. Papers.

33. Shelton *Mason County Journal*, 18 and 22 December 1930. The *Journal* gave prominent front-page space to articles supporting retention of the mill, while relegating the views of the oystermen to inside-page obscurity.

34. Ibid., 25 December 1930; F. E. Dark to Reed, 23 December 1930, Reed Papers; Reed to Mills, 26 December 1930, Simpson Logging Co. Papers.

35. Reed to Mills, 26 December 1930, Simpson Logging Co. Papers.

36. Shelton *Mason County Journal*, 23 March and 16 April 1931. "The real goal in the present fight," editor Grant Angle stated, "is not only to retain the pulp mill in Shelton but to make this location safe for other industries." Shelton *Mason County Journal*, 30 March 1931.

37. Ibid., 11 and 18 July 1932; Reed to Frank E. Holman, 22 and 26 March 1932, Mark E. Reed Personal Papers, Simpson Reed & Co.; S. W. Anderson, "Memo regarding Simpson Logging Company," September 1943, copy in author's possession.

38. Federal Writers Program, *The New Washington, A Guide to the Evergreen State*, p. 540.

39. *Historical Statistics*, pp. 313, 317; Reed to Herbert Hoover, 26 November 1926, Simpson Logging Co. Papers; Reed to W. A. Whitman, 1 December 1926, Reed Papers.

40. L. L. Knapp to Reed, 13 December 1926; Spring to Reed, 12 October 1926; Reed to David T. Mason, 9 April 1928, Simpson Logging Co. Papers; Reed to E. M. Rogers, 16 December 1926, St. Paul & Tacoma Lumber Co. Papers; Reed to C. C. Crow, 30 October 1925, Reed Mill Co. Papers.

41. Reed to R. M. Calkins, 25 November 1929; Reed to Whitman, 8 December 1926, Reed Papers; Reed to Fox, 16 December 1926, Reed Mill Co. Papers.

42. George S. Long et al. to Simpson Logging Co., 19 January 1926; Reed to Schott, 26 May 1926, Simpson Logging Co. Papers; Reed to Wilson, 23 October 1928, Reed Papers; *Timberman* 27(February 1926):38.

43. Reed to J. J. Hewitt, 1 September 1927; Reed to Calkins, 25 November 1929, Reed Papers; Reed to Frost Snyder, 3 July 1927; Snyder to Reed, 24 August 1927, Simpson Logging Co. Papers; Edwin T. Coman, Jr. and Helen M. Gibbs, *Time, Tide and Timber*, pp. 293-94; *Timberman* 31(June 1930):190.

44. *Timberman* 28(April 1927):33; Shelton *Mason County Journal*, 29 March 1927; Reed to A. A. Scott, 4 May 1927, Reed Papers; Reed to Snyder, 21 November 1927, Simpson Logging Co. Papers. "We are now running four days a week only," an officer of the Clear Fir Lumber Company informed Reed, "both for the good of the industry and ourselves, primarily for ourselves as we lack space in which to pile all the lumber we are cutting." C. C. Corse to Reed, 25 March 1927, Simpson Logging Co. Papers.

45. Reed to E. C. Kaune, 24 October 1928; Reed to Govey, 12 February 1928, Simpson Logging Co. Papers; Reed to Clarke, 24 November 1928, Reed Papers; Shelton *Mason County Journal*, 16 February 1928.

46. W. Reed Draft Memoirs.

47. Reed to Clarke, 24 November 1928, Reed Papers; Reed to Scott, 7 August 1928; Reed to Snyder, 23 October 1928, Simpson Logging Co. Papers.

48. Reed to Long, 15 May 1928; Reed to Snyder, 5 September and 23 October 1928; Reed to David Davis, 10 May 1928, Simpson Logging Co. Papers; Shelton *Mason County Journal*, 21 May and 25 October 1928; William C. Butler to Reed, 31 May 1928, Reed Papers.

49. Merrill to Reed, 8 and 15 April 1929; Reed to Merrill, 11 April 1929, Merrill & Ring Lumber Co. Papers; Polson to Reed, 5 April 1929; Albert Johnson to Reed, 17 April 1929, Simpson Logging Co. Papers.

50. Merrill to Reed, 15 and 16 April 1929, Simpson Logging Co. Papers.

51. Reed to Merrill, 17 April 1929, Merrill & Ring Lumber Co. Papers; Merrill to Reed, 16 and 18 April 1929; Reed to W. H. Abel, 25 April 1929; Reed to Johnson, 22 April 1929, Simpson Logging Co. Papers; Shelton *Mason County Journal*, 2 May 1929.

52. Kreienbaum to D. Meredith, 30 September 1929, Reed Mill Co. Papers; Reed to Whitman, 7 November 1929; Reed to Scott, 14 January 1929, Simpson Logging Co. Papers.

53. Reed to Butler, 26 March 1929; Reed to Whitman, 28 December 1929, Simpson Logging Co. Papers. "Seemingly," William Butler told Reed, "it is no longer necessary that marginal producers should continually embarrass the industry." Butler to Reed, 15 July 1929, Simpson Logging Co. Papers.

54. Reed to Wilson, 23 October 1928, Reed Papers; Reed to W. B. Greeley, 20 June 1928; Long to Reed, 30 June 1928; Greeley to Reed, 3 July 1928, Simpson Logging Co. Papers.

55. Reed to Greeley, 5 July 1928, Simpson Logging Co. Papers.

56. Reed to Whitman, 7 November 1929, Simpson Logging Co. Papers.

57. Shelton *Mason County Journal*, 21 June 1927.

58. Roscoe A. Balch to Reed, 14 December 1928; Reed to Balch, 17 December 1928; W. H. Parsons to Reed, 28 October 1929; Reed to

Parsons, 13 July 1929; Joshua Green to Reed, 14 May 1928, Reed Papers; Shelton *Mason County Journal*, 17 December 1928.

59. Long to Reed, 6 August and 24 September 1929; Reed to John W. Blodgett, 10 March 1930, Simpson Logging Co. Papers.

60. Reed to Long, 15 October 1929; Reed to Blodgett, 10 March 1930, Simpson Logging Co. Papers.

61. Reed to Blodgett, 10 March 1930; Reed to Long, 15 October 1929, Simpson Logging Co. Papers.

62. *West Coast Lumberman* 48(15 August 1925):18.

63. Reed to Wolfe's Laboratories, 17 April 1930; William T. Phy to Reed, 3 May 1928; Reed to Calkins, 25 November 1929, Reed Papers; Reed to Whitman, 6 April and 5 September 1929, Simpson Logging Co. Papers; W. Reed Draft Memoirs.

Notes to Chapter 6

1. Joan Hoff Wilson, *American Business and Foreign Policy, 1920-1933*, pp. 66-69; William Starr Meyers, ed., *The State Papers and Other Public Writings of Herbert Hoover*, 1:13-14; Harris Gaylord Warren, *Herbert Hoover and the Great Depression*, pp. 87-88; J. Richard Snyder, "Hoover and the Smoot-Hawley Tariff," *Annals of Iowa* 41(Winter 1973):1175-76.

2. Summary of Shingle Industry Data, n.d., Wesley L. Jones Papers, Manuscripts Collection, University of Washington Library; A. C. Edwards to Mark E. Reed, 26 February 1926, Simpson Logging Co. Papers, Simpson Timber Co.; U.S. Tariff Commission, *Report to the President on Lumber, 1932*, pp. 1-3; U.S. Tariff Commission, *Summary of Tariff Information, 1929*, pp. 918-20.

3. Reed to C. E. Dant, 18 February 1929, Reed Mill Co. Papers, Simpson Logging Co.; W. Yale Henry to Wesley L. Jones, 1 May 1930, Jones Papers; Reed to Richard Condon, 19 March 1929; William C. Butler to Reed, 8 November 1929, Simpson Logging Co. Papers.

4. E. G. Griggs to James Tyson, 21 December 1928, Simpson Logging Co. Papers; E. E. Schattschneider, *Politics, Pressures and the Tariff*, pp. 154-56; *Timberman* 28(December 1926):36.

5. Shelton *Mason County Journal*, 1 April 1929; Griggs to Tyson, 21 December 1928; Tyson to Griggs, 3 January 1929; Tyson to Reed, 1 January 1929, Simpson Logging Co. Papers; Griggs to Reed, 28 September 1927, St. Paul & Tacoma Lumber Co. Papers, Manuscripts Collection, University of Washington Library.

6. Tyson to Griggs, 3 January 1929, Simpson Logging Co. Papers.

7. Dant to Reed, 14 February 1929, Reed Mill Co. Papers; Condon to Reed, 28 March 1929; Reed to Condon, 1 April 1929, Simpson Logging Co. Papers.

8. Reed to Butler, 26 March and 3 April 1929, Simpson Logging Co. Papers.

9. Reed to C. Bascom Slemp, 20 May 1929; Reed to Butler, 3 April 1929; Condon to Reed, 28 March 1929, Simpson Logging Co. Papers; Reed to Dant, 18 February 1929, Reed Mill Co. Papers.

10. *Hoover State Papers*, 1:31-37; Condon to Reed, 17 April 1929, Simpson Logging Co. Papers.

11. House Committee on Ways and Means, *Hearings, Tariff Readjustment—1929*, 70:2, pp. 9168-69, 9475, 9607.

12. Reed to Slemp, 20 May 1929; Condon confidential report, n.d., Simpson Logging Co. Papers.

13. Condon confidential report, n.d.; Lin H. Hadley to Reed, 1 June 1929; Reed to Hadley, 25 May 1929, Simpson Logging Co. Papers.

14. *Congressional Record*, 71:1, p. 2106; Reed to Condon, 13 May 1929; William S. Bennet to Dant, 25 May 1929; Hadley to Reed, 1 June 1929, Simpson Logging Co. Papers.

15. John W. Summers to Reed, 17 June 1929; Hadley to Reed, 1 June 1929, Simpson Logging Co. Papers; *Timberman* 30(May 1929):36.

16. Reed to Slemp, 1 June 1929; Reed to S. M. Hauptman, 10 June 1929, Simpson Logging Co. Papers.

17. Edgar A. Hirsch to C. H. Kreienbaum, 22 April 1929, Reed Mill Co. Papers; Walter E. Edge to Jones, 1 August 1929; R. Roosa to Jones, 26 June 1929, Jones Papers; Condon to Reed, 19 February 1930, Simpson Logging Co. Papers.

18. Butler to Reed, 27 May 1929; Frank H. Lamb to Reed, 5 May 1929; Reed to Jones, 23 May 1929, Simpson Logging Co. Papers; *New York Times*, 18 May 1929.

19. Jones to G. L. Neff, 16 September 1929, Jones Papers; Reed to Summers, 22 June 1929, Simpson Logging Co. Papers. "The more I see of the tariff," Senator Hiram Johnson of California wrote several months later, "the more I realize old General Hancock's assertion in the campaign of 1880, that it was a mere local issue in which selfishness predominated. Hancock was bitterly assailed for his statement at that time, but its verity is now generally accepted." Hiram W. Johnson to Hiram W. Johnson, Jr., 1 March 1930, Hiram W. Johnson Papers, Bancroft Library, University of California, Berkeley. I am indebted to Professor Robert E. Burke of the University of Washington for providing me with copies of material in the Johnson Papers.

20. Butler to Reed, 22, 23 and 27 May and 18 June 1929; Reed to Jones, 23 May 1929; Jones to Reed, 29 May 1929, Simpson Logging Co. Papers; *New York Times*, 13 May 1929.

21. Condon to Jones, 6 August 1929; Jones to Roland H. Hartley, 12 February 1930, Jones Papers.

22. Butler to Reed, 23 May and 3 July 1929, Simpson Logging Co. Papers; Edwin G. Ames to Millard T. Hartson, 3 November 1920, Edwin G. Ames Papers, Manuscripts Collection, University of Washington Library.

23. Reed to George S. Long, 28 May 1929; Reed to Jones, 25 May and 10 June 1929; Reed to Butler, 25 May 1929; Butler to Reed, 23 May 1929, Simpson Logging Co. Papers. "The action you are able to obtain from your brother Senators," warned Condon, "will be conclusive in our coming political campaigns, both personal and general." Condon to Jones, 6 August 1929, Jones Papers.

24. Jones to Reed, 29 May 1929; C. C. Dill to Reed, 6 June 1929; Reed to Dill, 30 May and 26 August 1929; Reed to Condon, 12 June 1929; Reed to Edwards, 5 August 1929; Reed to Butler, 5 July 1929, Simpson Logging Co. Papers; Dill to Reed, 15 December 1928, Mark E. Reed Papers, Manuscripts Collection, University of Washington Library.

25. Reed to Jones, 10 June 1929; Jones to Reed, 13 and 24 June 1929; Condon to Reed, 20 June 1929, Simpson Logging Co. Papers; Senate Committee on Finance, *Hearings, Tariff Act of 1929*, 71:1, p. 53; *West Coast Lumberman* 56(July 1929):70.

26. Jones to Reed, 24 June and 5 July 1929; Jones to Condon, 7 June 1929, Simpson Logging Co. Papers; Jones to James Couzens, 5 July 1929; Couzens to Jones, 2 August 1929, Jones Papers; *New York Times*, 1 August 1929. For Canadian reaction to the tariff deliberations, see Richard D. Kottman, "Herbert Hoover and the Smoot-Hawley Tariff," *Journal of American History* 62(December 1975):609-35.

27. Reed to Butler, 5 August 1929; Jones to Reed, 5 July 1929, Simpson Logging Co. Papers.

28. Reed to Jones, 8 August 1929; Butler to Reed, 7 August 1929, Simpson Logging Co. Papers. Historians have never doubted Smoot's total devotion to protection. He was, notes F. W. Taussig, "an out-and-out protectionist of the most intolerant stamp." F. W. Taussig, *The Tariff History of the United States*, p. 496.

29. Reed to Jones, 8 August 1929; Reed to Butler, 5 August 1929, Simpson Logging Co. Papers; Condon to Jones, 6 and 7 August 1929, Jones Papers.

30. Butler to Reed, 11 July 1929; Reed to Butler, 5 August 1929, Simpson Logging Co. Papers.

31. Condon to Jones, 19 August 1929, Jones Papers; Reed to Condon, 23 September 1929; Reed to Russell Hawkins, 30 September 1929; Hawkins to Reed, n.d., Simpson Logging Co. Papers.

32. Reed to Butler, 7 September 1929; Reed to Condon, 23 September 1929; Condon to Long, 17 September 1929; Hawkins to Reed, 30 August 1929; Reed to Hawkins, 30 September 1929, Simpson Logging Co. Papers.

33. Jones to Reed, 2 October 1929; Reed to Hawkins, 30 September 1929; Butler to Reed, 26 September 1929, Simpson Logging Co. Papers.

34. Butler to Reed, 3 July and 21 and 26 September 1929; Hawkins to Reed, 30 August 1929; Reed to Jones, 3 September 1929; Reed to

Condon, 23 September 1929; Condon to Long, 17 September 1929; Reed to Butler, 20 September 1929, Simpson Logging Co. Papers.

35. Reed to Butler, 5 August 1929; Butler to Reed, 10 October 1929, Simpson Logging Co. Papers. "There are a great many members of the senate," observed an important lumberman, "who are apparently indifferent to the fact that the manufacturer loses money, that is a mere incident." John W. Blodgett to Hawkins, 25 November 1929, Simpson Logging Co. Papers. Also see Taussig, *Tariff History of the United States*, pp. 496-98; John D. Hicks, *Republican Ascendancy, 1921-1933*, pp. 220-21.

36. Reed to Jones, 18 June 1929; Butler to Reed, 3 July, 7 August, 21 September and 8 November 1929; Jones to Reed, 24 June 1929; Reed to Condon, 3 September 1929; Reed to Hawkins, 21 October 1929, Simpson Logging Co. Papers.

37. Butler to Reed, 7 August and 9 September 1929; Reed to Butler, 5 August 1929; Reed to Edwards, 5 August 1929; Reed to Hawkins, 21 October 1929, Simpson Logging Co. Papers.

38. Reed to Summers, 10 June 1929; Reed to Hawkins, 4 November 1929; C. C. Crow to Hawkins, 1 December 1929, Simpson Logging Co. Papers; Seattle *Business Chronicle*, 9 December 1928.

39. *Seattle Times*, 6 October 1929; Reed to Jones, 31 October 1929; Jones to Reed, 5 November 1929; Reed to Hawkins, 4 November 1929, Simpson Logging Co. Papers.

40. Jones to Reed, 2 and 24 October 1929, Simpson Logging Co. Papers; Johnson to H. Johnson, Jr. and Archibald M. Johnson, 18 October 1929, H. Johnson Papers; Bronson W. Cutting to Edward L. Stafford, 30 October 1929, quoted in Jordan A. Schwarz, *The Interregnum of Despair*, p. 7.

41.   Jones to Reed, 29 August 1929; Reed to Jones, 3 September 1929; Reed to Butler, 18 November 1929, Simpson Logging Co. Papers; Jones to H. J. Bratlie, 16 September 1929; Bratlie to Jones, 20 September 1929, Jones Papers.

42. Reed to Jones, 7 and 19 October 1929; Jones to Reed, 2 October 1929, Simpson Logging Co. Papers. Reed noted that "cedar which at one time was considered our most valuable wood is now our least valuable and has been for a number of years," Reed to Jones, 26 September 1929, Simpson Logging Co. Papers.

43. *Congressional Record*, 71:1, pp. 5446, 5453.

44. Butler to Reed, 8 November 1929; Hawkins to Reed, 13 November 1929; Reed to Butler, 13 November 1929, Simpson Logging Co. Papers.

45. *Congressional Record*, 71:1, p. 5509; Hawkins to Reed, 13 November 1929; Dill to Reed, 18 November 1929, Simpson Logging Co. Papers.

46. Reed to Hawkins, 18 November 1929; Reed to Blodgett, 20 November 1929; Dill to Reed, 18 November 1929, Simpson Logging Co. Papers.

47. Butler to Reed, 4 December 1929; Reed to Long, 5 December 1929; Reed to Hawkins, 2 December 1929, Simpson Logging Co. Papers.

48. Crow to Jones, 25 December 1929, Jones Papers; Blodgett to Long, 10 December 1929, Simpson Logging Co. Papers.

49. Reed to Long, 8 and 18 November 1919; Long to Reed, 31 December 1929; Blodgett to Reed, 18 January 1930; Reed to Butler, 18 November 1929, Simpson Logging Co. Papers.

50. Reed to Hawkins, 2 December 1929; Long to Reed, 25 November and 31 December 1929; Blodgett to Reed, 18 January 1930, Simpson Logging Co. Papers. In response to this warning Reed exclaimed that "if it comes to pass in our governmental affairs where an interested American citizen, acting on the square, cannot appear before the members of the Congress of the United States and set forth the necessities for congressional action, as he seems them in the interest of his business, then we are riding for a fall in governmental affairs." Reed to Blodgett, 13 January 1930, Simpson Logging Co. Papers.

51. Butler to Reed, 4 December 1929; Reed to Minot Davis, 10 January 1930, Simpson Logging Co. Papers; Shelton *Mason County Journal*, 10 March 1930.

52. Reed to George A. Bergstrom, 27 January 1930; Condon to Reed, 19 February 1930, Simpson Logging Co. Papers.

53. Jones to Reed, 28 February 1930; Reed to Blodgett, 10 March 1930; Reed to Jones, 11 March 1930; Blodgett to Reed, 18 January 1930, Simpson Logging Co. Papers. Governor Hartley wrote to Jones that many of his friends were upset over "what they called your apparent timid attitude in this matter." Hartley to Jones, 6 February 1930, Jones Papers.

54. *Congressional Record*, 71:2, pp. 5669-70, 5687; *New York Times*, 21 March 1930. On Chinese labor in British Columbia, see Harold M. Stilson, Jr. and Edwood R. Maunder, "Red Cedar Shingles & Shakes," *Journal of Forest History* 19(July 1975):121.

55. *Congressional Record*, 71:2, p. 6015; Johnson to A. Johnson, 25 March 1930, H. Johnson Papers.

56. Jones to D. C. Botting, 1 April 1930; Jones to Seattle Cedar Lumber Manufacturing Co., 31 March 1930, Jones Papers; Summers to Reed, 17 June 1929, Simpson Logging Co. Papers.

57. J. H. Bloedel to congressmen, 12 April 1930; Condon to Joseph Irving and Reed, 12 April 1930; Blodgett to Reed, 18 and 28 April 1930; Reed to Blodgett, 19 April and 3 May 1930, Simpson Logging Co. Papers; F. J. Wood to Jones, 26 April 1930, Jones Papers.

58. Blodgett to Reed, 8, 14 and 25 1930; n.d.; Reed to Blodgett, 3 May 1930; Reed to Condon, 20 May 1930; Condon to Reed, 16 May 1930, Simpson Logging Co. Papers; Jones to Condon, 17 May 1930, Jones Papers.

59. *Congressional Record*, 71:2, pp. 10635, 10789-90; Condon to Reed, 28 May 1930, Simpson Logging Co. Papers; Lamb to Jones, 16 May 1930; Alex Polson to Jones, 17 June 1930, Jones Papers; *West Coast Lumberman* 58 (January 1931):34; Hicks, *Republican Ascendancy*, p. 221.

60. *Hoover State Papers*, 1:314-18; Herbert Hoover, *The Memoirs of Herbert Hoover*, vol. 2, *The Cabinet and the Presidency, 1920-1933*, p. 296; Taussig, *Tariff History of the United States*, pp. 499-500; Hicks, *Republican Ascendancy*, p. 221; Broadus Mitchell, *Depression Decade*, pp. 73-76; Wilson, *American Business and Foreign Policy*, pp. 88-98.

61. Long to Reed, 17 June 1930; Reed to Long, 18 June 1930, Simpson Logging Co. Papers; Jones to Neff, 13 May 1930, Jones Papers. Failure to secure a tariff cost Northwest congressmen considerable political support. Alfred J. Hillier, "Albert Johnson, Congressman," *Pacific Northwest Quarterly* 36(July 1945):210; Keith Murray, "Issues and Personalities of Pacific Northwest Politics, 1889-1950," *Pacific Northwest Quarterly* 41(July 1950):229.

62. Jones to Reed, 14 March 1930, Simpson Logging Co. Papers.

Notes to Chapter 7

1. Shelton *Mason County Journal*, 26 June 1930; William G. Reed Draft Memoirs, n.p., copy in author's possession; Mark E. Reed to Coleman C. Vaughan, 19 July 1930, Mark E. Reed Papers, Manuscripts Collection, University of Washington Library.

2. George L. Drake and Elwood R. Maunder, *A Forester's Log*, pp. 9, 136-37; W. Reed Draft Memoirs.

3. Shelton *Mason County Journal*, 18 May 1931; Alex Polson to Reed, 16 May 1931; Reed to Polson, 18 May 1931, Simpson Logging Co. Papers, Simpson Timber Co.

4. John Kenneth Galbraith, *The Great Crash, 1929*, pp. 93-132, 182-91; Reed to C. B. Blethen, 15 July 1932, Mark E. Reed Personal Papers, Simpson Reed & Co.; Reed to C. H. Kreienbaum, 10 April 1929; Reed to Lee L. Doud, 2 December 1929, Simpson Logging Co. Papers.

5. Reed to R. M. Calkins, 10 December 1929, Reed Papers.

6. Newspaper clipping, Mark E. Reed folder, Washington State Biography File, Northwest Collection, University of Washington Library; Reed to Calkins, 10 December 1929; Reed to W. H. Parsons, 30 September 1929, Reed Papers; W. Reed Draft Memoirs.

7. Reed to Doud, 2 November 1929; W. A. Whitman to Reed, 5 February 1930; Reed to Whitman, 11 March 1930; Reed to J. A. Swalwell, 25 November 1929, Simpson Logging Co. Papers; Reed to Katheryn Wilson, 16 June 1930, Reed Papers.

8. W. Reed Draft Memoirs; Reed to E. A. Sims, 21 May 1930; William S. Westover to Reed, 15 February 1930, Reed Papers.

9. *Timberman* 31(June 1930):36; Reed to Kreienbaum, 4 June 1930, Reed Mill Co. Papers, Simpson Timber Co.; Reed to Sims, 21 May

1930, Reed Papers; Shelton *Mason County Journal*, 5 June 1930; *Business Week* (7 May 1930):13.

10. Reed to Sims, 21 May 1930; Reed to Ed Davis, 4 September 1930, Reed Papers; *Timberman* 31(June 1930):36.

11. Reed to E. Davis, 4 September 1930, Reed Papers.

12. Reed to Whitman, 12 December 1930; Reed to H. A. Brokaw, 12 December 193 1930; Minot Davis to Reed, 12 November 1930, Simpson Logging Co. Papers.

13. "Some of the other operators competitive with ours," Reed noted, "are down to as low as a $2.00 minimum." Reed to Frost Snyder, 16 December 1930; Reed to William C. Butler, 25 July 1931; Butler to Reed, 24 July 1931, Simpson Logging Co. Papers; Reed to Lawrence Richey, 18 April 1932, Reed Personal Papers; George Drake oral history interview with Elwood R. Maunder, 19 January 1968, Forest History Society, pp. 4-5.

14. Shelton *Mason County Journal*, 2 July 1928; Andrew Mellon quoted in Galbraith, *Great Crash*, p. 197; Reed to F. R. Clarke, 24 November 1930, Reed Papers; Reed to Brokaw, 12 December 1930; Reed to Snyder, 16 December 1930, Simpson Logging Co. Papers; *Simpson Diamond* 3(October-November 1963):4; Drake 1968 interview with Maunder, pp. 4-5.

15. Reed to E. P. Blake, 11 April 1932; George L. Drake to George H. Fields, 3 June 1933, Reed Personal Papers; Reed to Clarke, 24 November 1930, Reed Papers.

16. C. H. Kreienbaum and Elwood R. Maunder, "Forest Management and Community Stability," *Forest History* 12(July 1968):11.

17. Ibid., p. 12; Drake and Maunder, *Forester's Log*, pp. 130-31; W. Reed Draft Memoirs; Shelton *Mason County Journal*, 15 August 1932.

18. Kreienbaum and Maunder, "Forest Management and Community," p. 12.

19. Reed to John W. Blodgett, 31 August 1931; Reed to Snyder, 16 June 1931; Charles S. Keith to Reed, 2 June 1931; C. E. Dant to Reed, 25 May 1931, Simpson Logging Co. Papers; Kreienbaum to Earl Kalk, 27 May 1931, Reed Mill Co. Papers; *Business Week* (7 October 1931):14; U.S. Bureau of the Census, *Historical Statistics of the United States, Colonial Times to 1957*, pp. 313, 317; C. H. Kreienbaum and Elwood R. Maunder, *The Development of a Sustained-Yield Industry*, pp. 62-67.

20. *Timberman* 33(March 1932):65; Reed to Snyder, 3 July 1931; Reed to David Davis, 29 June 1931; Kreienbaum to Reed, 25 June 1931, Simpson Logging Co. Papers.

21. Reed to Kiplinger Washington Agency, 20 February 1932, Reed Personal Papers; *Historical Statistics*, pp. 313, 317; *West Coast Lumberman* 60 (February 1933):16; Reed to A. J. Morley, 23 July 1932; William G. Reed to D. Davis, 7 April 1932, Simpson Logging Co. Papers; Kreienbaum to Reed, 4 December 1931; Kreienbaum to William B. Greeley, 6 February 1932, Reed Mill Co. Papers.

22. Reed to R. D. Merrill, 29 June 1932; Merrill to Reed, 27 June 1932; Kreienbaum to Reed, 9 April 1932, Simpson Logging Co. Papers; Reed to Merrill, 28 June 1932; T. Jerome memorandum, 13 May 1932, Merrill & Ring Lumber Co. Papers, Manuscripts Collection, University of Washington Library.

23. Reed to Merrill, 25 and 28 June 1932, Merril & Ring Lumber Co. Papers; W. Reed to D. Davis, 14 October 1932, Simpson Logging Co. Papers.

24. Reed to Merrill, 28 June 1932, Merrill & Ring Lumber Co. Papers; Reed to Snyder, 19 July 1932, Simpson Logging Co. Papers.

25. Reed to Snyder, 19 July 1932, Simpson Logging Co. Papers.

26. M. Davis to Keith, 18 June 1931; M. Davis to Reed, 30 March 1931; Reed to Blodgett, 12 November 1929, Simpson Logging Co. Papers.

27. Shelton *Mason County Journal*, 2 February 1931; Kreienbaum to Reed, 20 June 1930, Reed Mill Co. Papers; Merrill to Reed, 29 May and 15 September 1930; Snyder to Reed, 13 June 1930, Simpson Logging Co. Papers. Kreienbaum believed that "many of our large lumbermen and timbermen have lost faith in the future possibility of the industry and their one object is to unload their properties, through a merger, by selling to the public and turning the management over to some one else." Kreienbaum to Reed, 7 November 1930, Simpson Logging Co. Papers.

28. Reed to J. D. Tennant, 17 May and 1 September 1930, Simpson Logging Co. Papers.

29. Shelton *Mason County Journal*, 9 April 1931; Minutes of Trustees Meetings, 20 and 21 May, 2 September and 11 December 1931, Douglas Fir Export Co. Papers, Oregon Historical Society; Reed to C. H. Springer, 28 October 1931; Reed to Keith, 6 and 16 June 1931, Simpson Logging Co. Papers; Kreienbaum to Reed, 21 May 1931, Reed Mill Co. Papers.

30. Shelton *Mason County Journal*, 14 May 1931; Reed to Keith, 16 June 1931, Simpson Logging Co. Papers; Kreienbaum to W. D. Veazey, 20 April 1933, Reed Personal Papers; Kreienbaum and Maunder, *Development of a Sustained-Yield Industry*, pp. 32-38.

31. M. Davis to Reed, 3 March and 27 May 1931; Reed to Frederick Weyerhaeuser, 11 July 1931; Reed to J. H. Bloedel, 6 July 1931, Simpson Logging Co. Papers; W. Reed Draft Memoirs.

32. Reed to Butler, 9 April 1931, Simpson Logging Co. Papers.

33. Reed to Blodgett, 12 October 1931; Blodgett to Reed, 26 August and 6 October 1931; Bloedel to Reed, 16 September 1931, Simpson Logging Co. Papers; *Business Week* (11 March 1931):14.

34. Reed to Blodgett, 31 August 1931; Blodgett to Reed, 19 May 1931; Reed to M. Davis, n.d.; 31 March 1931; Reed to Butler, 31 August 1931; Simpson Logging Co. Papers; Rodney C. Loehr, ed., *Forests for the Future*, p. 90. While the Oregon operators "would freely

criticize the architecture and construction of St. Peters in Rome," observed Blodgett, "they would hesitate to design and construct a henhouse." Blodgett to Reed, 19 May 1931, Simpson Logging Co. Papers.

35. Kreienbaum to Reed, 15 August 1931, Reed Mill Co. Papers; Reed to Blodgett, 31 August 1931, Simpson Logging Co. Papers. "Clearly," the acerbic Butler commented, "none of the present organization of the Weyerhaeuser Timber Company on the Coast have either the personality or the capacity for the job." Butler to Reed, 24 July 1931, Simpson Logging Co. Papers. George Long had died in mid-1930.

36. Reed to Weyerhaeuser, 11 July 1931; Weyerhaeuser to Reed, 15 July 1931; Carl M. Stevens to Reed, 31 July 1931, Simpson Logging Co. Papers.

37. Reed to Stevens, 3 August 1931; Reed to Butler, 31 August 1931; Bloedel to Reed, 8 September 1931; Stevens to Reed, 9 October 1931, Simpson Logging Co. Papers. On Weyerhaeuser's involvement with the proposed merger, also see Ralph W. Hidy, Frank Ernest Hill, and Allan Nevins, *Timber and Men*, p. 435.

38. Reed to Laird Bell, 7 March, 5 April, 21 June, and 18 July 1932; Bell to Reed, 18 June and 13 July 1932; Reed to James Tyson, 31 December 1932, Simpson Logging Co. Papers.

39. Reed to Bell, 7 and 15 March 1932; Bell to Reed, 19 March 1932, Simpson Logging Co. Papers.

40. Bloedel to Reed, 31 October 1931; R. A. Wiley to Reed, 6 July 1932, Simpson Logging Co. Papers; Sims to Reed, 14 April 1930; H. S. Temper to Reed, 27 May 1930; Geoffrey Winslow to Reed, 28 May 1930, Reed Papers; R. M. Hardy to Reed, 31 March 1932, Reed Personal Papers; Seattle *Argus*, 23 January 1932; Shelton *Mason County Journal*, 27 June 1932; William S. Forth, "Wesley L. Jones." (Ph.D. dissertation), pp. 730, 798.

41. Reed to Mat Mattison, 6 April 1932, Reed Personal Papers; Seattle *Argus*, 23 January 1932.

42. Shelton *Mason County Journal*, 9 August 1927; Ralph A. Horr to W. W. Scruby, 8 February 1932; Mattison to Reed, 10 April 1932; Fred A. Adams to Reed, 20 April 1932, Reed Personal Papers; Butler to Reed, 11 April 1932, Simpson Logging Co. Papers; Seattle *Argus*, 21 May 1932.

43. Reed to Butler, 8 December 1931, Simpson Logging Co. Papers.

44. Harold L. Ickes to Reed, 12 March 1932; Reed to Ickes, 16 March 1932, Reed Personal Papers.

45. Reed to Raymond Benjamin, 19 May 1932; Parsons to Reed, 9 June 1932; Reed to William E. Humphrey, 23 May 1932; Reed to Ed Benn, 30 March 1932, Reed Personal Papers.

46. Reed to Wesley L. Jones, 28 May 1932, Simpson Logging Co. Papers; Shelton *Mason County Journal*, 4 July 1932; Reed to Albert Johnson, 21 March 1932; Reed to Polson, 15 July 1932, Reed Personal

Papers; Reed to Norman B. Gibbs, 17 May 1930, Reed Papers; Reed to Asahel Curtis, 28 October 1931, Asahel Curtis Papers, Manuscripts Collection, University of Washington Library.

47. Shelton *Mason County Journal*, 4 July 1932.

48. Ibid., 11 and 25 July 1932; Seattle *Argus*, 30 July 1932; Reed to Henry Suzzallo, 20 October 1932, Henry Suzzallo Papers, Manuscripts Collection, University of Washington Library.

49. Seattle *Argus*, 23 and 30 July, and 13 August 1932.

50. Reed to Butler, 30 June 1932, Simpson Logging Co. Papers; Reed to Theodore B. Bruener, 16 August 1930, Reed Papers; Reed to Blethen, 15 July 1932, Reed Personal Papers. With the daily press "pimping for Roosevelt," commented the *Argus*, "it is difficult for Seattleites to obtain the proper perspective." Seattle *Argus*, 6 August 1932.

51. Shelton *Mason County Journal*, 15 September 1932; Seattle *Argus*, 24 September 1932; Frank I. Sefrit to S. A. Perkins, 20 September 1932, S. A. Perkins Papers, Washington State Historical Society.

52. Reed to Merrill, 4 November 1932, Merrill & Ring Lumber Co. Papers; Shelton *Mason County Journal*, 20 October 1932; Reed to fellow lumbermen, 28 October 1932, Reed Mill Co. Papers.

53. Reed to Suzzallo, 20 October 1932, Suzzallo Papers; Reed to Arthur B. Govey, 24 October 1932, Simpson Logging Co. Papers; Sefrit to Perkins, 20 September 1932, Perkins Papers.

54. Reed to Merrill, 4 November 1932, Merrill & Ring Lumber Co. Papers; Robert L. Cole, "The Democratic Party in Washington State, 1919-1933," (Ph.D. dissertation), pp. 291-94; Fayette F. Krause, "Democratic Party Politics in the State of Washington During the New Deal," (Ph.D. dissertation), pp. 62-63; Shelton *Mason County Journal*, 10 November 1932; Reed to Humphrey, 18 November 1932, Reed Personal Papers.

55. Reed to Humphrey, 18 November 1932, Reed Personal Papers. "Not Democrats but DEPRESSION won the last election," a defeated congressman explained. "The poorest Democrats won over the best Republicans." John W. Summers to Reed, 14 January 1933, Reed Papers. Reed financed the move back to the state of another defeated incumbent, Representative Albert Johnson. Johnson to Reed, 27 February 1933; Reed to Johnson, 2 March 1933, Reed Personal Papers.

56. Seattle *Argus*, 26 November 1932; *Timberman* 34(December 1932):77.

57. Reed to Snyder, 19 December 1932; Bell to Reed, 4 January 1933, Simpson Logging Co. Papers.

58. Bell to Reed, 4 and 21 January 1933; Tyson to Reed, 12 January 1933, Reed to Bell, 11 January 1933; M. Davis to Reed, 7 January 1933, Simpson Logging Co. Papers.

59. Reed to Bell, 11 January 1933; Butler to Reed, 27 January 1933; Butler to Bell, 30 January 1933, Simpson Logging Co. Papers.

60. Reed to Butler, 28 January 1933, Reed Personal Papers.

61. Reed to Herbert L. Bovenizer, 7 January 1933; Reed to Robert A. Le Roux, 22 June 1933, Reed Papers; Reed to Snyder, 28 February 1933, Reed Personal Papers; *Timberman* 34(August 1933):54; Snyder to Reed, 27 May 1933, Simpson Logging Co. Papers.

62. Reed to Le Roux, 22 June 1933, Reed Papers; Reed to Kreienbaum, 5 June and 5 July 1933, Reed Mill Co. Papers.

63. Reed to J. J. Underwood, 15 April 1933, Reed Personal Papers.

64. Kreienbaum to Leon R. Scott, 19 May 1933, Reed Mill Co. Papers; *Timberman* 34(June 1933):7-8.

65. Reed to Snyder, 7 June 1933; Reed to Saul Haas, 15 April 1933, Simpson Logging Co. Papers; Reed to Kreienbaum, 9 June 1933, Reed Mill Co. Papers; J. C. Castner to Reed, 18 April 1933, Reed Papers.

66. Emergency National Committee Minutes, 10 and 23 July 1933, Reed Mill Co. Papers; *West Coast Lumberman* 60 (August 1933):3-5; *Business Week* (29 July 1933):8. En route to Chicago, Reed stopped in Walla Walla to receive an honorary degree from Whitman College. The college extolled Reed, "whose large enterprises in lumber and banking have helped develop and stabilize the business life of this state, whose experience with problems of taxation and legislation have enabled him to render invaluable service to all whose patriotism and statesmanship are expressed by interest and constructive activity in public affairs both local and national." *West Coast Lumberman* 60(July 1933):9; Stephen B. L. Penrose to Reed, 11 April 1933, Reed Papers.

67. Emergency National Committee Minutes, 4 July 1933; Memorandum of Conference with Recovery Administration, 8 July 1933; Code of Fair Competition for the Lumber and Timber Industries, 10 July 1933, Reed Mill Co. Papers; Loehr, ed., *Forests for the Future*, pp. 100, 116-19.

68. Kreienbaum to Edgar A. Hirsch, 3 August 1933; Reed to Kreienbaum, 9 June 1933, Reed Mill Co. Papers; *Timberman* 34(September 1933):7; *West Coast Lumberman* 60(September 1933):3. Simpson became the most vocal critic of the code in the Northwest. Kreienbaum and Maunder, *Development of a Sustained-Yield Industry*, pp. 67-85; Drake 1968 interview with Maunder, p. 12.

69. At least four other lumbermen died as a result of dysentery contracted while working on the N.R.A. code. W. Reed Draft Memoirs; Shelton *Mason County Journal*, 28 and 31 August, and 4 and 7 September 1933; *West Coast Lumberman* 60(August 1933):5; Kreienbaum and Maunder, *Development of a Sustained-Yield Industry*, p. 98; George Drake oral history interview with Elwood R. Maunder, 22-23 February 1967, Forest History Society, pp. 145-46; Reed folder, Washington State Biography File.

70. Dubuar Scrapbook, no. 109, pp. 37-38, Northwest Collection, University of Washington Library; Mark E. Reed folder, Meany Pioneer File, Northwest Collection, University of Washington Library; *Town Crier* 28(30 September 1933):3; *West Coast Lumberman* 60(September 1933):19; *Timberman* 34(September 1933):8, 47; Shelton *Mason County Journal*, 7 September 1933.

Bibliography

Unpublished Sources

Manuscript Collections

Edwin G. Ames Papers. University of Washington Library.
Thomas Burke Papers. University of Washington Library.
Asahel Curtis Papers. University of Washington Library.
Douglas Fir Export Company Papers. Oregon State Historical Society.
Louis F. Hart Papers. Washington State Archives.
Roland H. Hartley Papers. Washington State Archives.
Knute Hill Papers. Washington State University Library.
Hiram W. Johnson Papers. Bancroft Library. University of California, Berkeley.
Lon Johnson Papers. Washington State University Library.
Wesley L. Jones Papers. University of Washington Library.
Ernest Lister Papers. Washington State Archives.
Edmond S. Meany Papers. University of Washington Archives.
Merrill and Ring Lumber Company Papers. University of Washington Library.
Austin Mires Papers. Washington State University Library.
S. A. Perkins Papers. Washington State Historical Society.
Port Blakely Mill Company Papers. University of Washington Library.
Mark. E. Reed Papers. University of Washington Library.
Mark E. Reed Personal Papers. Simpson Reed & Company.
Reed Mill Company Papers. Simpson Timber Company.
Simpson Logging Company Papers. Simpson Timber Company.
Simpson Timber Company Papers. Simpson Reed & Company.
St. Paul and Tacoma Lumber Company Papers. University of Washington Library.
Henry Suzzallo Papers. University of Washington Library.
Washington State Federation of Labor. University of Washington Library.

Other Primary Materials

Anderson, S. W. "Memo Regarding Simpson Logging Company," September 1943. Copy in author's possession.
Cohen, Arthur G. "Resume of Legislative Actions on Appropriations for Higher Educational Institutions." Northwest Collection. University of Washington Library.

Drake, George. Oral History Interviews with Elwood r. Maunder. Nov. 1958; Feb. 1967; Jan. 1968. Forest History Society. Santa Cruz.

Dubuar Scrapbooks. Northwest Collection. University of Washington Library.

General Information Notebook. Simpson Reed & Company.

Reed Family Information Book. Simpson Reed & Company.

Reed, Mark E., et al. "A Statement by the 'Majority.' " Northwest Collection. University of Washington Library.

――――. Folder. Meany Pioneer File. Northwest Collection. University of Washington Library.

――――. Folder. Washington State Biography File. Northwest Collection. University of Washington Library.

Reed, William G. Draft Memoirs. Copy in author's possession.

――――, ed. "The Katheryn Wilson Memoirs." Simpson Reed & Company.

Theses and Dissertations

Allen, Howard W. "Miles Poindexter: A Political Biography." Ph.D. dissertation, University of Washington, 1959.

Cole, Robert L. "The Democratic Party in Washington State, 1919-1933: Barometer of Social Change." Ph.D. dissertation, University of Washington, 1972.

Cravens, Hamilton. "A History of the Washington Farmer-Labor Party, 1928-1924." M.A. thesis, University of Washington, 1962.

Dick, Wesley A. "Visions of Abundance: The Public Power Crusade in the Pacific Northwest in the Era of J. D. Ross and the New Deal." Ph.D. dissertation, University of Washington, 1973.

Fitts, James. L. "The Washington Constitutional Convention of 1889." M.A. thesis, University of Washington, 1951.

Forth, William S. "Wesley L. Jones: A Political Biography." Ph.D. dissertation, University of Washington, 1962.

Gunns. Albert F. "Roland Hill Hartley and the Politics of Washington State." M.A. thesis, University of Washington, 1963.

Krause, Fayette F. "Democratic Party Politics in the State of Washington During the New Deal: 1932-1940." Ph.D. dissertation, University of Washington, 1971.

Meany, Edmond S., Jr. "The History of the Lumber Industry in the Pacific Northwest to 1917." Ph.D. dissertation, Harvard University, 1935.

Pullen, Douglas R. "The Administration of Washington State Governor Louis F. Hart, 1919-1925." Ph.D. dissertation, University of Washington, 1974.

Rakestraw, Lawrence. "A History of Forest Conservation in the Pacific Northwest, 1891-1913." Ph.D. dissertation, University of Washington, 1955.

Saltvig, Robert D. "The Progressive Movement in Washington." Ph.D. dissertation, University of Washington, 1966.

Sparks, William O. "J. D. Ross and Seattle City Light, 1917-1932." M.A. thesis, University of Washington, 1964.

Steen, Harold K. "Forestry in Washington to 1925." Ph.D. dissertation, University of Washington, 1969.

Tattersall, James N. "The Economic Development of the Pacific Northwest to 1920." Ph.D. dissertation, University of Washington, 1960.

Tripp, Joseph F. "Progressive Labor Laws in Washington State (1900-1925)." Ph.D. dissertation, University of Washington, 1973.

Published Sources

Books

Adams, Kramer A. *Logging Railroads of the West Coast.* Seattle: Superior Publishing Company, 1961.

Andrews, Ralph W. *Heroes of the Western Woods.* New York: E. P. Dutton and Company,1960.

Angle, Grant C., and William D. Welsh. *A Brief Historical Sketch of Shelton Washington.* Shelton: Shelton Chamber of Commerce, 1940.

Bagley, Clarence B. *History of Seattle, From the Earliest Settlement to the Present Time.* Chicago: S. J. Clarke Publishing Company, 3 vols. 1916.

Bancroft, Hubert Howe. *History of Washington, Idaho and Montana, 1845-1889.* San Francisco: The History Company, 1890.

Blankenship, Mrs. George E. *Early History of Thurston County, Washington.* Olympia: Privately published, 1914.

Bernstein, Irving. *The Lean Years: A History of the American Worker, 1920-1933.* Boston: Houghton Mifflin Company, 1966.

Brier, Howard M. *Sawdust Empire, The Pacific Northwest.* New York: Alfred A. Knopf, 1958.

Clark, Norman H. *The Dry Years: Prohibition and Social Control in Washington.* Seattle: University of Washington Press. 1965.

———. *Mill Town: A Social History of Everett Washington, from Its Earliest Beginnings on the Shores of Puget Sound to the Tragic and Infamous Event Known as the Everett Massacre.* Seattle: University of Washington Press, 1970.

———. *Washington, A Bicentennial History.* New York: W. W. Norton and Company, 1976.

Coman, Edwin T., Jr., and Helen M. Gibbs. *Time, Tide and Timber: A Century of Pope & Talbot.* Stanford: Stanford University Press, 1949.

Cox, Thomas R. *Mills and Markets: A History of the Pacific Coast Lumber Industry to 1900.* Seattle: University of Washington Press, 1974.

Deegan, Harry W. *History of Mason County,* rev. ed. Shelton: Privately published, 1960.

Drake, George L., and Elwood R. Maunder. *A Forester's Log: Fifty Years in the Pacific Northwest.* Santa Cruz: Forest History Society, 1975.

Federal Writers Program. *The New Washington: A Guide to the Evergreen State,* rev. ed. Portland: Binfords and Mort, 1950.

Galbraith, John Kenneth. *The Great Crash, 1929.* Boston: Houghton Mifflin Company, 1954.

Hawthorne, Julian, ed. *History of Washington, the Evergreen State.* New York: American Historical Publishing Company, 2 vols., 1893.

Hicks, John D. *Republican Ascendancy, 1921-1933.* New York: Harper and Brothers, 1960.

Hidy, Ralph W., Frank Ernest Hill, and Allan Nevins. *Timber and Men: The Weyerhaeuser Story.* New York: The Macmillan Company, 1963.

Holbrook, Stewart. *Burning an Empire: The Story of American Forest Fires.* New York: The Macmillan Company, 1945.

————. *Green Commonwealth: A Narrative of the Past and a Look at the Future of One Forest Products Community.* Seattle: Dogwood Press, 1945.

Hoover, Herbert. *The Memoirs of Herbert Hoover.* Vol. 2. *The Cabinet and the Presidency, 1920-1933.* New York: The Macmillan Company, 1952.

Hyman, Harold M. *Soldiers and Spruce: Origins of the Loyal Legion of Loggers and Lumbermen.* Los Angeles: Institute of Industrial Relations, University of California, 1963.

Hynding, Alan. *The Public Life of Eugene Semple: Promoter and Politican of the Pacific Northwest.* Seattle: University of Washington Press, 1973.

James, Dave. *Big Skookum: A Study of 100 Logging Years in Mason County, 1853-1953.* Seattle: Simpson Timber Company, 1953.

Jensen, Vernon H. *Lumber and Labor.* New York: Farrar and Rinehart, 1945.

Johansen, Dorothy O., and Charles M. Gates. *Empire on the Columbia: A History of the Pacific Northwest,* 2nd ed. New York: Harper & Row, 1967.

Kreienbaum, C. H., and Elwood R. Maunder. *The Development of a Sustained-Yield Industry: The Simpson-Reed Lumber Interests in the Pacific Northwest, 1920s to 1960s.* Santa Cruz: Forest History Society, 1972.

Landeen, William M. *E. O. Holland and the State College of Washington, 1916-1944.* Pullman: State College of Washington, 1958.

Loehr, Rodney C., ed. *Forests for the Future: The Story of David T. Mason, 1907-1950.* St. Paul: Minnesota Historical Society, 1952.

Lumbermen's and Logger's Guide, 1919. Tacoma: Bernard Brereton, 1919.

Meyers, William Starr, ed. *The State Papers and Other Public Writings of Herbert Hoover.* New York: Kraus Reprint Company, 1970.

Mitchell, Bradus. *Depression Decade: From New Era through New Deal, 1929-1941.* New York: Holt, Rinehart and Winston, 1947.

Nesbit, Robert C. *"He Built Seattle": A Biography of Judge Thomas Burke.* Seattle: Univerisity of Washington Press, 1961.

Newell, Gorton. *So Fair a Dwelling Place: A History of Olympia and Thurston County, Washington.* Olympia: Olympia News Publishing Company, 1950.

————. *Rogues, Buffons & Statesmen.* Seattle: Hangman Press, 1975.

Phillips, James W. *Washington State Place Names*. Seattle: University of Washington Press, 1971.

R. L. Polk & Co.'s *Olympia City and Thurston County Directory, 1902-3*. Tacoma: R. L. Polk & Co., 1902.

Reed, Thomas M. *Pioneer Masonry: A History of the Early Days of Freemasonry on the Pacific Coast*. Seattle: J. M. Taylor Printing Company, 1903.

Renfro, Alfred T. *The Fourteenth Session: A Brief History of the Men who represented the Million and a Half People of the State of Washington in the Legislature of 1915*. Seattle, 1915.

Ross, Herman W., and Richard Seelye Jones. *The Fifteenth Session: A Biographical and Pictorial History of the Washington State Legislature, 1917*. Seattle, Ross and Jones, 1917.

Sale, Roger. *Seattle, Past to Present*. Seattle: University of Washington Press, 1976.

Schattschneider, E. E. *Politics, Pressures and the Tariff: A Study of Free Private Enterprise in Pressure Politics, as Shown in the 1929-1930 Revision of the Tariff*. New York: Prentice-hall, 1935.

Schwarz, Jordan A. *The Interregnum of Despair: Hoover, Congress, and the Depression*. Urbana: University of Illinois Press, 1970.

Snowden, Clinton A. *History of Washington: The Rise and Progress of an American State*. New York: The Century History Company, 6 vols., 1909.

Spencer, Lloyd and Lancaster Pollard. *A History of the State of Washington*. New York: The American Historical Society, 4 vols, 1937.

Sweetman, Maude. *What Price Politics: The Inside Story of Washington State Politics*. Seattle: White and Hitchcock Corporation, 1927.

Taussig, F. W. *The Tariff History of the United States*, rev. ed. New York: G. P. Putnam's Sons, 1931.

Tyler, Robert L. *Rebels of the Woods: The I.W.W. in the Pacific Northwest*. Eugene: University of Oregon Press, 1967.

Vinnedge, Robert W. *The Pacific Northwest Lumber Industry and Its Development*. New Haven: Yale University School of Forestry, 1923.

Warren, Harris Gaylord. *Herbert Hoover and the Great Depression*. New York: Oxford University Press, 1959.

Wilson, Joan Hoff. *American Business and Foreign Policy, 1920-1933*. Lexington: University Press of Kentucky, 1971.

Articles

Allis, S. "As Seen in a Logging-Camp," *Overland Monthly*, 36 (September (1900):195-208.

Angle, Grant C. "Sol Simpson, Pioneer Logger," *Simpson Lookout* 5 (May 1951):2, 10.

Beckman, Victor H. "Lumber Resources of Washington," *Pacific Monthly* 19 (April 1908):385-89.

Berner Richard C. "The Port Blakely Mill Company, 1876-89," *Pacific Northwest Quarterly* 57 (October 1966):158-71.

Boas, Ralph Philip. "The Loyal Legion of Loggers and Lumbermen," *Atlantic Monthly* 127 (February 1921):221-26.

Conklin, Edwin P. "Logging on Puget Sound, As Illustrated in the Lives of Sol Simpson and Mark E. Reed," *Americana Illustrated* 29 (April 1935):256-83.

Ficken, Robert E. "President Harding Visits Seattle," *Pacific Northwest Quarterly* 67 (July 1975):105-14.

———. "Mark E. Reed: Portrait of a Businessman in Politics," *Journal of Forest History* 20 (January 1976):4-19.

Fielde, Adele M. "Lumbering in the State of Washington," *Independent* 63 (7 November, 1907):1108-12.

Gates, Charles M. "A Historical Sketch of the Economic Development of Washington since Statehood," *Pacific Northwest Quarterly* 39 (July 1948):214-32.

Hillier, Alfred J. "Albert Johnson, Congressman," *Pacific Northwest Quarterly* 36 (July 1945):193-211.

Hodgson, Allen H. "Going After that Forty Per Cent," *Pacific Pulp and Paper Industry* 1 (July 1927):11-13, 48.

Holbrook, Stewart H. "The Logging Camp Loses Its Soul," *Sunset* 56 (June 1926):19-21, 62.

Hovey-King, Alvin. "The Lumber Industry of the Pacific Coast," *American Monthly Review of Reviews* 27 (March 1903):317-23.

Kottman, Richard D. "Herbert Hoover and the Smoot-Hawley Tariff: Canada, A Case Study," *Journal of American History* 62 (December 1975):609-35.

Kreienbaum, C. H. "Price Warfare in Waterborne Markets," *Timberman* 32 (April 1931):109.

———, and Elwood R. Maunder. "Forest Management and Community Stability: The Simpson Experience," *Forest History* 12 (July 1968):6-19.

Lyford, C. A. "Standing Timber Yield Tax Proposal for State of Washington," *West Coast Lumberman* 60 (January 1933):18-19.

Lyman, W. D. "The State of Washington," *Atlantic Monthly* 87 (April 1901):505-15.

Mason, David T., and Elwood R. Maunder. "Oral History Excerpts: Memoirs of a Forester," *Forest History* 13 (April-June 1969):28-39.

Meany, Edmond S. "Western Spruce and the War," *Washington Historical Quarterly* 9 (October 1918):255-58.

Murray, Keith. "Issues and Personalities of Pacific Northwest Politics, 1889-1950," *Pacific Northwest Quarterly* 41 (July 1950):213-33.

Oliphant, J. Orin. "Legislative Reapportionment in Washington," *Washington Historical Quarterly* 22 (January 1931):3-25.

Ralph, Julian. "Washington: The Evergreen State," *Harper's New Monthly Magazine* 85 (September 1892):594-607.

Reid, Bill G. "Fraklin K. Laine's Idea for Veteran's Colonization, 1918-1921," *Pacific Historical Review* 33 (November 1964):447-61.

Richardson, Elmo R. "Olympic National Park: Twenty Years of Controversy," *Forest History* 12 (April 1968):6-15.

Roush, J. F. "Legislative Reapportionment in Washington State," *Pacific Northwest Quarterly* 28 (July 1937):263-300.

Snyder, J. Richard. "Hoover and the Hawley-Smoot Tariff: A View of Executive Leadership," *Annals of Iowa* 41 (Winter 1973):1173-89.

Stevens, Carl M. "The Taxation of Forest Property in the State of Washington," *Journal of Forestry* 22 (May 1924):464-72.

Stilson, Harold M., Jr., and Elwood R. Maunder, "Red Cedar Shingles & Shakes: The Labor Story," *Journal of Forest History* 19 (July 1975): 114-24.

Tenney, W. A. "Evolution of the Northwest," *Overland Monthly* 35 (April 1900):321-32.

Vassault, F. I. "Lumbering in Washington," *Overland Monthly* 20 (July 1892):23-32.

Government Documents

U.S. Congress. *Congressional Record.* 1929-1930.

U.S. Congress. House. Committee on Ways and Means. *Hearings, Tariff Readjustment—1929.*

U.S. Congress. Senate. Committee on Finance. *Hearings, Tafiff Act of 1929.*

U.S. Congress. Senate. Committee on Reforestation. *Hearings.* 1923.

U.S. Department of Commerce. Bureau of the Census. *Historical Statistics of the United States, Colonial Times to 1957.* Washington, D. C.: Government Printing Office, 1961.

U.S. Department of Commerce and Labor. Bureau of Corporations. *The Lumber Industry.* 1913.

U.S. Department of Labor. Bureau of Labor Statistics. *Monthly Labor Review.* 1929.

U.S. Tariff Commission. *Summary of Tariff Information, 1929.*

U.S. Tariff Commission. *Report to the President on Lumber, 1932.*

Washington State. *An Official Report of the Resources of the State.* 1894.

Washington State. *Biennial Report of the Board of State Land Commissioners to the Governor of the State,* 1896.

Washington State. Bureau of Statistics, Agriculture and Immigration. *Agricultural, Manufacturing and Commercial Resources and Capabilities of Washington, 1901.*

Washington State. Bureau of Statistics, Agriculture and Immigration. *A Review of the Resources and Industries of Washington, 1909.*

Washington State. Department of State. Bureau of Statistics and Information. *The Logged-Off Lands of Western Washington.* 1911.

Washington State. *House Journal.* 1915-1917.

Newspapers

New York Times, 1929-30.

Olympia *Morning Olympian,* 1925-26.

Olympia *Pacific Tribune,* 1866, 1891.

Olympia *Washington Standard*, 1892, 1893, 1898, 1901, 1902.
Seattle *Argus*, 1917, 1921, 1923, 1925, 1926, 1928, 1929, 1932.
Seattle *Business Chronicle*, 1929.
Seattle Post-Intelligencer, 1921, 1923, 1925, 1926, 1927, 1929.
Seattle Star, 1923, 1926.
Seattle Times, 1921, 1923, 1925, 1926, 1927, 1929.
Seattle Union Record, 1923, 1926.
Shelton *Mason County Journal*, 1899-1933.
Spokane *Spokesman-Review*, 1923, 1925, 1926.
Tacoma News Tribune, 1923, 1925, 1926.

Periodicals

Business Week, 1930, 1931, 1933.
Camp and Mill News, 1922, 1923, 1924, 1926.
Four L Bulletin, 1919-23.
Literary Digest, 1924.
Pacific Mason, 1897.
Pacific Pulp and Paper Industry, 1927.
Simpson Diamond, 1963.
Simpson Lookout, 1951.
Sunset, 1916.
Timberman, 1906-33.
Town Crier, 1933.
West Coast Lumberman, 1914-33.
West Shore, 1877, 1888.

Index